When Will
Jesus
Bring the
Pork Chops?

*Also by George Carlin
in Large Print:*

Napalm & Silly Putty

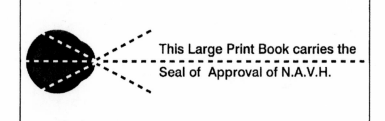

When Will Jesus Bring the Pork Chops?

George Carlin

Thorndike Press • Waterville, Maine

Published in 2005 by arrangement with Hyperion, an imprint of Buena Vista Books, Inc.

Thorndike Press® Large Print Core.

The tree indicium is a trademark of Thorndike Press.

The text of this Large Print edition is unabridged.
Other aspects of the book may vary from the original edition.

Set in 16 pt. Plantin by Christina S. Huff.

Printed in the United States on permanent paper.

Library of Congress Cataloging-in-Publication Data

Carlin, George.
    When will Jesus bring the pork chops? / by George Carlin.
        p. cm.
    ISBN 0-7862-7346-1 (lg. print : hc : alk. paper)
    1. American wit and humor.   2. Large type books.
    I. Title.
PN6165.C36 2005
818´.5402—dc22   2004027402

This book is dedicated to my amazing daughter, Kelly: keeper of the sacred DNA, citizen of the universe, and one of America's few really good Buddhist poker players.

As the Founder/CEO of NAVH, the only national health agency solely devoted to those who, although not totally blind, have an eye disease which could lead to serious visual impairment, I am pleased to recognize Thorndike Press★ as one of the leading publishers in the large print field.

Founded in 1954 in San Francisco to prepare large print textbooks for partially seeing children, NAVH became the pioneer and standard setting agency in the preparation of large type.

Today, those publishers who meet our standards carry the prestigious "Seal of Approval" indicating high quality large print. We are delighted that Thorndike Press is one of the publishers whose titles meet these standards. We are also pleased to recognize the significant contribution Thorndike Press is making in this important and growing field.

Lorraine H. Marchi, L.H.D.
Founder/CEO
NAVH

★ Thorndike Press encompasses the following imprints: Thorndike, Wheeler, Walker and Large Print Press.

Acknowledgments

Everlasting thanks to my editor, Gretchen Young, who withstood a last barrage of changes and pulled everything together. She also did an outstanding job protecting me from certain evil people in the publishing company who were jealous of my nice teeth and never stopped plotting against me.

All love to my troll-mate, the sweet Sara Jane.

Major funding for this book was made possible by deliberately starving a family of four in Tennessee.

"Of course the people don't want war. But after all, it's the leaders of the country who determine the policy, and it's always a simple matter to drag the people along whether it's a democracy, a fascist dictatorship, or a parliament, or a communist dictatorship. Voice or no voice, the people can always be brought to the bidding of the leaders. That is easy. All you have to do is tell them they are being attacked, and denounce the pacifists for lack of patriotism, and exposing the country to greater danger."

— Hermann Göring
At The Nuremberg Trials

"All tears are the same."

— Irish Woman

"So little time. So little to do."

— Oscar Levant

"The main obligation is to amuse yourself."
— S. J. Perelman

"Today's another day. Time to play."

— Sally Wade

Preface

I'm an outsider by choice, but not truly. It's the unpleasantness of the system that keeps me out. I'd rather be in, in a good system. That's where my discontent comes from: being forced to choose to stay outside.

My advice: Just keep movin' straight ahead. Every now and then you find yourself in a different place.

George's Holiday Message

Since this book comes out in the fall, I'd like to take advantage of this early opportunity to wish all of you an enjoyable Christmas season and a happy New Year filled with good fortune. Of course, I realize this can't happen for everyone. Some of you are going to die next year, and others will be crippled and maimed in accidents, perhaps even completely paralyzed. Still others will be stricken with diseases that can't be cured, or will be horribly scarred in fires. And let's not forget the robberies and rapes — there'll be lots of them. Therefore, many of you will not get to enjoy the happy and fortunate New Year I'm wishing for you. So just try to do the best you can.

A Note of Appreciation

From the Desk of:

Spot Wade

On the occasion of the publication of his new book, *When Will Jesus Bring the Pork Chops?*, I want to wish the author good luck and let the readers know that as my rep and personal assistant — hired to deny rumors of my marriage and subsequent same-sex divorce to Sir Elton John's dog, Arthur, and how now I'm an expectant dad — George Carlin was easy to work with and followed instructions well — although he was often tardy, with lame excuses like "other things to do."

Similar to that of a cocker spaniel, who wants nothin' more than our complete and undivided attention, his personality is pleasant, well-tolerated, and meets with my approval — except for the time when, like Jesus, he forgot to bring the pork chops. But now's not the time to dwell on food. Well . . . maybe it is.

At any rate, I'm proud that one of my employees — especially you, Mr. Carlin — has demonstrated that you're more than just a flash in the pan, as is so often the case with seared tuna. And by the way — as long as we're still talkin' about food — regardin' Jesus bringin' the pork chops, lemme know when they finally arrive. We'll eat them religiously, and enjoy a fine glass of wine.

What are you lookin' at?

A Modern Man

I'm a modern man,
digital and smoke-free;
a man for the millennium.

A diversified, multi-cultural,
post-modern deconstructionist;
politically, anatomically and ecologically incorrect.

I've been uplinked and downloaded,
I've been inputted and outsourced.
I know the upside of downsizing,
I know the downside of upgrading.

I'm a high-tech low-life.
A cutting-edge, state-of-the-art,
bi-coastal multi-tasker,
and I can give you a gigabyte in a nano-
second.

I'm new-wave, but I'm old-school;
and my inner child is outward-bound.

I'm a hot-wired, heat-seeking,
warm-hearted cool customer;

voice-activated and bio-degradable.
I interface with my database;
my database is in cyberspace;
so I'm interactive, I'm hyperactive,
and from time to time I'm radioactive.

Behind the eight ball, ahead of the curve,
ridin' the wave, dodgin' the bullet,
pushin' the envelope.

I'm on point, on task, on message,
and off drugs.

I've got no need for coke and speed;
I've got no urge to binge and purge.

I'm in the moment, on the edge,
over the top, but under the radar.

A high-concept, low-profile,
medium-range ballistic missionary.

A street-wise smart bomb.
A top-gun bottom-feeder.

I wear power ties, I tell power lies,
I take power naps, I run victory laps.

I'm a totally ongoing, big-foot, slam-dunk
rainmaker with a pro-active outreach.

A raging workaholic, a working rageaholic;
out of rehab and in denial.

I've got a personal trainer,
a personal shopper,
a personal assistant,
and a personal agenda.

You can't shut me up;
you can't dumb me down.

'Cause I'm tireless, and I'm wireless.
I'm an alpha-male on beta-blockers.

I'm a non-believer,
I'm an over-achiever;
Laid-back and fashion-forward.
Up-front, down-home;
low-rent, high-maintenance.

I'm super-sized, long-lasting,
high-definition, fast-acting,
oven-ready and built to last.

A hands-on, footloose, knee-jerk head case;
prematurely post-traumatic,
and I have a love child who sends me hate-
    mail.

But I'm feeling, I'm caring,

17

I'm healing, I'm sharing.
A supportive, bonding, nurturing
primary-care giver.

My output is down, but my income is up.
I take a short position on the long bond,
and my revenue stream has its own cash flow.

I read junk mail, I eat junk food,
I buy junk bonds, I watch trash sports.

I'm gender-specific, capital-intensive,
user-friendly and lactose-intolerant.

I like rough sex; I like tough love.
I use the f-word in my e-mail.
And the software on my hard drive
is hard-core — no soft porn.

I bought a microwave at a mini-mall.
I bought a mini-van at a mega-store.
I eat fast food in the slow lane.

I'm toll-free, bite-size, ready-to-wear,
and I come in all sizes.

A fully equipped, factory-authorized,
hospital-tested, clinically proven,
scientifically formulated medical miracle.

I've been pre-washed, pre-cooked, pre-heated,
pre-screened, pre-approved, pre-packaged,
post-dated, freeze-dried, double-wrapped
and vacuum-packed.

And . . . I have unlimited broadband capacity.

I'm a rude dude, but I'm the real deal.
Lean and mean.
Cocked, locked and ready to rock;
rough, tough and hard to bluff.

I take it slow, I go with the flow;
I ride with the tide, I've got glide in my stride.

Drivin' and movin', sailin' and spinnin';
jivin' and groovin', wailin' and winnin'.

I don't snooze, so I don't lose.
I keep the pedal to the metal
and the rubber on the road.
I party hearty, and lunchtime is crunch time.

I'm hangin' in, there ain't no doubt;
and I'm hangin' tough.
Over and out.

Euphemisms: It's a Whole New Language

Euphemistic language turns up in many areas of American life in a variety of situations. Not all euphemisms are alike, but they have one thing in common: They obscure meaning rather than enhance it; they shade the truth. But they exist for various reasons.

Sometimes they simply replace a word that makes people uncomfortable. For instance, the terms *white meat, dark meat* and *drumstick* came into use because in Victorian times people didn't like to mention certain body parts. No one at the dinner table really wanted to hear Uncle Herbert say, "Never mind the *thighs*, Margaret, let me have one of those nice, juicy *breasts*." It would've made them uncomfortable.

And at the same time, for the same reason, *belly* became *stomach*. But even *stomach* sounded too intimate, so they began saying *tummy*. It's actually a bit sad.

I first became aware of euphemisms when I was nine years old. I was in the living room with my mother and my aunt Lil when I mentioned that Lil had a *mole* on her face.

My mother was quick to point out that Lil didn't have a mole, she had a *beauty mark.*

That confused me because, looking at Lil, the beauty mark didn't seem to be working. And it confused me further, because my uncle John also had a brown thing on his face, and it was clearly not a beauty mark. And so on that day, I discovered that on some people what appeared to be moles were actually beauty marks. And as it turned out, they were the same people whose *laugh lines* looked a lot like *crow's-feet.*

By the way, that whole beauty-mark scam worked so well that some women routinely began using eyebrow pencils to apply fake beauty marks — a "fake mole" being something no self-respecting woman would ever think of giving herself. Somehow, I can't imagine Elizabeth Taylor turning to Joan Crawford and saying, "Lend me your eyebrow pencil, Joanie, I'm gonna put a fake mole on my face."

By the way, it was only a few years after the Aunt Lil incident that I took comfort in the fact that some people apparently thought my ugly *pimples* were nothing more than minor *skin blemishes.*

Another role euphemisms play is to simply put a better face on things, to dress up existing phrases that sound too negative. *Nonprofit* became *not-for-profit,* because nonprofit sounded too much as though someone didn't know what they were doing. Not-for-profit makes it clear that there was never any intention of making a profit in the first place.

But some words that are euphemized aren't even vaguely negative, they're merely considered too ordinary. For that reason, many things that used to be *free* are now *complimentary.* Asking the hotel clerk if the newspapers are free makes you sound like a mooch, but "Are the newspapers complimentary?" allows you to retain some small bit of dignity. This is the reason some hotels offer their guests *complimentary continental breakfasts,* while others give their customers *free doughnuts.*

If you're one who would enjoy a closer look at euphemisms, you'll find a number of sections in the book that will interest you. I broke the euphemisms into segments, because they play such a large and varied role in American speech. And I call it The New Language, because it's certainly new to me; I know I didn't grow up with it. And that's my larger point: that it's gotten worse over time. There were probably a few early signs I noticed, but I knew the problem was getting serious when I began to hear ordinary people refer to *ideas* as *concepts.*

More to come.

Stiff Upper Lip, You Know

Imagine two different commercial airliners taking long, fatal plunges directly into the ground from high altitudes. One is a British Airways plane filled with staid English diplomats and upper-class landed gentry. The other plane is Alitalia, filled with uneducated Sicilian, Greek and Turkish peasants. As the two planes dive toward certain destruction, which one do you think will have the louder screaming and the more colorful praying, cursing and blasphemy? You get one guess. Hint: It isn't the British plane.

Eye Blaster: Get One Now

Are your eyes dry and itchy? It's possible you may have dry, itchy eyes. Don't take a chance. Call now for Eye Blaster, a special, self-powered unit that blasts hot, refreshing steam directly into the eyes to relieve symptoms fast.

Just plug in the Eye Blaster and wait forty-five minutes for full heat and steam pressure to build up. Then blast the scalding hot steam directly into your eyes for thirty to forty minutes. Submerge your head immediately in ice water for fifteen minutes, then repeat the steam treatment. Repeat these steps seven times and then take a breather. Do not use more than fifteen times in one twenty-four-hour period. Children under five should not use Eye Blaster unsupervised. When using on pets, tie pet to a chair before blasting. Safe for old people. Doctor approved, but not eye doctors. Call now.

Hand Me My Purse

Boxing is an activity in which each of two men, by delivering a series of repeated, sharp blows to the head, attempts to render the other senseless, leaving him lying on the floor, unable to act rationally, defend himself or even stand up. If one of the two men is knocked down and beaten into an only partially blank and helpless mental state, the other is made to stand aside and the contest is halted momentarily, while the damaged man regains just enough strength to stand up and have the beating continue — to the point where he is again lying on the floor, this time completely immobile and functionless. Afterward, the two men embrace in a display of good sportsmanship.

Remember Your Uncle John?

Hi Billy. I'm Uncle John. I came up to say goodnight. You remember your Uncle John, don't you? You remember the time I took you down to the beach and we set the hot dog stand on fire and three people died? Wasn't that fun? Remember runnin' away from the police? And how we hid in the sewer and Uncle John got poo-poo all over him? And he wiped it on your coat? You remember? And then I took you to the bar and got drunk and vomited on the jukebox? And sparks started flyin' out of the jukebox and a fire started? And all the people were screamin'? Remember that? Remember the screamin'? And the ambulances? Wasn't that fun?

And do you remember that other time? The time I took you to the circus? The lion got loose and ate a monkey? Wasn't that fun? And they had to kill the lion? And the monkeys got real sad, so they had to kill the monkeys, too? Wasn't that fun? And then the man fell off the trapeze and smashed into the ground, and they had to kill him? And all the other trapeze people got real sad and they had to kill them too? Hah? Wasn't that fun?

Why are you cryin', Billy? Please don't cry. If you stop cryin', I'll take you to the rodeo. Wouldn't that be fun? Maybe someone will get trampled, or gored. They've got horsies and cows, too, you know. Maybe they'll have to kill a horsie. Or a cow. And if they kill a cow, maybe we'll get to eat him in a hamburger. Wouldn't that be fun? Please don't cry.

Remember the time you fell outta my car? Remember, you were lookin' out the window, and we went around a corner real fast to keep from hittin' that lady? And you went flyin' out the window and hit the pole, head first? And the doctor had to sew your head up with a big needle? I've got a boat now, Billy. You wanna go out on my boat? I promise I'll be careful. Are you asleep yet? Billy? Please stop cryin'.

Count the Superfluous Redundant Pleonastic Tautologies

My fellow countrymen, I speak to you as co-equals, knowing you are deserving of the honest truth. And let me warn you in advance, my subject matter concerns a serious crisis caused by an event in my past history: the execution-style killing of a security guard on a delivery truck. At that particular point in time, I found myself in a deep depression, making mental errors which seemed as though they might threaten my future plans. I am not over-exaggerating.

I needed a new beginning, so I decided to pay a social visit to a personal friend with whom I share the same mutual objectives and who is one of the most unique individuals I have ever personally met. The end result was an unexpected surprise. When I reiterated again to her the fact that I needed a fresh start, she said I was exactly right; and, as an added plus, she came up with a final solution that was absolutely perfect.

Based on her past experience, she felt we needed to join together in a common bond for a combined total of twenty-four hours a day, in order to find some new initiatives. What a novel innovation! And, as an extra bonus, she presented me with the free gift of a tuna fish. Right away I noticed an immediate positive improvement. And although my recovery is not totally complete, the sum total is I feel much better now knowing I am not uniquely alone.

The Control Freaks

Hello. We're the ones who control your lives. We make the decisions that affect all of you. Isn't it interesting to know that those who run your lives would have the nerve to tell you about it in this manner? Suffer, you fools. We know everything you do, and we know where you go. What do you think the cameras are for? And the global-positioning satellites? And the Social Security numbers? You belong to us. And it can't be changed. Sign your petitions, walk your picket lines, bring your lawsuits, cast your votes, and write those stupid letters to whomever you please; you won't change a thing. Because we control your lives. And we have plans for you. Go back to sleep.

They Came From Out of the Sky

I find it discouraging — and a bit depressing — when I notice the unequal treatment afforded by the media to UFO believers on the one hand, and on the other, to those who believe in an invisible supreme being who inhabits the sky. Especially as the latter belief applies to the whole Jesus-Messiah-Son-of-God fable.

You may have noticed that, in the media, UFO believers are usually referred to as *buffs,* a term used to diminish and marginalize them by relegating them to the ranks of hobbyists and mere enthusiasts. They are made to seem like kooks and quaint dingbats who have the nerve to believe that, in an observable universe of trillions upon trillions of stars, and most likely many hundreds of billions of potentially inhabitable planets, some of those planets may have produced life-forms capable of doing things that we can't do.

On the other hand those who believe in an eternal, all-powerful being, a being who demands to be loved and adored unconditionally and who punishes and rewards according to his whims are thought to be worthy, upright, credible people. This, in spite of the large numbers of believers who are clearly close-minded fanatics.

To my way of thinking, there is every bit as much evidence for the existence of UFOs as there is for the existence of God. Probably far more. At least in the case of UFOs there have been countless taped and filmed — and, by the way, unexplained — sightings from all over the world, along with documented radar evidence seen by experienced military and civilian radar operators.

This does not even begin to include the widespread testimony of not only highly trained, experienced military and civilian pilots who are selected for their jobs, in part, for their above-average eyesight and mental stability, but also of equally well-trained, experienced law-enforcement officers. Such pilots and law-enforcement people are known to be serious, sober individuals who would have quite a bit to lose were they to be associated with anything resembling kooky, outlandish beliefs. Nonetheless, they have taken the risk of revealing their experiences because they are convinced they have seen something objectively real that they consider important.

All of these accounts are ignored by the media.

Granted, the world of UFO-belief has its share of kooks, nuts and fringe people, but have you ever listened to some of these religious true-believers? Have you ever heard of any extreme, bizarre behavior and outlandish claims associated with religious zealots? Could any of them be considered kooks, nuts or dingbats? A fair person would have to say yes.

But the marginal people in these two groups don't matter in this argument. What matters is the prejudice and superstition built into the media coverage of the two sets of beliefs. One is treated reverently and accepted as received truth, the other is treated laughingly and dismissed out of hand.

As evidence of the above premise, I offer one version of a typical television news story heard each year on the final Friday of Lent:

"Today is Good Friday, observed by Christians worldwide as a day that commemorates the crucifixion of Jesus Christ, the Son of God, whose death redeemed the sins of mankind."

Here is the way it *should* be written:

"Today is Good Friday, observed worldwide by Jesus buffs as the day on which the popular, bearded cultural figure, sometimes referred to as *The Messiah,* was allegedly crucified and — according to legend — died for mankind's so-called sins. Today kicks off a 'holy' weekend that culminates on Easter Sunday, when, it is widely believed, this dead 'savior' — who also, by the way, claimed to be the son of a sky-dwelling, invisible being known as God — mysteriously 'rose from the dead.'

"According to the legend, by volunteering to be killed and actually going through with it, Jesus saved every person who has ever lived — and every person who ever *will* live — from an eternity of suffering in a fiery region popularly known as hell, providing — so the story goes — that the person to be 'saved' firmly believes this rather fanciful tale."

That would be an example of unbiased news reporting. Don't wait around for it to happen. The aliens will land first.

The Two Commandments

I have a problem with the Ten Commandments. Here it is: Why are there ten? We don't need that many. I think the list of commandments was deliberately and artificially inflated to get it up to ten. It's clearly a padded list.

Here's how it happened: About five thousand years ago, a bunch of religious and political hustlers got together to figure out how they could control people and keep them in line. They knew people were basically stupid and would believe anything they were told, so these guys announced that God — God personally — had given one of them a list of ten commandments that he wanted everyone to follow. They claimed the whole thing took place on a mountaintop, when no one else was around.

But let me ask you something: When these guys were sittin' around the tent makin' all this up, why did they pick ten? Why ten? Why not nine, or eleven? I'll tell you why. Because ten sounds important. Ten sounds official. They knew if they tried eleven, people wouldn't take them seriously. People would say, "What're you kiddin' me? The Eleven Commandments? Get the fuck outta here!"

But ten! Ten sounds important. Ten is the basis for the decimal system; it's a decade. It's a psychologically satisfying number: the top ten; the ten most wanted; the ten best-dressed. So deciding on ten command-ments was clearly a marketing decision. And it's obviously a bullshit list. In truth, it's a political document, artificially inflated to sell better.

I'm going to show you how you can re-duce the number of commandments and come up with a list that's a bit more logical and realistic. We'll start with the first three, and I'll use the Roman Catholic version be-cause those are the ones I was fed as a little boy.

- I AM THE LORD THY GOD, THOU SHALT NOT HAVE STRANGE GODS BEFORE ME.
- THOU SHALT NOT TAKE THE NAME OF THE LORD THY GOD IN VAIN.
- THOU SHALT KEEP HOLY THE SABBATH.

Okay, right off the bat, the first three com-mandments — pure bullshit. "Sabbath day," "Lord's name," "strange gods." Spooky lan-guage. Spooky language designed to scare and control primitive people. In no way does superstitious mumbo jumbo like this apply to the lives of intelligent, civilized hu-mans in the twenty-first century. You throw out the first three commandments, and you're down to seven.

- HONOR THY FATHER AND MOTHER.

This commandment is about obedience and respect for authority; in other words it's simply a device for controlling people. The truth is, obedience and respect should not be granted automatically. They should be earned. They should be based on the parents' (or the authority figure's) performance. Some parents deserve respect. Most of them don't. Period. We're down to six.

Now, in the interest of logic — something religion has a really hard time with — I'm going to skip around the list a little bit:

- THOU SHALT NOT STEAL.
- THOU SHALT NOT BEAR FALSE WITNESS.

Stealing and lying. Actually, when you think about it, these two commandments cover the same sort of behavior: dishonesty. Stealing and lying. So we don't need two of them. Instead, we combine these two and call it "Thou shalt not be dishonest." Suddenly we're down to five.

And as long as we're combining commandments I have two others that belong together:

- THOU SHALT NOT COMMIT ADULTERY.
- THOU SHALT NOT COVET THY NEIGHBOR'S WIFE.

Once again, these two prohibit the same sort of behavior; in this case, marital infidelity. The difference between them is that coveting takes place in the mind. And I don't think you should outlaw fantasizing about someone else's wife, otherwise what's a guy gonna think about when he's flogging his dong?

But marital fidelity is a good idea, so I suggest we keep the idea and call this commandment "Thou shalt not be unfaithful." Suddenly we're down to four.

And when you think about it further, honesty and fidelity are actually parts of the same overall value. So, in truth, we could combine the two honesty commandments with the two fidelity commandments, and, using positive language instead of negative, call the whole thing "Thou shalt always be honest and faithful." And now we're down to three.

- THOU SHALT NOT COVET THY NEIGHBOR'S GOODS.

This one is just plain stupid. Coveting your neighbor's goods is what keeps the economy going: Your neighbor gets a vibrator that plays "O Come All Ye Faithful," you want to get one, too. Coveting creates jobs. Leave it alone.

You throw out coveting and you're down to two now: the big, combined honesty/fidelity commandment, and the one we haven't mentioned yet:

- THOU SHALT NOT KILL.

Murder. The Fifth Commandment. But, if you give it a little thought, you realize that religion has never really had a problem with murder. Not really. More people have been killed in the name of God than for any other reason.

To cite a few examples, just think about Irish history, the Middle East, the Crusades, the Inquisition, our own abortion-doctor killings and, yes, the World Trade Center to see how seriously religious people take Thou Shalt Not Kill. Apparently, to religious folks — especially the truly devout — murder is negotiable. It just depends on who's doing the killing and who's getting killed.

And so, with all of this in mind, folks, I offer you my revised list of the Two Commandments:

First:

- THOU SHALT ALWAYS BE HONEST AND FAITHFUL, ESPECIALLY TO THE PROVIDER OF THY NOOKIE.

And second:

- THOU SHALT TRY REAL HARD NOT TO KILL ANYONE, UNLESS, OF COURSE, THEY PRAY TO A DIFFERENT INVISIBLE AVENGER THAN THE ONE YOU PRAY TO.

Two is all you need, folks. Moses could have carried them down the hill in his pocket. And if we had a list like that, I wouldn't mind that brilliant judge in Alabama displaying it prominently in his courthouse lobby. As long as he included one additional commandment:

- THOU SHALT KEEP THY RELIGION TO THYSELF!!!

The Filthy, Dirty News

Announcer: It's six o'clock, time for *Action-6 News* with Leslie Crotchmonger and Dick Hopshteckler. Here's Leslie with today's top stories.

L: Good evening. First the headlines:

- A giant man shits on Philadelphia.
- An old man shows his soiled anus to a waitress at an Olive Garden.
- A small dog eats a man's balls and dies.
- A crippled couple is arrested for fucking on a roller coaster.

Now the stories behind the headlines: In Philadelphia today, a giant man dropped his huge pants and squatted over Independence Hall. He then unleashed a . . .

(Dick reaches over and grabs Leslie's script.)

D: Fuck you, you cunt, you did the headlines.

L: Lick my asshole, you dimwitted prick. My name comes first on the opening announcement.

D: That's because you blew the news director.

L: At least I didn't blow a homeless guy who has the siff.

D: Oh yeah? Well, he wouldn't have the siff if you didn't fuck him in the Dumpster out back.

L: Eat my box.

D: Not without a gas mask, Dearie.

L: Keep fuckin' with me, Little Dick, and I'll tell your wife about the Cub Scouts you went down on.

D: Leslie, the way we're acting is crazy. Let's put all this petty, personal stuff behind us and act like professionals. What do you say?

L: Good idea. I agree.

D: So, what's coming up at six o'clock?

L: How the fuck should I know? What do you think I am, a fuckin' psychic?

D: No way! If you were psychic, you would've known you were gonna wind up with labia that hang down like satchel handles.

L: Thanks, Dick, that's real clever. By the way, doesn't that get to you? Being called Dick?

D: Being called Dick is a lot better than being called Dick Licker.

L: Eat shit, raisin balls! I hope you swallow a turd. Well, folks, that's it for *Action-6 News.* Don't miss *News at Eleven* tonight as Rod Holder interviews a nun who's been receiving obscene phone calls from a man who says he wants to chew her bush during a funeral mass.

Announcer: *Action-6 News* has been brought to you by First Bank, meeting community needs since 1849. First Bank: Experience Out the Ass.

That's the Spirit

I don't understand these people who call themselves spiritual advisors. Franklin Graham, the unfortunate son of Billy Graham, is George Bush's spiritual advisor. Bill Clinton had Jesse Jackson.

Here's the part I don't understand: How can someone else advise you on your spirit? Isn't spirit an intensely personal, internal thing? Doesn't it, by its very nature, elude definition, much less analysis? What kind of advice could some drone who has devoted his life to the self-deception of religion possibly give you about your spirit? It sounds like a hustle to me.

Guys Called Junior

I have no respect for any man who allows people to call him Junior; I immediately think he's a chump and a loser. To me, Junior means lower than, lesser than, beneath. Putting "Junior" on a kid's name is just a way for a father to control and demean his son and prevent him from having an identity of his own. I don't like that whole cult-of-the-father thing in the first place. But apparently some guys' self-esteem is just low enough that they accept it. I have no respect for them.

Pro sports is full of these hopelessly Daddy-addicted athletes who wouldn't think of taking a shit without their fathers' approval. I especially have no respect for the ones whose fathers coached them in high school or college, or whose fathers played the same position they did. When I hear the sons of coaches and former athletes talking on television, they sound to me like parent-pleasers and ass-kissers. Why don't they grow up?

Guys & Dolls: Part 1

Ladies First

I notice a lot of this "comedy" they have on television is about relationships. Do you ever see this stuff? Relationship comedy? Well, I don't know much about relationships, but over the years I've noticed a few things about the two sexes, and I'd like to discuss them. Men and women: the big, hairy, noisy male creatures, and the smaller, smoother, but nonetheless also quite noisy, female creatures.

Here's all you need to know about men and women: Women are crazy, men are stupid. And the main reason women are crazy is that men are stupid. It's not the only reason, but it's a big one. And by the way, if you don't think men are stupid, check the newspaper. Ninety-nine percent of all the truly horrifying shit going on in this world was initiated, established, perpetrated, enabled or continued by men. And that includes the wave and the high five, two of history's truly low points.

But as I say, besides knowing that men are stupid, it's also important to remember that women are crazy. And if you don't think

44

women are crazy, ask a man. That's the one thing men aren't stupid about; they know for sure, way down deep in their hearts, that women are straight-out fuckin' nuts.

But it doesn't just happen; it isn't an accident. Women have good reason to be nuts, the main one being that in the course of life, compared with men, they have far more to put up with; they bear greater burdens. Think of it this way: In the Big Cosmic Cafeteria, as human beings move down the chow line of life and reach that section where the shit is being spooned out, women are given several extra portions.

And please understand, my motives here are not selfish or personal. I'm not saying all this stuff to get in good with women — although an occasional blow job would be nice. But it's not a requirement. It's optional. BJO: Blow Job Optional. No, I just think it should be evident to any person who's being honest — and thinking clearly — that women carry a lot more of life's baggage than men.

To begin with, they're smaller and weaker, so they get slapped, punched, raped, abused and, in general, get the shit beaten out of them on a rather regular basis. By men, of course, who are stronger. If women were stronger, this wouldn't be happening. Men would not raise a hand if they thought the balance was more equal; they would back down quickly. Then again, if women were stronger, they would probably be beating the shit out of men just for the fun of it. It's only fair.

Appearance is Everything

Another major problem for women: They have to look good all the time — or at least they think they do. So they'll be attractive to their male protectors. "Gotta look good tonight, Joey's gonna beat the shit out of me. Maybe I can get a nice kick in the fuckin' mouth. Gotta look my best."

And looking one's female best requires a lot of things. Start with cosmetics. Just think of all the products and procedures a woman is forced to deal with in the world of cosmetics: cleansers, toners, foundation, blush, face powder, lipstick, lip gloss, lip liner, eyeliner, eye shadow, eyebrow pencil, mascara, nail polish, nail polish remover, manicures, pedicures, fake fingernails, fake eyelashes . . .

Gimme Some Skin

. . . face cream, neck cream, eye cream, thigh cream, foot cream, day cream, night cream, cold cream, wrinkle remover, makeup remover, hand lotions, body lotions, bath oils, bath beads, shower gels, bubble baths, scented baths, perfumes, colognes, toilet water, astringents, moisturizers, emulsions, exfoliants, peels, scrubs, depilatories, body wraps, facial masks . . .

Hair Hair!

. . . shampoos, conditioners, bleaches, dyes, rinses, tints, perms, straighteners, wigs, falls, rats, extensions, combs, barrettes, bobby pins, hairpins, hairnets, hair curlers, scrunchies, ribbons, bows, tiebacks, headbands . . .

Procedures

. . . streaking, frosting, teasing, spraying, moussing, blow drying, cutting, layering, curling, eyelash curling, eyebrow plucking, armpit shaving, leg shaving, crotch shaving, crotch waxing, leg waxing, eyebrow waxing . . .

And a purse! A big fuckin' purse so she can carry all this shit around with her. Especially the makeup, which must be close at hand at all times. "Gotta have my makeup. In case I run into Joey and he wants to beat the shit outta me. I gotta look my best. Maybe he'll punch me repeatedly in the kidneys and the stomach so it doesn't mark up my face. He's so thoughtful."

I Have Nothing to Wear

And, my friend, I hope you're aware that when we talk about women looking good, we're also talking about clothing. Clothing is what generates all this shopping shit that occupies so much of a woman's time. Because the truth is, women have to buy, own and wear an unbelievably bewildering number of garments:

Take It Off!!!

Slips, half-slips, camisoles, thongs, panties, pantyhose, stockings, half hose, knee-highs, anklets, socks, leg warmers, garter belts, girdles, corsets, training bras, padded bras, sports bras, nursing bras, push-up bras, strapless bras, Wonderbras, bustiers, teddies, petticoats, peignoirs, negligees, nightgowns, shorties, muumuus, body stockings . . .

Top to Bottom

. . . blouses, sweaters, jerseys, pullovers, halter tops, miniskirts, maxiskirts, slacks, suits, sunsuits, business suits, pants suits, culottes, capris, shorts, short shorts, hot pants, formal gowns, bridal gowns, evening gowns, street dresses, sundresses, cocktail dresses, housedresses, housecoats, winter coats, fall coats, spring coats, hats and scarves . . .

Baubles & Bangles

. . . brooches, pins, necklaces, pendants, medallions, lockets, bracelets, ankle bracelets, earrings, wedding rings, engagement rings, friendship rings, thumb rings, toe rings and (optional, of course) nipple, nose and labia rings.

And let's not even begin to talk about shoes. Oh, God! Sorry girls! I take it back. But at least let's keep it brief: tennis shoes, sandals, open-toes, slingbacks, mules, wedgies, flats, half-heels and . . . high heels. High heels that damage a woman's feet, ankles and knees, but make her ass and legs look great, so how can you blame a guy for the occasional rape? "Hey, the bitch was askin' for it, she was wearin' high heels."

Down the Aisle

Now, generally, all this obsession with appearance has one purpose. It's supposed to lead to romance and — it is devoutly wished by some — a wedding. A wedding is another one of those good deals women get: The man "takes a wife," the woman is "given away," her family pays for the whole thing, and everyone stands around hoping she gets pregnant immediately.

Knock Knock!

Pregnant! Hey, another terrific treat for the gals! A chance to gain forty pounds, puke in the morning, walk like a duck, get sore tits and develop a nice case of hemorrhoids. What a deal! And such attractive clothing. Plus, she can't get up off the couch without help. Well, it's her own fault. This wouldn't have happened if she had taken her birth contol pill or used her diaphragm. Notice: her pill, her diaphragm.

And Baby Makes Work

But think of how fulfilling it can be. After all, now she has a baby; a baby she gets to raise practically alone. And if she decides to be a stay-at-home mom, she gets to cook, clean, sew, scrub, scour, wax, wash, dry, iron, do the shopping, drive the van and entertain the guests. She's a housewife! An unpaid, in-family domestic servant. Admittedly, that description is a bit more in line with the old model. The new model is so much better: She "gets a fuckin' job so she can be bringin' somethin' in." But, somehow, she still winds up being an unpaid, in-family domestic servant — after she gets home from the job.

You know, the job? Where she gets paid less than men for the same work, does not rise beyond a certain level in the company and gets harassed all day long by some oversexed moron with a lump in his pants.

Probably better just to stay home where she doesn't have to be bothered with that pesky paycheck crap, and there's none of that nonsense about Social Security, pension plans and unemployment money in case of divorce. Just alimony and child support . . . if the ex-husband can be located. The ex who probably thought she was looking a little used up and dumped her for someone whose milk glands hadn't sagged yet.

Can't forget those milk glands, can we, girls? Tits! Two tits, sticking straight out of your chest; in some cases sticking *straight* out. Well, for a few years, anyway. Yes, girls, just by virtue of being female, you get to walk around all your life with two vulnerable milk glands hanging out in front of you like lanterns. And if, somehow, you should get the idea that men don't approve of the size and shape of those milk glands, you'll find plenty of social pressure to have them artificially "enhanced." Such enhancement usually will be performed and supervised by men.

Here's another physical treat for females: periods! Cramping, bloating and bleeding five days a month. Fifteen percent of the time. And you can add the time spent with premenstrual syndrome. PMS. Men gave it that name. If women had named it, it would be called "My several days of shrieking and crying and depression, just before my several days of bleeding, cramping and bloating." Men don't quite see it from that angle. Men experience PMS as a problem for them. "What's the matter, Joey? You don't look so good." "Ahhhh, my wife's got the PMS."

Here are some more special female advantages in case you haven't had enough: pap smears, mammograms, hysterectomies, mastectomies, miscarriages, abortions, labor pains, childbirth pain, episiotomies, stretch marks and breast-feeding. And postpartum depression. Can't imagine why she wouldn't feel good. And just to top it all off, menopause. Menopause! More strange behavior and exciting physical sensations.

And in exchange for all this, in exchange for all this abuse from nature, what is the woman's payoff? Why, she's allowed to get into the lifeboat first. At least theoretically. How often do you think that really happens?

Oh, and let's not forget, many men are quite willing to hold the door open for her. In fact, some men are quite impressed with their willingness to do this; they brag about it: "Yeah, I beat the shit out of her a lot, but when she runs from one room to the other, I always hold the door open."

I'll tell you what a bad deal women got: They're in the majority on this planet, and they still wound up with the shitty end of the stick. That's how big a hosing they got.

Oh, and one other inequity I neglected to mention; very unequal. But this one works in women's favor: They live longer than men. And remember this happens in spite of all the shit they have to put up with. So who do you think is tougher? Men or women? Why don't you guess. And don't forget, women have the huge added burden of having to put up with men.

Free Breast Examinations

As a public service, the Hell's Angels will be conducting free breast examinations this weekend at their clubhouse behind the Chrome Sprocket Bar. If you prefer privacy, the Bikers' Mobile Breast Patrol will be happy to perform their services in the privacy of your bedroom. Pelvic examinations and pap tests are also available but usually take a little longer.

It's a Female Problem

Beside a dusty road, in the open air, a physically repulsive man dressed in filthy doctor clothes stands at a rusted out examination table wearing a coal miner's hat and heavy work gloves. A woman lies in front of him on the examination table, her legs extending out from under a torn sheet, the ankles resting in stirrups. Nearby, an unattractive "nurse" sits at a desk picking her nose and wiping it on a lamp. Women squat nearby on tree stumps, reading magazines, waiting their turns. Just above this tableau is a large sign reading DISCOUNT ROADSIDE GYNE-COLOGY.

Smooth Flight

I really enjoyed my recent airplane trip to Africa; everything went just perfectly. I had no trouble at all making reservations a month in advance, and I had my tickets in hand, including seat selection, a week before the flight. I even ordered a special vegetarian meal. I left home early the day of the flight and arrived at the airport with several minutes to spare. My friend dropped me off at the curb and left immediately.

My one bag, which was a light one, was easy to carry and did not have to be checked. I was able to take it on board and save time at each end. I walked into the terminal. There was no line at the security area, my carry-on bag passed inspection, and I didn't ring any bells walking through the metal detector. Looking for my gate number on the departures board and spotting it without breaking stride, I headed for Gate 1, the nearest gate. With just a few minutes left until takeoff, I walked the few steps to the gate and boarded the plane.

The seat I had reserved was right next to the window, and the seat next to me was unoccupied; plenty of room to spread out. I was in first class with only three other passengers. The two female flight attendants were pleasant . . . and very attractive. They said my special meal was on board. I had plenty of legroom, and all my seat controls worked perfectly; seat-back tilt, contour button, leg rest, light switch, even the stereo controls.

Everything continued flawlessly. The plane's door was closed exactly on time, and we taxied immediately to the end of the runway. Pausing barely an instant, we began our takeoff roll, which sounded and felt extremely smooth. There was very little vibration; just a steady increase in power and speed as we became airborne and gently glided up. I felt no bumps or strain, and we quickly leveled off to a quiet cruise speed at our assigned altitude. Then the plane went into a steep dive and crashed into the ground, killing all but two of us.

Fortunately, my cosurvivor was a fantastic-looking woman; a registered nurse who had taken survival courses. After a quick check, we realized neither of us was hurt, and then I remembered I still had two joints tucked into my sock. We got high and made love several times. The sex was great for both of us and we promised to see each other often if we somehow managed to get out of there. The only condition on her part was that there be no commitment of any kind between us; she wanted to be independent. I agreed.

After a short time, we found some sandwiches and beer. We ate and drank and laughed for about an hour and then we noticed that a signal-flare gun had landed nearby. We fired off one flare, and, almost immediately, saw a small private plane flying overhead. They spotted us and began to circle. They made a low pass at us, waggling their wings, and then headed off, presumably to get help. Thank God, everything was still going smoothly.

That's when the gorilla showed up.

If Looks Could Kill

I don't think it's right that ugly women should be allowed to get plastic surgery and get fixed up to look real nice. I think if you're born ugly you ought to stay that way. That should be it. It's not right to let people get fixed up. It's creepy to think that you could possibly find yourself fucking some woman you picked up because you thought she was great-looking, but underneath she's really ugly. She got her nose fixed, her lips, her eyes; she got nipped and tucked and liposuctioned, and the surgeon did a good job — he didn't overdo it — and now she looks really great. But underneath it all, she's horrible-looking and you're actually fucking a pig; someone you wouldn't even ask for change of a dollar if you could see her real face. It's not right. Ugliness should be a permanent condition.

The Continuing Story of Mary & Joseph: "It's a boy"

Mary: Joe, we're gonna have a baby.

Joe: What? That's impossible. All I ever do is put it between your thighs.

Mary: Well, I don't know. Something must've gone wrong.

Joe: Who says you're pregnant?

Mary: An angel appeared to me in the backyard and said so.

Joe: An angel?

Mary: An angel of God. His name was Gabriel. He had a trumpet and he appeared to me in the backyard.

Joe: He what?

Mary: He appeared to me.

Joe: Was he naked?

Mary: No. I think he had on a raincoat. I don't really know. He was glowing so brightly.

Joe: Mary, you're under a lot of stress. Why don't you take a few days off from the shop. The accounts can wait.

Mary: I'm telling you, Joe. This Angel Gabriel said that God wanted me to have his baby.

Joe: Did you ask for some sort of sign?

Mary: Of course I did. He said tomorrow morning I'd start getting sick.

Joe: But why should God want a kid?

Mary: Well, Gabriel said that according to Luke it's kind of an ego thing. Plus, he promised the Jews a long time ago, it's just that he never got around to it. But now that he feels *ready* for children he doesn't want to just make them out of clay or dust. He wants to get humans involved.

Joe: Well, is he going to help toward raising the kid? God knows we can't do it alone. I could use a bigger shop, and maybe he could throw a couple of those nice crucifix contracts my way. The Romans are nailin' up everything that walks.

Mary: Honey, Gabriel said not to worry. The kid would be a real winner. A public speaker and good with miracles.

Joe: Well, that's a relief. Anyway, I guess now that you're officially pregnant I can start puttin' it inside you.

Mary: I'm sorry, honey. God wants it to be strictly a virgin birth.

Joe: I don't get it.

Mary: That's right, Joe.

Joe: Don't I get to do anything?

Mary: He wants you to come up with a
name for the kid.

Joe: Jesus Christ!

Mary: Joe, you're so heavy.

Guys & Dolls, Part 2

Man, Oh Man!

To my way of thinking, men have only one
real problem: other men. That's where all the
trouble starts. A long time ago, men gave
away their power. To other men: princes,
kings, wizards, generals and high priests.
They gave it away, because they believed
what these other men told them. They
bought the okeydoke. The bullshit. Men always buy the okeydoke when it comes from
other men.

Some stranger probably stood up at a
campfire and said, "All right, boys, from
now on, I'm the king. The sun is my father,
the moon is my mother and they're the ones
who tell me when to throw the virgins into
the volcano. I'll be expecting all of you to
bow deeply when you see me, and give me

half your crops. Plus I'm allowed to fuck your wife. And don't forget, if I want to I can concentrate real hard and make your head explode."

And the other men around the campfire nodded their heads and said to one another, "This guy makes a lot of sense." A man will always buy the bullshit, because a man is not too bright.

But I'm not suggesting a man doesn't have a great deal to put up with. He does. First of all, a man has to make believe he knows what he's doing at all times. And while he's doing whatever it is he's doing, he has to make believe he doesn't need any help.

He has to make believe he can fix *anything*. And if he can't fix it now, he'll fix it later. And if he can't fix it later, he has a friend who can fix it, and if not, it was no good to start with, it's not worth fixing, and besides, he knows where he can get something better, much cheaper, but they're all outta them right now, and besides, they're closed. This is the male disease. It's called being full of shit.

The male disease includes the need to be in charge at all times. In charge, in control, in command. A "real man" sees himself as king of the hill, leader of the pack, captain of the ship. But all the while, in order to fit in and belong, he has to act like all the other men and do what they do, so he'll be accepted. And get a good job and a promotion and a raise and a Porsche, and a wife. A wife who will immediately trade in the Porsche on a nice, sensible Dodge van with folding seats so they can be like all the other boring families. The poor fuck. The poor stupid fuck.

His manliness also requires that he refuse to go to a doctor or a hospital unless it can be demonstrated to him that he has, in fact, been clinically dead for six months. "No sense goin' to the hospital, honey, I don't seem to be in a coma." Therefore, he must learn to ignore pain. "It doesn't really hurt. Bleeding from six holes in the head doesn't really hurt. Just gimme the remote and get me a beer. And get the fuck outta here."

Most men learn this stupid shit from their fathers. Fathers teach their sons not to cry. "Don't let me hear you cryin' or I'll come up there and give you something to cry about!" Great stuff, hah? All the problems in the world — repeat, *all* the problems in the world — can be traced to what fathers do to their sons.

So, little boys learn to hide their feelings,

and society likes that because, that way, when they get to be eighteen, they'll be able to go overseas and kill strangers without feeling anything. And of course, that bargain includes a certain reluctant willingness to have their balls shot off: "Honey, I have to go overseas and have my balls shot off, or else the rest of the guys will think I'm too afraid to go overseas and have my balls shot off." The poor fucks. The poor stupid fucks.

And so, as a result of all this repression of feelings, the extent of the average man's emotional expression is the high five. Or sometimes, when really deep feelings emerge, both hands. The high ten. This is raw emotion. And that's about all they're capable of. And they have Dad to thank. Thanks, Dad.

But wait! Don't think dads can't be fun at times, too. After all, dads introduce their sons to the Wonderful World of Men — the male subcultures. The really tough-guy, masculine, he-man stuff. No wimps, no pussies, no softies.

There are five deadly male subcultures and they all overlap: the car and machinery culture, the police and military culture, the outdoors and gun culture, the sports and competition culture and the drug and alcohol culture. And, as a bonus, I'm gonna throw in one more: the "Let's go get some pussy and beat the shit outta queers" culture. As I say, they all overlap. Many men belong to all six.

This male universe is, of course, detectable by analyzing its combustible chemical formula: gasoline, gunpowder, alcohol and adrenaline. A chemistry rendered even more lethal by that ever-present, ever-delightful accelerant: testosterone. Talk about substance abuse! If it's chemical dependency you're interested in, you might want to look into testosterone. TESS-TAHSS-TER-OWN!! — the most lethal substance on earth. And it does not come from a laboratory, it comes from the scrotum; a scrotum located, interestingly enough, not far from the asshole. How fitting.

And, as it happens, all these male subcultures share a particular set of features: homophobia, coupled with an oddly ironic, complete, childlike trust in male authority. Men are attracted to powerful men. They also share a strong fear and dislike of women. This in spite of a pathological obsession with pussy. TESS-TAHSS-TER-OWN!!

So why are men like this? I think the overriding problem for men is that in life's main event, reproduction, they're left out; women do all the work. What do men contribute? Generally, they're just looking for a quick parking space for some sperm. A couple of hits of hot jism, and the volume on the TV goes right back up. It's my belief that most of these flawed male chromosomes should not be allowed to go forward for even one more unfortunate generation. But such is biology.

And so, excluded as they are from reproduction, men must find other ways to feel useful and worthwhile. As a result, they measure themselves by the size of their guns, the size of their cars, the size of their dicks and the size of their wallets. All contests that no man can win consistently.

And let me tell you why all this happened. Because women are the source of all human life. The first human being came from the belly of a female. And all human fetuses begin as females. The brain itself is basically female until hormones act on it to make it structurally male.

So, in reality, all men are modified females. Where do you think those nipples came from, guys? You're an afterthought. Maybe that's what's bothering you. Is that what's on your mind, Bunkie? That would explain the hostility: Women got the good job, men got the shitty one. Females create life, males end it. War, crime and violence are primarily male franchises. Man-shit.

It's nature's supreme joke. Deep in the womb, men start out as the good thing and wind up as the crappy thing. Not all men, just enough. Just enough to fuck things up. And the dumbest part of it all is that not only do men accept all this shit . . . they do it to themselves.

By the way, I'm not letting women completely off the hook. After all, the one part of the lower anatomy that is the same in both sexes is the asshole. But women who are assholes aren't called that. They're named for a different part of their lower anatomy. They're called cunts. Isn't it nice that cunts and assholes are next-door neighbors?

Ninety-Nine Things You Need to Know

There are ninety-nine things you need to know:

Number one: There are more than ninety-nine things you need to know.

Number two: Nobody knows how many things there are to know.

Number three: It's more than three.

Number four: There is no way of knowing how many things you need to know.

Number five: Some of the things you need to know are things you already know.

Number six: Some of the things you need to know are things you only think you know.

Number seven: Some of the things you need to know are things you used to know and then forgot.

Number eight: Some of the things you need to know are things you only *thought* you forgot and actually still know.

Number nine: Some of the things you

need to know are things
you know but don't really
know you know.

Number ten: Some of the things you need
to know are things you don't
yet know you need to know.

Number eleven: Some of the things you
think you need to know
are things you probably
don't really need to
know.

Number twelve: Some of the things you
need to know are things
known only by people
you don't know.

Number thirteen: Some of the things you
need to know are things
nobody knows.

Number fourteen: Some of the things you
need to know are
things that are un-
knowable.

Number fifteen: Some of the things you
need to know are things

that can only be imag-
ined.

Number sixteen: At any time the list of
things you need to know
can be abruptly sus-
pended.

Now you know.

Euphemisms: Shell Shock to PTSD

Earlier in the book, in the first section on this
subject of euphemistic language, I mentioned several reasons we seem to employ so
much of it: the need to avoid unpleasant real-
ities; the need to make things sound more important than they really are; marketing
demands; pretentiousness; boosting employee self-esteem; and, in some cases, just
plain, old political correctness.

But no matter their purpose, the one
thing euphemisms all have in common is
that they soften the language. They portray
reality as less vivid. And I've noticed Americans have a problem with reality; they prefer

to avoid the truth and not look it in the eye. I think it's one of the consequences of being fat and prosperous and too comfortable. So, naturally, as time has passed, and we've grown fatter and more prosperous, the problem has gotten worse. Here's a good example:

There's a condition in combat — most people know it by now. It occurs when a soldier's nervous system has reached the breaking point. In World War I, it was called *shell shock*. Simple, honest, direct language. Two syllables. Shell shock. Almost sounds like the guns themselves. Shell shock!!

That was 1917. A generation passed. Then, during the Second World War, the very same combat condition was called *battle fatigue*. Four syllables now. It takes a little longer to say, stretches it out. The words don't seem to hurt as much. And *fatigue* is a softer word than *shock*. Shell shock. Battle fatigue. The condition was being euphemized.

More time passed and we got to Korea, 1950. By that time, Madison Avenue had learned well how to manipulate the language, and the same condition became *operational exhaustion*. It had been stretched out to eight syllables. It took longer to say, so the impact was reduced, and the humanity was completely squeezed out of the term. It was now absolutely sterile: operational exhaustion. It sounded like something that might happen to your car.

And then, finally, we got to Vietnam. Given the dishonesty surrounding that war, I guess it's not surprising that, at the time, the very same condition was renamed *post-traumatic stress disorder.* It was still eight syllables, but a hyphen had been added, and, at last, the pain had been completely buried under psycho-jargon. Post-traumatic stress disorder.

I'd be willing to bet anything that if we'd still been calling it *shell shock,* some of those Vietnam veterans might have received the attention they needed, at the time they needed it. But it didn't happen, and I'm convinced one of the reasons was that softer language we now prefer: The New Language. The language that takes the life out of life. More to come.

Elegy for "Millennium"

You don't hear the word *millennium* much anymore, do you? It's kind of sad. Here's a word that lies around for long periods of time looking for work, but never really doing very much. Then, every thousand years, things suddenly pick up and there's a flurry of activity. The word is on everyone's lips, and is heard in almost every conversation. It stays red-hot for several years, enjoying its popularity — seeing its name in newspapers and magazines, making appearances on radio and TV. But then a peak is reached, and, after a while, things begin to slow down. The activity tapers off, and before long, it's once again relegated to history books, academic journals and reference works. Goodbye, poor *millennium*. I'm going to miss you. When you return, I may not be here to welcome you back.

Who, Me? Hate?

I saw two bumper stickers on a car: HATE IS NOT A FAMILY VALUE and VALUE ALL FAMILIES. What is the purpose of having things like this on your car? Certainly it's not to change someone else's opinion of family life at a red light. More likely, the purpose is to inform us that the driver doesn't hate anyone, and that he considers himself pure and virtuous and better than the rest of us. So it's actually self-righteousness. The driver apparently forgot that the seven deadly sins include both anger *and* pride.

Jacko Beats Them All

I don't care if Michael Jackson freaked off with little boys or not. It doesn't bother me. Fuck those kids. And fuck their greedy parents too. What's important to me is that Michael is the greatest entertainer who ever lived. Bar none. Watch him dance; pay attention to the showmanship. No one ever came close.

Elvis was a bogus white guy with sex appeal and good looks who ripped off a lot of great black music, watered it down, and made it safe for lame whites who couldn't handle the experience of raw, emotional black music. Never grew as an artist; remained an entertainer. Fuck Elvis.

Sammy Davis Jr.? Nice try. Ordinary dancer, ordinary singer, second-rate impressionist. I also didn't like the insincere sincerity. But he was a nice man, personally; I give him credit for that.

Frank Sinatra? Great singer of songs, among the best. Superb musician. Grew as an artist. No showmanship, though. Arrogant, too. And mean to ordinary people. Fuck him.

Michael Jackson buries them all. I say give him a bunch of kids and let him dance.

Let's Get Real, Here

I've decided to cash in on TV's reality-show trend. I have several ideas, but they may need some work before I approach the networks. Here's what I'm working on:

Island Cuisine

This idea grew out of *Survivor*, but I have a new twist: You put twelve people on a barren island, and you let them starve to death. You make sure they get no food, but you provide plenty of fresh drinking water — you don't want them to die of thirst, you want them to starve to death.

That would be entertaining enough, but here's the fun. You make sure half the contestants are large, aggressive, physically fit individuals, and the other half are small, mild-mannered and physically weak. Then you wait them out and see who survives — and, more fun, you watch how they do it. The show is called *Guess Who's for Dinner*. The only part I haven't decided yet is whether to provide utensils.

Gettin' High and Havin' Fun

Here's another idea I think has a good shot: *Maniac on Drugs*. Each week you put a different homicidal maniac in a van filled with assault rifles and you provide him with large amounts of speed, crack, acid and PCP. Then you let him drive around New York City for several days, and you videotape everything he does. Naturally, you clear all this with the police, so they don't interfere with the smooth flow of the show. At the end of thirteen weeks, you take all the psychos, give them a fresh supply of drugs and turn them loose at Disney World with rocket-propelled grenades. Actually, now that I think about it, this idea is too good for the networks; I'm gonna put it on pay-per-view.

Here's a variation for the finale, in case the Disney people get squeamish. You give the maniacs the same drugs, but instead of grenade launchers, you go back to the assault rifles. Everything's the same, but this time you put them on an ordinary, nonstop passenger train from New York to Los Angeles. You strap video cameras to their heads and let them run loose on the train, allowing them to befriend the other passengers. Remember, it's nonstop, no one can get off. I guarantee you'd get some really great footage. By the way, to save a little money, this could also be done on a Greyhound bus. But you'd need a really good driver who isn't easily distracted.

Guys' Night Out

Here's the one I'm proudest of because it took the most thought. I call it *Lucky Bachelor.*

Our chosen guy is selected from letters sent in to the show. In step one, the lucky bachelor is sent out on three separate occasions to pick up women in cheap bars and bring each of them to a hotel where he tries to fuck them. If they go along easily, he then convinces them to commit a perverted act involving a floor lamp, a woodpecker and a box of rubber bands — an act most people would consider completely depraved. All this activity is videotaped.

In step two, we stop three men at random on the street, show them the videos and ask them which of the women the lucky bachelor should marry. That woman is called the designated bride. We then ask the two losing women to vote on which one of the three random street guys looks like the best fuck. That guy is called the designated, best-fuck street guy.

In step three, we take the two losing street guys and the two losing bar girls and feed them near-fatal doses of aphrodisiacs, put them in thong bathing suits and turn them loose in an adult sex shop with unlimited credit. This footage, strictly an added feature, could possibly be some of the liveliest on the show.

Now, the alert reader is probably wondering what happened to our original lucky bachelor. Well, in step four we arrange for him and the designated best-fuck street guy to stage a bare-knuckle fistfight — to the death — in the center aisle of St. Peter's in Rome during a papal high mass. The two men must keep fighting until one of them dies; it's important to the show. As a side feature, we keep a camera trained on the pope, and every time he falls asleep during the fight, we give the guys an extra hundred dollars.

The reason it's important that one of the two men dies is because the next day, in the same church, we're going to hold step five: a combination wedding and funeral. The loser of the fight gets the funeral, the winner gets to marry the designated hotel-fuck bride, with the remaining, losing bar and hotel participants serving as bridesmaids and pallbearers. We then give the newly-weds all the leftover drugs from *Maniac on Drugs* and send them on a honeymoon to some nice, conservative golfing resort on Hilton Head Island, where they are required to take large amounts of drugs and two weeks of golf and tennis lessons.

Looks Aren't Everything

This next one is a makeover show. My working title is *Try Looking Like That For a Change!* You start by picking three incredibly beautiful, successful supermodels and then, against their wills, you sedate them, strap them down and subject them to extensive plastic surgery. You give them big, misshapen noses; sagging eye-bags; and plenty of wrinkles and drooping skin on their faces. Then you pump enough fat into their asses, hips and thighs to make them really unhappy. When they come out of the anesthesia, the audience yells, "Try Looking Like That For a Change!" I'm so excited about this one that I'm working on a variation that involves involuntary sex-change surgery.

Wrap-Up

Well, that's about it. I suppose all that's left would be for me to tell you about a show called *Bowel Movement.* Basically, it's a show that involves a fixed-position camera, a toilet and a series of guys with diets organized primarily around beer and extra-spicy Mexican food. Perhaps it's better if I don't go into too much detail at this time. And you know something? This one might actually belong on cable.

That's it, folks. I've done all I can to develop a hit show. But the creative process can only go so far; the rest is up to you, the public, and I'm counting on your good taste.

We Just Wanna Watch

First, let me say that most people take these so-called tragedies like Columbine and Oklahoma City far too seriously. You have to remember, it's all part of the American way of life. If you live in America you have to go along with these things. You can't be sitting around whining, "Ohh, a lot of people got killed." These things happen, folks. People get killed.

But concerning the guys (it's always men) who commit these mass killings — and other less dramatic murders for that matter: After the sentence of death is passed, you will usually see the whining families of the "victims" insist on watching the execution up close, through a little window. They want to see the guy die. Don't these people know there's nothing to see? It's uneventful. An attendant gives the guy an injection; it's like watching someone get a flu shot. There's nothing to see. But they often get their wish and are allowed to witness what's little more than a medical procedure.

Now, my feeling is, if you're going to let people watch some guy get executed, it would make much more sense to put on a little show for these ghouls. Entertain them.

Place the guy in a small steel room and send in four or five of these sadistic prison guards with steel pipes and let them beat the guy to death. For about an hour. A constant, uninterrupted, sixty-minute clubbing would seem far more in keeping with our national values.

And, of course, this method would be much more satisfying to the families of these so-called victims; these fine, upstanding religious families who believe in a merciful God. They'd enjoy watching these psychotic, animalistic prison guards doing what comes naturally — administering a nice, brutal clubbing. Prison guards who, by the way, dare I say, are also all fine, upstanding religious people as well. Folks, if you're gonna do these things, don't settle for halfway measures. Do them right. Do them the Christian way.

Keep America Clean

As a public service, next weekend Boy Scouts will be picking up litter and trash from America's highways and dumping it in America's rivers. If you'd like to pitch in and help the Boy Scouts, bring some of your own trash from home and throw it out the window of your car as you drive along your favorite road. You'll be doing your part to keep the highways clean. By the way, if you have any ideas about cleaning up the rivers, let us know.

Get the Fuck Oot

I'm tired of these Canadians who have worked in the American news media for years and still haven't learned to pronounce the words *out* and *about*. Peter Jennings is one of them, and there are about three or four more. These people need to be taught that it's *OUT* and *uh-BOUT,* not *OOT* and *uh-BOOT.* I say if you can't learn the language, it's aboot time you got the fuck oot of here. Besides, Canadians are just disguised English people, and it's a well-known fact that all English people deserve to die.

Uncle Sam Wants You

Things I wonder about the FBI's list of the "Ten Most Wanted" criminals: When they catch a guy and he comes off the list, does number eleven automatically move up? And does he see it as a promotion? Does he call his criminal friends and say, "I made it, Bruno. I'm finally on the list"?

How about when a new, really dangerous guy comes along and they absolutely have to put him at the top of the list without delay? (Call it "Number one with a bullet," if you wish.) Doesn't everyone else have to move down a notch? And doesn't one guy get dropped off? How do they decide which guy to drop? Is it automatically number ten? And how does he feel about that? Does he feel slighted? Does he feel maybe it should've been someone else? Has anyone who was demoted ever killed the new guy to gain his spot back?

One last question: Does the FBI search harder for number three than they do for number seven? I would. Otherwise why have the numbers at all? These are the kinds of thoughts that keep me from making any real progress in life.

Too Many People

There are too many people. Period. There have *always* been too many people. From the beginning. If these diaper-sniffing Christian babymongers would stop having so many of these cross-eyed little kids, maybe the rest of us would have a chance to spread out and have a little fun. Excess children waste our natural resources. If this society wants me to conserve energy, it had better get some of these child-worshipping religious fanatics to stop having five, six or seven babies. When they do that, I'll start turning off the lights. And yes, I know the fertility rate is down. Good. It should go down even further. Every family should be allowed half a child. If that.

An L.A. Street Problem

Who are all these guys in their twenties, out on the streets skateboarding at two and three in the afternoon? Get off the streets and find work, motherfucker! And by the way, I'm not talking about X Games guys who are really good at it; that's different, that's a way of life. I'm talking about these skateboard fucks who look like they're actually *going* somewhere. As if the skateboard were a means of transportation. What the fuck's the deal with these guys?

Same with these Rollerblading and

scooter fucks. Why are these fully grown men out on the street, playing with children's toys during working hours? And wearing helmets, for chrissakes! Jesus, I would be so embarrassed to wear a helmet. Grow up, motherfucker. And, while you're at it, stay out of the range of my car; I might just decide to run some consumer tests on those helmets. I might also decide to clear the streets of all nonessential traffic. So get a job or play on the sidewalk with the rest of the kids.

Bits and Pieces

- I'm starting to get more compassionate. I gotta watch that.

- Children's Hospital in New York is quite an amazing place. On a recent visit, I saw two seven-year-olds performing a kidney transplant.

- Be careful whom you befriend. They will eventually ask you for something.

- When she was getting fucked by Roy Rogers, do you think Dale Evans ever screamed, "Giddyup, Roy"?

- Here's a dead-end business: a shoeshine stand at the beach.

- Mexico has a new holiday known as the "Name-Calling Fiesta." People dress up in colorful costumes and do a series of folk dances while they call each other "cocksucker" and "motherfucker." Then they all get drunk and eat a big meal.

- Michael Jackson missed his calling. If he

had become a Catholic priest, he could've spent thirty or forty years blowing all the little boys he wanted, and no one would have said a word.

- *Hard work* is a misleading term. Physical effort and long hours do not constitute hard work. Hard work is when someone pays you to do something you'd rather not be doing. Anytime you'd rather be doing something other than the thing you're doing, you're doing hard work.

- Cosmologists are just now beginning to accept the possibility that the big bang was actually caused by a huge explosion in a meth lab.

- "Hello. I'm Howard Finely, and I'm running for state's attorney general. This is my pledge to you: If I am elected, and someone breaks the law, I will personally go to his house and beat the shit out of him. Thank you."

- Why does it always take longer to get somewhere than it does to come back?

- What's with these recumbent bicycles? Listen, buddy, if you wanna take a nap, lie down. If you wanna ride a bike, buy a fuckin' bicycle.

- I prefer people with imagination: dictators, serial killers, schizophrenics, assassins, skinheads, drug lords, violent bikers, devil worshippers. To me, these are the interesting people. To get its edge back, I think what America really needs is more evil. Intense, unalloyed, concentrated evil.

- I was reading a fitness magazine that had an article about cross-training, and I realized this would have been a good idea for Jesus.

- People who see life as anything more than pure entertainment are missing the point.

- The future ain't what it used to be.

- Wouldn't it be fun if, all at once, everybody just forgot everything they knew?

- These professional child-worshippers say we should put the needs of children first. Why? What about the needs of adults? We come second? It's stupid. If you put the needs of children first, you're going to wind up with way too many diapers and lollipops and not nearly enough bongs and condoms.

- WHAT HAPPENED? Washington, Jefferson, Franklin, Madison, Adams, Hamilton. Things were going well. Then Ford, Quayle, Mondale, Agnew, Nixon, Clinton, Dole, Bush I, Bush II. What happened?

- This morning I had a great idea, but it was too late to put it into the book. I just wanted you to know this is where it would have gone.

  TRUE FACT: A radio commercial says that a certain diet pill works three times faster than starvation. Question: Are they guessing, or did they really run these tests?

- Here's something you can't do by yourself: practice shaking hands.

- Stop in today at Anne Bennington's Quality Cyst Removal. Regular cysts, five dollars. Really big, difficult cysts, a dollar a pound. Anne Bennington's:

Cyst removal for the discerning.

- THE OPTIMIST: "I have no friends, no family, no money, no food, no job, no credit, no luck, no hope and no future. However, I do have matches, toothpicks, chewing gum, paper clips, rubber bands, shoelaces and Scotch Tape. Maybe things aren't so bad."

- Am I the only one who thinks the Muppets weren't funny?

- If you have twins, a good idea is to sell one of them. What the hell, you've got two, why not pick up a few dollars?

- When child abuser Father John Geoghan was killed in prison, he was sixty-eight years old. If a psychic had attended his ordination forty years earlier and told his parents, "When John is sixty-eight, he will be strangled to death in prison while serving time for touching children's penises," at the very least there would have been a small commotion.

TRUE FACT: There is now a gay softball World Series.

- A children's museum sounds like a good idea, but I would imagine it's not easy to breathe inside those little glass cases.

- Why is it the only time you ever hear the word *figment* it's in relation to the imagination? Aren't there any other kinds of figments?

- If everyone in the world sat quietly at the same time, closed their eyes and concentrated as hard as they could on peace and goodwill, all the killing and cruelty in the world would continue. And probably increase.

- You know what you never see? A Korean guy with freckles and a big hook nose.

- I wonder when we pick up the telephone, does each of us get his own individual dial tone, or is there just one systemwide, master dial tone that each of us jumps on and off when we need it? These things eat at me.

- If a safe is unlocked, is it still a safe?

- Here's an optical illusion you can try at home. Take a pencil and make a small black dot in the middle of an ordinary piece of paper. Cover your left eye and stare at the dot from a distance of about two inches. You will see the Battle of Chancellorsville. If you don't, check the paper. Or maybe you made the dot wrong.

- Just because you don't have a lot of money to spend is no reason you shouldn't spend what little you have.

- A good promotional idea for a singles bar would be to have "Date-rape Friday." Drinks half-price, free GHB, free Plan-B pills, free RU-486 morning-after pills, free rape counseling and generous rebate coupons for an abortion clinic. That takes care of attracting the men; I'm still working on how to get some women to show up.

- I had no shoes, and I felt sorry for myself until I met a man with no feet. I took his shoes. Now I feel better.

- You know what would have been a smart thing to do in these developing countries that need electricity? To have tried large-scale experiments with alternative energy sources: solar, wind, geothermal, etc. We could have tested and tried to perfect these technologies on a large scale in places that need it. That would have been smart. That's why we didn't do it.

- You know what you never see? A really good-looking homeless couple.

- I've always wondered if the Library of Congress provides books in their public toilets to promote reading. I should think they wouldn't want to pass up a captive audience like that.

- A GENERIC JOKE: A person goes into a place and says something to another person. The second person says something back to the first person, who listens to that and then says something back to the second person. The thing he says back is really funny.

- Stick around. China's gonna win it all.

  TRUE FACT: In Moscow there's a professional entertainer who is described as a Hitler impersonator. Show biz.

- Get one now! Everybody has one!

They're almost gone! New, super-deluxe, jumbo, handy, portable, lightweight, convenient, collapsible, prewrapped, easy to use, guaranteed, available in all sizes in designer colors. Get one now! Won't rust tarnish, blister, crack or peel, but it will cause tumors.

Keepin' It Real in the Air

Off We Go, Into the Wild Blue Yonder

I think the safety instructions that airline flight attendants deliver before departure could be greatly improved if they were simply a bit more honest and complete. They should include graphic descriptions — accompanied by animated and live-action video — of the devastating physical damage done to the human body during a crash. They should cite examples of various anatomical mutilations. They should also include a detailed description of the damage done to the lungs and skin by fire and smoke inhalation, to demonstrate that surviving the impact of the crash alone is not always sufficient. People deserve the truth.

Then, how about a more relaxed, breezy pre-flight announcement made in the cadences of young people: "Hi. Listen, we'll be leaving soon? Then we're gonna fly a while and get there possibly this afternoon? Okay? Later on, we'll chow down, have some brews and maybe catch a movie? Okay? And hey, try not to ring your bell a lot and wake us up . . . unless something really scary is going on. Okay? Thanks. Oh, and by the way, the captain says do that thing with the belts."

Leveling Off

"Ladies and gentlemen, we're leveling off at our cruising altitude. That means the cockpit crew will soon be lighting up and enjoying a few hits of something really nice we picked up in Hawaii. After about six hits, they're gonna turn off the autopilot, take their hands off the controls and let the plane do what it wants for a couple of minutes. The captain suggests you keep your seat belts fastened unless you have a strong appetite for blunt trauma."

"The captain has just turned on the fasten-seat-belt sign. He didn't mean to, but the joint he was smoking fell in his lap, and when he jumped up, his head hit the switch."

"The captain has turned off the seat-belt sign. But he cautions you to stay alert, as sometimes these planes don't work as well as we'd like them to."

"The captain has just turned the seat-belt

sign on again. Of course, he also just stuffed a pound of walnuts up his nose, one by one, so you can decide for yourselves what you want to do about the belts."

Still Cruisin' Along

A socially responsible pilot: "On your right, you will see Las Vegas, where millions of visitors are fleeced out of their hard-earned money each year by huge, impersonal hotels originally built by brutal, criminal syndicates and now owned by brutal, criminal corporations. These large, impersonal hotels have no concern for service or quality, but merely wish to generate more gambling activity, because the advantage is heavily weighted toward the house. Whores and drugs are available at all hours."

A poetic pilot: "Off to your right you'll see the Colorado River as it snakes its way carefully through the ancient, multicolored walls of the Grand Canyon, echoing mutely the dreams and disappointments of countless generations of red-skinned people who inhabited the Great Southwest."

An interesting pilot: "There's the house

where John Gacy lived. If you look carefully, in his backyard you can see the top of the chute where he dropped the bodies of the twenty-six children he killed. Over on the right, we'll soon be coming up to the gas station where Ted Bundy picked up his twenty-third victim. Altogether, he is thought to have killed between thirty-six and fifty young women, almost all of whom parted their hair in the middle."

A political pilot: "Most of the farms you see used to belong to small farmers. But their land has been brutally repossessed by the greedy, grasping bankers, only to be bought up by huge agribusiness corporations who poison the land and produce tasteless food. These corporations receive billions of dollars a year from the taxpayers for no good reason except to enhance their wealth."

Pilot with the blues: "Ladies and gentlemen, I've been feeling kind of depressed lately, and I think you'll agree, we all share guilt for the world's suffering and deteriorating condition. Sometimes I ask myself, 'Is it all worthwhile?' Quite often, I give up hope completely and try to think of interesting ways of killing myself that would get my name on television." (Sounds of a struggle in the cockpit)

Comin' Down

"Ladies and gentlemen, we have just begun our gradual descent into the Indianapolis area, a descent similar in many ways to the gradual slide of the United States from a first-class world leader to an aggressive, third-rate debtor nation of overweight slobs, undereducated slob children and aimless elderly people who can't afford to buy medicine. The current conditions in Indianapolis: Temperature sixty-one degrees, partly cloudy skies, winds from the southwest and intense Midwestern boredom."

Tired of the Handi-Crap

Now, listen, I gotta tell you somethin' and I'm not gonna sugarcoat this because it is what it is. But boy, oh boy, am I gettin' tired of this handicapped business. Aren't you? Hah? Don't you think this handicapped shit has gone far enough?

And I'm like you, folks; normally I would feel sympathy for these people. But the first thing they tell you is that they don't want sympathy. You ever hear 'em say that? "I don't want your sympathy." And I say, fine, fuck you. No sympathy.

And by the way, if there are any handi-capped people reading this, I'm not talking about you, all right? I'm talking about the other handicapped people, the ones who'll never see this book. So don't get all excited and start rolling around causing trouble in your electric go-cart or whatever the fuck it is. Calm down. I'm on your side.

I Need My Space

And just to show you my heart's in the right place, I'm gonna start out by mentioning a few of the positive things about the handi-capped, okay? First of all, the big blue parking spaces. This was a great idea. I think most people would agree, those spaces come in mighty handy (which is where the word "handy-capped" came from in the first place — a lot of people don't know that). They're always right near the entrance to the store or the building, and I find that I can get in and out of the place in a hurry and complete my business with a minimum of delay.

Stalling Around

Another handicapped feature I enjoy are the extra-large toilet stalls in public restrooms; once again, an excellent idea. There's so much room in there to spread out; it's like a gymnasium. I can do some pushups, work on my kickboxing, try out a few dance steps. Occasionally I bring a picnic lunch. Nothing fancy; just a small salad, a bit of cheese, perhaps a delicate Bordeaux.

I find that once you're locked in there, you can pretty much do what you want. About the only limitations might be common decency and a sensible regard for personal safety. One time, I had a few friends over and we played cards all night. The good thing was when one of the players had to take a shit, he didn't have to drop out of the game for several hands. He simply traded places with the person who was using the toilet as a chair and it worked out great.

I mention all this because I want you to know I recognize some of the positive things that have grown out of this unfortunate obsession America has with the handicapped.

They're Easily Board

But on this subject I also have a few complaints to make, the main one being this business at the airport of letting the handicapped get on the plane early. I don't like the idea of people boarding ahead of me just because they've had a run of bad luck. It doesn't seem fair. I think if a person's had some bad luck, it should apply across the board to all segments of his life. We shouldn't be going around trying to selectively fix people's bad luck.

And what bothers me most about the process is, I'm not sure all these people are truly handicapped; some of them don't look that fucked up. I think there's a fairly hefty amount of bullshitting going on at the check-in counter.

Rollin', Rollin', Rollin'

The whole fiasco begins just before the flight, with the parade of wheelchairs. And apparently, just about anyone can get their hands on one of those airport wheelchairs. You know the ones I mean? The ones the airlines provide? Not a wheelchair some guy brings from home; I don't mind that. I figure if a guy's laid out money for his own wheelchair, he's probably legitimately fucked up. And I don't mind a guy gettin' ahead of me if he's legitimately fucked up. You know? Like if a huge chunk of his head is missing, or he's got a whole caved-in chest and two or three of his limbs don't work. Generally, in a case like that, I'm gonna give the guy the benefit of the doubt. I say roll his ass down the jetway and let's get the fuck outta town.

But, to me, some of these airline-wheel-chair people don't look that fucked up; they just look old — and my guess is they're lazy.

A lot of old people are lazy, because somehow when they hit their 80s or 90s, they think it's time to take it easy. Old people aren't "spry" and "full of ginger" anymore. Now they're all just lazy. And frankly, I think they're just tryin' to get a free ride to the gate.

Raising Canes

But let's get back to the actual process of boarding. As soon as the wheelchair derby is over the next thing you have to contend with is these people who show up with canes and crutches; what I call the quasi-handicapped. And even though I'm willing to cut the wheelchair people some slack, I'm not so easy on the cane folks. I'm convinced most of these jokers with canes don't really need them.

And once again it's the old people, tryin' to gain sympathy and get to the front of the line. It's obviously a scam; have you noticed, for instance, how suddenly these canes materialize? Out of nowhere? One minute everyone at the gate looks perfectly healthy, the next minute half of 'em have a limp. And before you know it there are twenty or thirty people leanin' on canes. I'm convinced that somewhere in the airport (which has now become a large mall with airplanes as a side attraction) there must be a little place where you can rent canes. "Canes for Planes."

But you know something? I'm not that upset. Not really. Because the best part about these "handicapped" people gettin' on the plane first is that they have to get off last. Fuck 'em, they always get off last. While they're still lookin' for their carry-on bags and rectal thermometers, I'm halfway into town. You see? Life has a way of evening things out.

Euphemisms: The March of Time

At we resume our look at the advance of euphemisms, we have to keep a close eye on the image-makers: advertisers, marketers, public-relations people. And to repeat an earlier point, it's important to remember that, over time, this trend toward softer language has only gotten worse.

It All Got Different

I don't know when the whole thing started, but I do know that at some point in my life, *toilet paper* became *bathroom tissue*. I wasn't consulted on this. I didn't get a postcard, I didn't get an e-mail, no one bothered to call. It just happened. One day, I simply found myself using bathroom tissue.

And then, just as my *loafers* were becoming *slip-ons*, my *sneakers* turned into *running shoes*, and in no time, my running *shoes* became *athletic footwear*. It was about then that a trip to the department store revealed that my lazy-slob uniform of *sweatpants* and *sweatshirt* were now located in a section called *Activewear*.

The world was changing. I saw *second-hand clothing* referred to as *vintage apparel;* I saw *toupees* advertised as *hair appliances,* in keeping, I would imagine, with the *dental appliances* that had long since replaced *false teeth*.

Ya Gotta Have a System

Of course, if you didn't want to wear a *hairpiece* or a *rug* (nice old-fashioned term), you could always look around for a good, reliable *hair-replacement system*. Keep an eye out for *systems,* folks, they're everywhere. The clerk who sold me my *answering machine* said I was purchasing a *voice-processing system;* a *mattress and box-spring set* is now called a *sleep system;* and the people who sell *mops* have not been resting. According to a commercial I saw recently, the Clorox ReadyMop is now America's favorite *mopping system*.

And if you think you can escape these systems by going for a drive, forget it; your car has been systematically (get it?) infiltrated, too. The *heater and air conditioner* became the *climate-control system,* your *brakes* have been replaced by a *braking system,* and *your seat belts and air bags* are now known as the *impact-mangement system.* You can't beat the system.

Marketers will always strive to make things sound more impressive than they really are; that's why *dashboards* became *instrument panels.* But how's this for laying it on thick? A magazine ad recently informed me that the cars depicted were equipped with leather *seating-surfaces.* When you get right down to it, you have to admit, marketing people have a ton of balls.

That's Entertainment

The upgrading continued: At home, I found myself watching *animation* instead of *cartoons.* And it turns out, all those TV shows I'd seen before were not really *reruns,* they were *encore presentations.* At about that time I noticed *soap operas* had begun billing themselves as *daytime dramas.*

Theaters felt overdue for an upgrade, too, so they became *performing arts centers,* or sometimes *performance spaces* — in keeping with the spirit of certain *nightclubs* who now speak of themselves as *party spaces.* (The really hip just call them *spaces*.) While all this was happening in smaller locations, the big arenas decided they wanted to be known as *events centers*.

Center is another word that's become important. Hospitals have long thought of themselves as *medical centers,* but now libraries have joined the chorus, calling themselves *learning resources centers*. And just to wrap this section up — and returning to show business for a moment — no matter what size the place where entertainment was being presented, at some point it was decided they would all just be called *venues*.

Systems, facilities, spaces, centers and venues: They're all words to keep an eye on in today's atmosphere of increasing self-importance.

You Want More Changes?

Profits became *earnings, personnel* became *human resources,* the *complaint department* became *customer relations*. People started offering *feedback* instead of *criticism; car sickness* turned into *motion discomfort; messengers* became *couriers; junk mail* morphed into *direct marketing; special delivery* was suddenly *pri-*

ority mail; and after all these years, I picked up the phone and discovered *information* was identifying itself as *directory assistance.* I don't even want to mention my dismay at the fact that every old-fashioned, shady *used-car* dealer in a plaid jacket was suddenly selling *certified pre-owned vehicles.*

By this time, the *dump* had become the *landfill.* I guess it was inevitable; the *garbagemen* who fill it had long since become *sanitation engineers,* and in some cities, *garbage collection* was going by the fancy (and misleading) name *environmental services.*

The changes even got me where I lived. According to the Census Bureau, my *apartment* had become a *dwelling unit,* and when I asked my *janitor* to put a *peephole* in the door, I discovered later that actually the *custodial engineer* had installed an *observation port.*

Change of pace: One day, a *bucktoothed* girl told me she had *overbite.* That was the day I traded in my *glasses* for *prescription eyewear.*

Of course, some of these language upgrades are more widespread than others; admittedly, they're not all universal. For instance, we still have *motels,* but some of them wanted to charge a little more, so they became *motor lodges.* We also still have *house trailers,* but if they're for sale and profits are involved, they become *motor homes, mobile homes, modular homes* or *manufactured housing.*

So apparently, what we thought all this time was a *trailer park* is actually a *manufactured-home community.* I guess the lesson is we never quite know what we're dealing with. Could it be that all these years on the *Jerry Springer* show we've actually been watching manufactured-home-community trash?

I Have a Drug (Store) Problem

I guess you've noticed a trip to the drugstore has changed a lot too; the products have all been transformed. To start with, the *medicine* I used to take is now called *medication.* (I have a hunch medication costs more than medicine.) *Mouthwashes* are *dental rinses, deodorants* have been joined on the shelf by *antiperspirants* (probably because *sweat* has become *nervous wetness*), a plain old bar of *soap* these days is being described variously as a *bath bar,* a *cleansing bar* and a *clarifying bar.* Can you imagine a mother saying, "Young man, if I hear that word out of you one more time, I'm going to wash your mouth out with a *clarifying bar*"? Doesn't sound right, does it?

The hair people have taken liberties, too: *hair spray* — too ordinary. Try *holding mist.* Of course, if you don't want holding mist, you can always turn to *shaping mousse* or *sculpting gel.* Anything to get you to pay a little more. *Cough drops* have grown up and turned into *throat lozenges,* some even calling themselves *pastilles* or *troches.* Guess what? Right! Two dollars more for lozenges, pastilles and troches.

I can remember, in television's early years, when *constipation* was called *occasional irregularity.* These days, in a kind of minor, reverse-euphemism trend, we're back to constipation, which parallels the recent TV comeback made by *diarrhea.* No more *lower gastric distress.* Diarrhea! "Gotta go, gotta go, gotta go, gotta go!" The new TV candor. (Even though you still can't say *shit.*) By the way, doctors used to claim that constipation could be relieved by eating more *roughage;* now they're pushing *fiber.* I still prefer roughage. If I want fiber, I eat a basket.

And hey, lady! Advancing age causing *vaginal friction?* Tell the pharmacist you have a *personal dryness problem.* I'm sure he has some sort of *intimate feminine-lubricating solution* to recommend. That's the way they describe crotch products now. Even a good old-fashioned *douche* has turned into a *feminine wash*. And remember *feminine hygiene sprays?* Personally, they didn't sound very tasty to me. If they had come in flavors they might have been more successful. Vagin-illa, crotch-ocolate, labia-lime. Just a thought. Anyway, the latest female product I've heard of is *protective underwear,* which, frankly, folks, I don't even want to think about. More later.

Tips for Serial Killers

Because I enjoy following the exploits of serial killers, I'm always hoping they never get caught. So I've compiled a list of suggestions to help them stay on the loose longer; that way they can provide me with maximum entertainment.

TO THE KILLERS: If you're looking for some form of perverted attention and publicity I can't help you. But if you just want to kill a lot of people, one by one, I'm your guy: Here's how you can maximize the time it will take the police to apprehend you.

- Make sure your victims are not all the same types. Kill a variety of people: tall, short, rich, poor, male, female, young, old. But don't kill them in any particular order. Do two old men in a row, then do a young woman, then a teenage boy. Mix blondes and brunettes and long hair and short. And don't bother with prostitutes.

- Vary the types of locations where you grab your victims and vary the times of day.

- Try to do the work in heavily populated areas where there are more murders to begin with.

- If at all possible, travel around the country and kill each victim in a different state. Never kill two people in the same city within a year. And don't travel in a straight line. Randomness is your greatest ally.

- Kill each of your victims in a completely different manner: Do some really weird ones, and then do some ordinary ones. Sexual, non-sexual; ritual, non-ritual. Don't specialize. Patterns are your enemy.

- Dispose of the bodies as far from the murder sites as possible, always at least a hundred miles. Bury some, burn some and dissolve others in lime and acid. If you encounter any chance witnesses to any part of the killings or the disposals, they should be killed and disposed of with a minimum of fuss. And be sure to dispose of them separately.

- When driving to the murder or especially the disposal sites, be careful not to break the law or have an accident. Use cash for everything. Don't stay in motels. Drive a late-model van-type vehicle you can sleep in, and don't park it where police might be expected to patrol. Have a large food supply and eat in the vehicle. If possible, change vehicles after every murder.

- Don't write notes to the police or taunt them in any way. It's dumb.

- Don't save newspaper clippings. In fact, don't even read the newspaper accounts.

- Don't keep souvenirs from any of the victims.

- Start watching the *CSI* shows on CBS and the *Law & Order* shows on NBC. Every now and then you will pick up some piece of information that will help you avoid mistakes.

Be smart and stay alive. Some of us are counting on you.

Wall Street Journal: Subscribe Now

The *Wall Street Journal* reminds you that your job as a businessman is to fuck the other guy before he fucks you. Sometimes you have to do such a complete job of fucking the other guy that he stays fucked for a long time, even to the point of going out of business and losing everything he owns. Quite often, the difference between getting fucked and being the one who does the fucking can be one small piece of business information, such as they're not making steam locomotives anymore, or the zeppelin travel market has begun to decline. Those two important business facts appeared recently in the *Wall Street Journal*. If you're a reptilian lowlife on your way up, stop getting fucked and start doing the fucking. Read the *Wall Street Journal*.

Crippled, Ugly and Stupid

In an earlier book, *Brain Droppings*, I wrote some things about politically correct language, but left out a few areas. I neglected three important groups of people who have had this awkward, dishonest language inflicted on them by liberals: I omitted those who are crippled, ugly or stupid. And so, to address these earlier omissions, I'd like to make a brief return visit to that playground of guilty white liberals: political correctness.

Political correctness is America's newest form of intolerance, and it is especially pernicious because it comes disguised as tolerance. It presents itself as fairness, yet attempts to restrict and control people's language with strict codes and rigid rules. I'm not sure that's the way to fight discrimination. I'm not sure silencing people or forcing them to alter their speech is the best method for solving problems that go much deeper than speech.

Therefore, those among you who are more politically sensitive than the rest of us may wish to take a moment here to tighten up those sphincter muscles, because I'm going to inject a little realism into the dream world of politically correct speech. Especially the words we use to describe one another.

Crippled Liberals

Perhaps you've noticed that when the politically correct, liberal rule-makers decide to rename a group of humans they view as victims, they begin by imparting a sense of shame to the group's existing name. And so, somewhere over the years, the word *cripple* has been discarded. No one mentions cripples anymore. That's because, in yet another stunning attempt to stand reality on its head, cripples have been assigned a new designation, the *physically challenged*. The use of *physically challenged* is an obvious attempt to make people feel better, the idea being, "As long as we can't cure these people, let's give their condition a more positive name, and maybe it will distract everyone." It's verbal sleight of hand.

The same is true of the ungainly phrase *differently abled*. I believe that if a person is going to insist on using tortured language such as differently abled, then he should be forced to use it to describe everyone. We're all differently abled. You can do things I can't do, I can do things you can't do. Barry Bonds can't play the cello, Yo-Yo Ma can't hit the curveball. They're differently abled.

It should be explained to liberals — patiently — that crippled people don't require some heroic designation; it's a perfectly honorable condition. It appears in the Bible: "Jesus healed the cripples." He didn't engage in rehabilitative strategies to improve the conditions of the physically disadvantaged. Can't these liberals hear how unattractive this language is? How poorly it sits on the ear? Personally, I prefer plain, descriptive language.

For instance — and this is a suggestion that will bother some, but I'm serious about it — why don't we just call handicapped people *defective?* We don't mind talking about birth defects; we don't flinch from that. We say, "Gunther has a birth defect." Isn't that a concession to the fact that people can be defective? Then what would be wrong with calling those people the *physically defective?* At what point in life does a person with a birth defect become a person who is differently abled? And why does it happen? I'm confused.

Ugly Language

Then there are those who don't quite measure up to society's accepted standards of physical attractiveness. The worst of that group are called ugly. Or at least they used to be. The P.C. lingo cops have been working on this, too.

And to demonstrate how far all this politically correct, evasive language has gone, some psychologists are actually now referring to ugly people as "those with severe appearance deficits." Okay? Severe appearance deficits. So tell me, psychologist, how well does that sort of language qualify for "being in denial"? These allegedly well-intentioned people have strayed so far from reality that it will not be a surprise for me to someday hear a rape victim referred to as an *unwilling sperm recipient*.

Back to ugly. Regarding people's appearance, the political-language police already have in place one comically distorted term: *lookism*. They say that when you judge a person, or rather, size them up (wouldn't want to judge someone; that would be judgmental) if you take their looks into account, you're guilty of lookism. You're a *lookist*.

And those valiant people who fight

lookism (many of them unattractive themselves) tell us that one problem is that in our society, those who get to be called beautiful and those who are called ugly are determined by standards arbitrarily set by us. Somehow, there is some fault attached to the idea that we, the people, are the ones who set the standards of beauty. Well, we're the ones who have to look at one another, so why shouldn't we be the ones who set the standards? I'm confused. I would say the whole thing was stupid, but that's my next topic, and it would sound like a cheap transition.

Stupid People

So, stupid. It's important to face one thing about stupidity: We can't get away from it. It's all around us. It doesn't take a team of professional investigators to discover that there are stupid people in the world. Their presence (and its effects) speaks for itself.

But where do these stupid people come from? Well, they come from American schools. But while they're attending these schools, they're never identified as stupid. That comes later, when they grow up. When they're kids, you can't call them stupid. Which may be contributing to the problem. Unfortunately, kids, stupid or otherwise, come under a sort of protective umbrella we've established that prevents them from being exposed to the real world until, at eighteen, their parents spring them on the rest of us, full grown.

There are stupid kids. And I do wish to be careful here how I negotiate the minefield of the *learning disabled* and the *developmentally disadvantaged* — in other words, "those with *special needs.*" (All of these being more examples of this tiresome and ridiculous language.) I just want to talk about kids who are stupid; not the ones with dings.

One of the terms now used to describe these stupid kids is *minimally exceptional.* Can you handle that? Minimally exceptional? Whatever happened to the old, reliable explanation, "The boy is slow"? Was that so bad? Really? "The boy is slow. Some of the other children are quick; they think quickly. Not this boy. He's slow." It seems humane enough to me. But no. He's minimally exceptional.

How would you like to be told that about your child? "He's minimally exceptional." "Oh, thank God for that! We thought he was just kind of, I don't know, slow. But minimally exceptional! Wow! Wait'll I tell our friends."

Political correctness cripples discourse, creates ugly language and is generally stupid.

I haven't quite finished this section. (I'm sure I needn't remind you P.C. people that "The opera isn't concluded until the *full-figured woman* offers her vocal rendering.") I know. I really had to strain to get that in. I'm thoroughly ashamed.

But before I leave this section, I wanted to make the point that, on a practical level, this language renders completely useless at least one perfectly good expression: "In the kingdom of the blind, the one-eyed man is king" becomes "In the kingdom of the visually impaired, the partially-sighted person is fully empowered." Sad, isn't it?

Location Location Location

I've noticed that when people speak these days, location seems important to them; and one location in particular: *there*. They say such things as *don't go there; been there, done that;* and *you were never there for me*.

They don't say much about *here*. If they

do mention here, they usually say, *"I'm outta here."* Which is really an indirect way of mentioning there, because, if they're outta here, then they must be going there, even though they were specifically warned not to. It seems to me that here and there present an important problem because, when you get right down to it, those are the only two places we have. Which, of course, is really neither here nor there.

So, let's first talk about don't go there. As we all know — painfully, by now — when you mention something someone thinks you shouldn't go into any further, they say, "Don't go there." What they fail to realize, of course, is that, technically, by the time they've told you not to go there, it's too late. You're already there, because you've already mentioned whatever it is they're uncomfortable with. At a time like that, what they should be saying is, "Don't stay there." Or, at the very least, "Please hurry back." Sort of like "Wish you were here."

The only time I would tell someone "Don't go there" is if they told me they were planning a trip to Iraq. If someone said, "We're going on our honeymoon to Fallujah," I would immediately say, "Don't go there."

By the way, when one of those TV

newsmen on MSNBC recently tried to get his co-anchor lady to react to some juicy celebrity rumor, she said to him, "I am *so* not going there." And I thought, "Why am I allowing a person like this to bring me the news?"

Being and Doing

Another phrase I don't care for is *been there, done that.* I, personally, am not so cocky. I prefer the modest approach. Instead of "Been there, done that," I will usually say, "Been nearby, done something similar." And by the way, most people don't seem to know the complete expression. I heard Drew Barrymore say it on *The Tonight Show*: "Been there, done that, got the T-shirt." It's a little smarter and it hasn't been overused yet.

Where Were You?

Staying with this subject of location, when someone is ending a long-term relationship, quite often they'll tell the other party, "You were never there for me." Here, again, what they may be forgetting is that possibly at some time in the past they had told that very same person, "Don't go there." So how can they blame the person for not being there when they themselves had issued specific instructions not to go there in the first place? It seems unfair.

So Move!

Additionally, many people who are ending relationships use another bothersome phrase: *moving on.* They'll say, "I found Steve in bed with a carnival worker and they were doing unpleasant things to a chipmunk. So I'm moving on." And I think to myself, "Actually, Steve sounds more like the one who's moving on."

Or they might say, "I'm leaving Armando. He beat me up yesterday in the frozen-food section of the supermarket. He struck me in the head repeatedly with a Stouffer's Lean Cuisine. I believe it was the Chicken Cordon Bleu. I'm moving on." Occasionally, I get impatient with these people. When they tell me they're moving on, I look at my watch and say, "Well, isn't it about time you got started? No sense standing around here, talking to me, when you could be out there . . . moving on."

I don't know, I guess it all works out, because when I run into the same person a few months later, they usually say, "I'm in a *whole different place* now." And I don't think they're referring to Pittsburgh.

Know Your Place

And by the way, speaking of geographic locations, why is San Francisco always said to be in the *Bay Area,* while Saudi Arabia is in the *Gulf Region?* Is a region really bigger than an area? And what about a *belt?* How big is a belt? The *Bible Belt* is bigger than the *Borscht Belt.* Maybe that's because there are more Christians than Jews. But that doesn't explain the *Rust Belt.* In the last several decades, a good deal of the U.S. population has moved from the Rust Belt to the *Sun Belt.* People changed belts. By the way, part of the Sun Belt runs right through the Bible Belt. That must be confusing.

Zoning Out

And let's not forget zones, especially *war zones*. The media like that phrase. If there's any kind of explosion at all, even a small gas heater, they'll say, "The living room looked like a war zone." Most of the time it's an overstatement. Because when you get right down to it, the only thing that looks like a war zone is a *combat area*.

Then there's the opposite of a war zone: a *demilitarized zone*. Korea has one of those, separating the North and South. A demilitarized zone sounds like a good idea, but I've noticed that wherever they have a demilitarized zone, there are always a lot of soldiers nearby. I guess that's in case the demilitarized zone suddenly becomes a combat area.

Now, the Gulf Region has been both a war zone and a combat area. That's because there were some countries who wanted to expand their *spheres of influence*. And also because of the big oil companies, who, of course, are in the *private sector*. The private sector is quite different from the *public arena*. Dick Cheney was in the private sector, then he moved to the public arena. Although many of his acts in the public arena have benefited his interests in the private sector.

Getting back a little closer to my own experience, on a recent visit to my hometown, New York City, I was walking through the area that we used to call the *Garment District*. I noticed that the local trade association now wanted people to call it the *Fashion Center*. Not everyone wanted that, just the ones who would like to raise the rents. Fashion Center is another example of how desperately people feel the need to upgrade themselves; they just want to feel better. They want to expand their *comfort zones.*

Your comfort zone is not the same as your *zone of privacy.* A few years ago, when the press was hounding Congressman Gary Condit about Chandra Levy's disappearance, he asked them to please grant him a *zone of privacy.* But of course, they couldn't do that. Because Gary Condit was in the public arena.

As I wind up our little journey through Location Land, I regret not getting to one other place: *where.* And if you wonder *where I'm going with this,* it's because you don't know *where I'm coming from.* Or maybe you simply don't know *where it's at.* Either way, I'm leaving now. *I need my space.*

Politician Talk #1:

Term Limits

When people mention term limits to me, I usually tell them the only politicians' terms I would like to limit are the ones they use when speaking. They have an annoying language of their own.

And I understand it's necessary for them to speak this way, because I know how important it is that, as they speak, they not inadvertently say something. And according to the politicians themselves, they don't *say* things, they *indicate* them: "As I *indicated* yesterday, and as I *indicated* to the president . . ."

And when they're not *indicating,* they're *suggesting:* "The president has *suggested* to me that as I *indicated* yesterday . . ." Sometimes instead of *indicating* or *suggesting,* they're *outlining* or *pointing things out:* "The president *outlined* his plan to me, and, in doing so, he *pointed out* that he has not yet *determined* his position."

Politicians don't *decide* things, they *determine* them. Or they make *judgments.* That's more serious: "When the hearings conclude, I will make a *judgment.* Or I may simply give you my *assessment*. I don't know yet, I haven't *determined* that. But when I do, I will *advise* the president."

They don't *tell*, they *advise;* they don't *answer*, they *respond;* they don't read, they *review;* they don't *form opinions*, they *determine positions;* and they don't *give advice*, they *make recommendations*. "I *advised* the president that I will not make a *judgment* until he has given me his *assessment*. Thus far, he hasn't *responded*. Once he *responds* to my initiative, I will *review* his *response, determine my position*, and *make my recommendations*."

And so it is, at long last, that after each has *responded* to the other's *initiatives*, and after they have *reviewed* their *responses*, made their *judgments, determined* their *positions* and *offered* their *recommendations*, they begin to approach the terrifying possibility that they now may actually be required to do something.

Of course, that would be far too simple, so rather than *doing something*, they *address the problem:* "We're *addressing the problem*, and we will soon *proceed to take action*."

Those are big activities in Washington: *proceeding* and *taking action*. But you may have noticed that, as they *proceed*, they don't always *take action;* sometimes they simply *move forward. Moving forward* is another one of their big activities.

"We're *moving forward . . . with respect to* Social Security." *With respect to* is lawyer talk; it makes things sound more important and complicated. So they're not *moving forward* on Social Security, they're *moving forward with respect to* Social Security. But at least they're *moving forward.* To help visualize this forward motion, you may wish to picture the blistering pace of the land tortoise.

Now, sometimes when they themselves are not *moving forward,* they're moving something else forward. Namely, *the process:* "We're *moving the process forward* so we can *implement* the provisions of the *initiative.*" *Implement* means *put into effect,* and an *initiative* is similar to a *proposal.* It's not quite a *measure* yet, but there's a possibility it may become a *resolution.*

Now, one may ask, "Why do we need all these *initiatives, proposals, measures* and *resolutions?*" Well, folks, it should be obvious by now: We need them in order to *meet today's challenges.* As I'm sure you've noticed, our country no longer has problems; instead we face *challenges.* We're always facing *challenges.* That's why we need people who can *make the tough decisions.* Tough decisions like: "How

133

much money can I raise in exchange for my integrity, so I can be reelected and continue to *work in government?*"

Of course, no self-respecting politician would ever admit to *working in government;* they prefer to think of themselves as *serving the nation.* This is one of the more grotesque distortions to come out of Washington. They say, *"I'm serving the nation,"* and they characterize their work as *public service.*

To help visualize this service they provide, you may wish to picture the activities that take place on a stud farm.

Politician Talk #2:

Trouble on the Hill

Continuing our review of the language of the elected, it seems that, linguistically, politicians hit their truest stride when they find themselves in trouble. At times like these, the explanations typically begin with a single word: *miscommunication.*

"How do you answer these felony charges, Senator?"

"The whole thing was a *miscommunication.*"

"But what about the tapes?"

"They took them out of context. They twisted my words." Nice touch. A person who routinely spends his time bending and torturing the English language telling us that someone has twisted his words.

But as the problem gets worse, and his troubles increase, he's forced to take his explanation in a new direction. He now tells us that *"The whole thing has been blown out of proportion."* And by the way, have you noticed with these blown-out-of-proportion people that it's always "the whole thing"? Apparently, no one has ever claimed that only a small part of something has been blown out of proportion.

But as time passes and the evidence continues to accumulate, our hero suddenly changes direction and begins using public-relations jujitsu. He says, *"We're trying to get to the bottom of this."* We. Suddenly, he's on the side of the law. *"We're trying to get to the bottom of this, so we can get the facts out to the American people."* Nice. The American people. Always try to throw them in; it makes it sound as if you actually care.

As the stakes continue to rise, our hero now makes a subtle shift and says, *"I'm willing to trust in the fairness of the American people."* Clearly, he's trying to tell us something: that there may just be a little fire causing all the smoke. But notice he's still at the *I-have-nothing-to-hide* stage.

But then, slowly, "I'm willing to trust in the fairness of the American people" progresses to *"There is no credible evidence,"* and before long, we're hearing the very telling, *"No one has proven a thing."*

Now, if things are on track in this drama, and the standard linguistic path of the guilty is being followed faithfully, "No one has proven a thing" will precede the stage when our hero begins to employ that particularly annoying technique: Ask-yourself-questions-and-then-answer-them:

"Did I show poor judgment? Yes. Was there inappropriate behavior? Yes. Do I wish this never happened? Of course. But did I break the law? That's not the issue."

The calendar is marching, however, and it soon becomes clear that our friend is most likely quite guilty, indeed. We know this, because he now shifts into that sublime use of the passive voice: *mistakes were made*. The beauty of mistakes were made is that it doesn't really identify who made them. You're invited to think what you wish. Bad advice? Poor staff work? Voodoo curse?

But it's too late. Mistakes were made quickly becomes *eventually I will be exonerated,* which then morphs into *I have faith in the American judicial system,* and the progression ends with that plaintive cry, *whatever happened to innocent until proven guilty?* Whatever happened to innocent until proven guilty; well, he's about to find out.

Eventually, in full retreat (and federal custody), he shuffles off in his attractive orange jumpsuit, and can be heard muttering that most modern of mea culpas: *"I just want to put this thing behind me and get on with my life."* And to emphasize how sincere he is, he announces, *"I'm taking responsibility for my actions."* How novel! Imagine; taking responsibility. He says it as though it were a recently developed technique.

Whenever I hear that sort of thing on the news, I always want to ask one of these I'm-taking-responsibility-for-my-actions people whether or not they'd be willing to take responsibility for *my* actions. You know, gambling debts, paternity suits, outstanding warrants. Can you help me out here, pal?

Regarding this whole put-this-thing-behind-me idea in general, here's what I'd like to do. I'd like to put this I-want-to-put-this-thing-behind-me-and-get-on-with-my-life thing behind *me* and get on with my *life*. May I repeat that for you? I'd like to put this I-want-to-put-this-thing-behind-me-and-get on-with-my-life thing behind *me* and get on with *my* life.

I think one of the problems in this country is that too many people are screwing things up, committing crimes and then getting on with their lives. What is really needed for public officials who shame themselves is ritual suicide. Hara-kiri. Like those Japanese business executives who mismanage corporations into bankruptcy. Never mind the lawyers and the public relations and the press conferences, get that big knife out of the kitchen drawer and do the right thing.

Politician Talk #3:

Senator Patriot Speaks

To take up a thread from an earlier section of this politico-lingo trilogy, we noted at the time the fact that most politicians operate under the delusion that what they're doing is serving the nation. Of course, if they really feel this way, they're more than simply misinformed, they're obviously not playing with a full bag of jacks.

So, citizens; a question. Do you think it's at all possible that these politicians whose judgment is so faulty that they actually believe they're serving the nation might be expected to indulge occasionally in some, oh, I don't know, exaggerated patriotism? Hah? Whaddya think? Maybe? Hah?

Well, fans, it's not just possible, it's downright inevitable. And should they be so indulging themselves on the Fourth of July, you'll want to be sure to have hip boots and shovels handy, because brown stuff is going to be piling up at an alarming rate. And I suggest you shovel fast, because your elected heroes will be squeezing every last ounce of counterfeit patriotism out of their blood-starved brains.

And so, as you see them rushing madly across the landscape, pushing all the buttons marked red, white and blue, be on the alert for phrases such as *Old Glory; Main Street; the stars and stripes; the heartland; all across this great land of ours; from Maine to California;* and, of course, *on American soil.* And don't forget all those *freedom-loving people around the world who look to us as a beacon of hope.* Those, I assume, would be the ones we haven't bombed lately. And you'd also better be ready to be reminded, over and over, that you live in a country that somehow fancies itself *leader of the free world.* Got that? Leader of the free world. I don't know when we're going to retire that stupid shit, but personally, I've heard it quite long enough.

And what exactly is the free world, anyway? I guess it would depend on what you consider the non-free world. And I can't find a clear definition of that, can you? Where is that? Russia? China? For chrissakes, Russia has a better Mafia than we do now, and China is pirating *Lion King* DVDs and selling dildos on the Internet. They sound pretty free to me.

Here are some more jingoistic variations you need to be on the lookout for: *The greatest nation on Earth; the greatest nation in the history of the world; and the most powerful nation on the face of the Earth.* That last one is usually thrown in just before we bomb a bunch of brown people. Which is every couple of years. And bombing brings me to the language used by politicians when referring to our armed forces.

Now, normally, during peacetime, politicians will refer to members of the military as *our young men and women around the world.* But since we're so rarely at peace for more than six months at a time, during wars Senator Patriot and his colleagues are fully prepared to raise the stakes. (Don't you just love that word, *colleagues?* It makes them sound so . . . I don't know, legitimate.) And so it is, that in times of combat, our young men and women around the world quickly become *our brave young fighting men and women stationed halfway around the world in places whose names they can't pronounce*. And for added emotional impact, they may also mention that these military folks spend a lot of time *wondering if they'll ever see their loved ones again*. That one gets people right in the belly button. And should the speaker be going for maximum emotional effect, he will deliver the above passage, substituting *sons and daughters* for *men and women*.

And isn't that reference "places whose names they can't pronounce" a lovely little piece of subtle racism? That's an all-American, red-meat bonus they throw in for you.

Here's another way politicians express their racist geographic chauvinism: *young men and women stationed in places the average American can't find on a map*. I've always thought it was amusing — and a bit out of character — for a politician to go out of his way to point out the limited amount of intelligence possessed by the American people. Especially since his job security depends on that very same limitation. It would also appear to contradict that other well-traveled and inaccurate standby: *The American people are a lot smarter than they're given credit for.*

Amazingly, politicians have mastered the art of uttering those words with a perfectly straight face, even though the proposition is stated precisely backward. Judging from the results of focus groups, polls and election returns that I've seen, and watching the advertising directed at Americans, I'd say the American people are a lot *dumber* than they're given credit for. As one example, just look at the individuals they keep sending to their statehouses and to Washington to represent them. Look also at what they've done to their once-beautiful country and its landscape.

Wrapping up this modest review of patriotic political language, I think it's safe to conclude that the degree of a politician's insincerity can best be measured by how far around the world our soldiers are, and whether or not any of them is able to pronounce the name of the place. And whether or not their neighbors back home can find it on a map.

Zero Tolerance

I get weary of this zero tolerance bullshit. It's annoying. To begin with, it's a fascist concept; it's what Hitler and Stalin practiced. It allows for no exceptions or compassion of any kind. All is black and white — no gradations. But even more important, it doesn't solve anything. The use of such a slogan simply allows whichever company, school or municipality is using it to claim they're doing something about a problem when, in fact, nothing is being done at all and the problem is being ignored. It's a cosmetic non-solution designed to impress simpletons. Whenever you hear the phrase zero tolerance, remember, someone is bullshitting you.

Dempsey's Department Store: Drop In Today

Shoppers! For a limited time only, Dempsey's Department Store is offering a complete line of cheap crap at extremely high prices. Come in today and be treated rudely by our poorly trained clerks. Remember, at Dempsey's we're not just talking about the high cost of living, we're doing something about it: We're raising our prices.

Enjoy a Pleasant Diurnal Experience

I'm not sure you've noticed it, but I'm always trying to improve society. And in my relentless pursuit, I feel the time may finally have arrived for me to address "Have a nice day." I think we can agree it has gotten completely out of hand.

Just to give you some background on my long-standing interest in this subject, when I was a young man we didn't have "Have a nice day." It isn't that we didn't have nice days, of course — offhand I can remember several, most of them in 1949 — but somehow, we had them without any prompting. No coaching was necessary. The nice days just sort of happened. Perhaps at that time the days were simply nicer, and we took them for granted. It could be that today's days leave much to be desired and actually need a little help. But if that's true,

I'm not convinced that "Have a nice day" is the best solution.

And so, in my ongoing effort to elevate human experience, I think I have come up with an improved version of "Have a nice day." It's an alternative system of well-wishing, and frankly, something I hope will become the next big trend.

But before I tell you about it, it's important to remind you that there is a limiting factor at work here: Most people have very little control over what sort of day they're going to have. For instance, when one person says, "Have a nice day," the other may well be thinking, "I've just been diagnosed with hypertrophic cardiomyopathy, and I'm also coughing up thick black stuff." In this case the well-wisher's words will fall on deaf ears.

And so, I feel that perhaps, in the interest of realism, instead of being directed arbitrarily to have a nice day, people should simply be encouraged to do the best they can.

It is also probably unrealistic to expect someone to have a nice day all day long. How often does that happen? The day is simply too long and comprises too many parts. One's day may start off well enough, but quite often the niceness is difficult to sustain over an extended period of time.

And so, instead of the now standard, and far too general, "Have a nice day," I have devised a new, more specific system of selective, short-term well-wishing that puts much less pressure on the recipient. In my system, the time of day a person offers good wishes determines what should be said.

As an example, under my method, if I run into an acquaintance at 9 a.m., I'm likely to say, "Have a satisfying midmorning." I believe in getting someone off to a good start, and it's a modest enough goal to suggest at such an early hour. Had the encounter taken place a bit earlier, I may have been inclined to offer a simple, yet cheerful, "Here's wishing you a refreshing post-sleep phase."

And, turning the clock back even further, if the two of us had been out late and parted at three in the morning, I'm sure I would have told him to "Have yourself a stimulating pre-dawn." As you can see, I'm fully prepared for any time of day.

Twelve noon, you ask? "May your midday be crammed with unfettered joy and myriad delights." Two in the afternoon? "I hope you experience a rewarding post-lunch."

Likewise as the day draws to a close. Can you guess what I tell a person at five-thirty in the afternoon? "Enjoy your sundown."

It's short, it's pleasant, it doesn't demand a lot. Here's one for the same time of day which I reserve for more serious-minded friends: "Have a profound dusk." I like it. I feel it shows a certain respect for the other fellow's depth of soul. Or — and this is a particular favorite of mine — "Have a challenging twilight." I enjoy giving the other person something to struggle with just as happy hour is getting under way.

By the way, I have a playful side as well. If my friend is a Scottish person I may say, "Have a bonnie gloaming." But not too often; I don't like to show off my command of foreign languages.

Well, folks, I hope you've enjoyed this little explanation of my new system, but more important, I hope you'll put it to work in your daily lives. And so now, dear reader, as we prepare to take our leave, you may be tempted to think I'll be hard-pressed to offer a parting wish that hasn't already been suggested. Don't underestimate me.

You see, I'm not limited to the short form. Occasionally, in an expansive mood, I get carried away and my rhetoric becomes ornate. And so, as we part, let me state that I hope you have a memorable tomorrow, including, but not limited to, the promising, golden hours of morning, the full, rich bloom of afternoon, and, of course, the quiet, gentle hours of evening, when time, pausing for an instant and breathing a small sigh, rushes forward to greet the newly forming day.

I hope you appreciate the extra effort.

Let's Kill a Tree for the Kids

Regarding public Christmas displays: At some point, someone who worked at Rockefeller Center must have said, "Boys, I have a great idea for Christmas. Let's kill a beautiful tree that's been alive for seventy-five years and bring it to New York City. We'll stand it up in Rockefeller Plaza and conceal its natural beauty by hanging shiny, repulsive, man-made objects on it, and let it stand there slowly dying for several weeks while simple-minded children stare at it and people from Des Moines take pictures of it. That way, perhaps we can add our own special, obscene imprint to Christmas in Midtown."

A Sore Point

Regarding the criticism of Al Gore's actions upon being elected president in 2000 and realizing that the Bush family would do everything in its power to reverse the results illegally: I recall at the time hearing some of the usual morons in this country refer to President-elect Gore as a sore loser because he sought legal redress in the courts.

Sore loser? You bet your fuckin' ass! What on earth is wrong with being a sore loser? It shows you cared about whatever the contest was in the first place. Fuck losing graciously — that's for chumps. And losers, by the way.

Americans have just flat-out lost their spirit; you see it everywhere. Have you ever watched these hockey assholes? When the game is over, they're forced to line up and shake hands with one another after spending three hours smashing each other in the mouth with sticks. Biggest load of shit I ever witnessed. Whatever happened to "In victory, magnanimity; in defeat, defiance." So said Frederick the Great.

Euphemisms: Write If You Get Work

Marx My Words

These days, people who have jobs are called *members of the workforce*. But I can't help thinking the Russian Revolution would have been a lot less fun if the Communists had been running through the streets yelling, "Members of the workforces of the world, unite!"

And I'm sure Marx and Lenin would not be pleased to know that, today, employees who refuse to work no longer go out on strikes. They *engage in job actions* that result in *work stoppages*. And if a work stoppage lasts long enough, the company doesn't hire *scabs*, it brings in *replacement workers*.

Ready, Aim, Non-Retain!

When it comes to firing people, companies try desperately to depersonalize the process so that no human being is ever seen to fire another. The language is extremely neutral, and whatever blame there is goes to something called *global market forces.* Fuckin' foreigners!

And these companies go through some truly exotic verbal gymnastics to describe what's taking place — although I'm not sure it makes the individuals in question feel any better. After all, being *fired, released* or *terminated* would seem a lot easier to accept than being *non-retained, dehired* or *selected out.*

Nor would I be thrilled to be told that, because the company was *downsizing, rightsizing* or *scaling down,* I was part of an *involuntary force-reduction.* I really don't care that my company is *reshaping* and *streamlining,* and that, in order to *manage staff resources,* a *focused reduction* is taking place, and I'm one of the workers being *transitioned out.* Just fire me, please!

I read somewhere that apparently one company's senior management didn't understand the fuss about this issue. After all, they said, all they were doing was *eliminating the company's employment security policy* by *engaging in a deselection process* in order to *reduce duplication.*

P.S. By the way, when those deselected people begin to look for new jobs, they won't have to be bothered reading the *want ads.* Those listings are now called *employment opportunities.* Makes you feel a lot better, doesn't it?

Euphemisms:

What Do You Do for a Living?

American companies now put a great deal of effort into boosting their employees' self-esteem by handing out inflated job titles. Most likely, they think it also helps compensate for the longer hours, unpaid overtime and stagnant wages that have become standard. It doesn't.

However, such titles do allow an ordinary *store clerk* to tell some girl he's picking up at a bar that he's a *product specialist.* Or a *retail consultant.* If it turns out she's a store clerk, too, but her store uses different euphemisms, then she may be able to inform him that she's a *sales counsellor.* Or a *customer service associate.* And, for a while there, they're under the impression that they actually have different jobs.

These are real job titles, currently in use to describe employees whose work essentially consists of telling customers, "We're all out of medium." Nothing wrong with that, but it's called store clerk, not retail consultant, and not customer service associate. Apparently, stores feel they can charge more for merchandise sold by a customer service associate than they can for the same junk sold by a clerk. By the way, if a clerk should be unhappy with his title, he can always move to a different store, where he may have a chance of being called a *product service representative*, a *sales representative* or a *sales associate*.

And I hope you took note of that word *associate*. That's a hot word with companies now. I saw a fast-food employee mopping the floor at an In-N-Out Burger and — I swear this is true — his name tag said "associate." Okay? It's the truth. Apparently, instead of money, they now give out these bogus titles.

At another fast-food place, Au Bon Pain, I noticed the *cashier's* name tag said *hospitality representative*. The cashier. The name tag was pinned to her *uniform*. The people who sell these uniforms now refer to them as *career apparel*. Or — even worse — *team wear*. I had to sit down when I heard that. Team wear.

Teams are also big in business; almost as big as associates. In Los Angeles's KooKooRoo restaurants the employee name tags say "team member." At a Whole Foods supermarket, I talked to the head of the meat department about ordering a special item; I figured he was the *head butcher*. But his name tag identified him as the *meat team leader*. Throw that on your résumé. I guess the people under him would have been *meat team associates*. I didn't stick around to ask.

So it's all about employee morale. And in a lot of companies, as part of morale-building, the *employees* are called *staff*. But it's all right, because most *customers* are now called *clients*. With those designations, I guess the companies can pay the staff less and charge the clients more.

I'm not sure when all this job-title inflation began, but it's been building for a while. At some point in the past thirty years *secretaries* became *personal assistants* or *executive assistants*. Many of them now consider those terms too common, so they call themselves *administrative aides*.

Everyone wants to sound more important these days:

Teachers became *educators*,
drummers became *percussionists*,
movie directors became *filmmakers*,
company presidents became *chief executive officers*,

family doctors became *primary-care providers,*

manicurists became *nail technicians,*

magazine photographers became *photojournalists,*

weightlifters became *bodybuilders*

and *bounty hunters* now prefer to be called *recovery agents*

And speaking of lifting, those *retail-store security people* who keep an eye on shoplifters are known as *loss-prevention managers.* Still more to come. Later.

Schmuck School: Call Now!

Why not be a schmuck? A licensed, practicing schmuck. Or, if you qualify, a CPS, a certified public schmuck. It may not seem like it when you look around, but there's actually a shortage of schmucks in America. As a result, there's big money in schmucking. The average schmuck earns $28,000 a year, plus benefits. And there are openings for schmucks in every field: The government is run by schmucks; big business is run by schmucks; and the retail field is crawling with schmucks. And, more and more, people are becoming independent, freelance schmucks on their own. Call the Schmuck Technical Institute today and get our free booklet, *Hey Putz, Be a Schmuck!* Most people only manage to be schmucks at parties, but here's your chance to become a full-time, year-round schmuck. Give us a call. Don't be a schmuck, be a schmuck.

In the Future:

- The human life span will be extended to 200 years, but the last 150 will be spent in unremitting pain and sadness.

- No one will take drugs, but people will still buy them and conceal them from the police.

- Children will be required to attend school only when something comes up in conversation they do not understand.

- All people will speak the same language, but no one will speak it well.

- Science will develop exotic flowers capable of producing music. Most of these plants will be exploited by record companies.

- All farming will cease and the land will be used for loitering.

- Although people will not keep pets of any kind, someone will still occasionally step in dogshit.

- A race of people living in the center of the Earth will be discovered when one of them comes out to buy a sunlamp.

- Miners will exploit the ocean floor, and, when trapped in a mine, the wives who gather to wait at the entrance will be forced to tread water.

- A team of astronauts will attempt to harness a comet and never be seen again.

- The human body will develop fins and gills, and beach property will increase tenfold in value.

- Man will learn to control the weather with a large hammer.

- A time machine will be built, but no one will have time to use it.

- At birth, religions will charge people an initial fee of $50,000 and then pretty much leave them alone.

- All the knowledge in the world will be contained on a single, tiny silicon chip which someone will misplace.

- People will be born with just enough money to last until they get seriously ill.

- The speed of the Earth's rotation will increase and everyone less than five feet tall will be flung off into space, including Paul Anka.

- The sun's light will diminish until it is the equivalent of a forty-watt bulb, and people with highly developed squinting skills will have a survival advantage.

- Every part of the human body will become replaceable, but all parts will be back-ordered six months.

- A utopian society ruled by women will emerge, and there will be peace and plenty for all. However, many men will still act like macho assholes.

- People will change clothes every six minutes but still never be quite happy with their appearance.

- Cities will be built under huge glass domes which, in time, will be completely covered by graffiti.

- Chickens will operate on gasoline and, surprisingly, many of them will get good mileage.

- Genetic scientists will develop vegetables too big to be transported and they will have to be eaten right at the farm.

- The insane will no longer be housed in asylums; instead, they will be displayed in department store windows.

- The oceans will dry up, and people will find things they dropped in the toilet many years ago.

- There will be no doctors or medicines of any kind and everyone will be really sick.

- Eventually, it will no longer be necessary to forecast the future, because time will disappear and everything will happen at once.

Dig This!

Whenever we go into some country we've bombed, burned and occupied, we always find mass graves full of dead people who were killed by the deposed dictator before we got there. And everybody in the United States acts like they're real surprised and disgusted. But when you think about it, what's a guy supposed to do with all those bodies after he's killed a couple of thousand people? Dig a separate hole for each one? Put up little markers with their names on them? Get real, for chrissakes. The whole idea of killing a couple of thousand people all at once, in one place, is to save time. Besides, all the United States ever does is complain a little, take a picture and then leave. So what's the fuckin' difference?

Fall Down, Go Boom!

You know what I find interesting? Land mines. Here are a few great statistics. Listen to this:

There are 340 different types of land mines made by a hundred different companies. Every day — that's every day — roughly six thousand fresh mines are placed in the ground. Right now, there are 110 million land mines in seventy-two countries; and every twenty-two minutes, one of them explodes. Seventy-five mines explode every day, and each month seven hundred people are maimed or killed. That's twenty-six thousand people a year. Don't you find that interesting?

Mines cost only three dollars to make and to put in the ground. But they cost a hundred dollars to disarm and remove. If you tried to remove them all, it would cost $33 billion and it would take eleven hundred years. They cost three dollars apiece, and they last indefinitely. Wouldn't it be nice if other products could make that claim?

Here's another funny statistic: In Cambodia, one out of every 236 civilians is missing a limb or an eye from an exploded land mine. Cambodia now has thirty thousand people with at least one missing limb. And they still have 4 million mines in the ground.

It makes you wonder whether or not some unlucky, one-legged Cambodian guy has ever stepped on a land mine with his good leg. I'll bet it's happened. I'll bet anything there's some guy in Cambodia who has hit the lottery twice.

I tried to think of what would be the most entertaining way of setting off a land mine, and I decided it would be to land on one while doing a cartwheel. Wouldn't that be weird to see? Makes you wonder if the high-school cheerleading squads in Cambodia keep mine detectors handy.

These are the kinds of thoughts I have when I'm sitting home alone and things are slow.

Be a Doctor: Act Now!

Be a doctor in just three weeks! Yes, thanks to our accelerated learning program, you can be a doctor in just three weeks — and you only have to study twenty minutes a day. Or become a dentist in just one afternoon. Don't like your present job? Don't fit into the current job market? Be a doctor. Or a dentist. It's easy. Call now and we'll include a nursing course for your wife. In fact, we can make your wife a nurse over the phone. Call Accelerated Medical School now! Don't be an asshole. Be a doctor.

Who Knows?

A: "I don't know. Or at least I don't know if I know. And I don't even know if I care to know if I know."

B: "I don't know what you mean."

A: "You know, I mean I don't *know* what I mean. You know what I mean?"

B: "What do you mean you don't know what you mean? I don't know what you mean."

A: "I mean, you know, I don't know."

B: "You don't know? You mean that?"

A: "I don't know."

A Continuing News Story All in One Place

Chicago, May 1: Police announced today

they have found evidence of a murder-dismemberment. In a North Side Dumpster, they have found a right arm, a left leg and the eyebrows of an adult white male. Police say the eyebrows are bushy and had recently been plucked. According to spokesmen, the search for additional body parts will continue.

May 6: Here is further news on that North Side dismemberment. Police have now found a set of blond sideburns, a lower lip, two matching buttocks, a middle finger, a knee and two and a half grams of armpit hair. As yet they have no identification, but sources say they're glad that at least it's still only one person they appear to be finding.

May 12: More on the dismemberment story: The police theory that they were dealing with only one body was shattered today when they discovered forty-four male nipples in a vending machine. Twenty-six of the nipples have hair, eighteen do not. One of them has a nipple ring inscribed LONNIE AND MARIE. They have also come across a belly button, a calf and several hundred warts, all found in a Hooters parking lot. Lint from the belly button leads police to believe the navel's owner was wearing a plaid shirt. The investigation continues.

May 23: Here is the latest from the North

Side: Police are now puzzled as to just how many bodies are involved. Today they found an Adam's apple, a hunchback, six heels, a pair of un-matching nostrils, a large bag of freckles, two dozen additional belly buttons, a blond goatee, half a neck, and a suitcase full of knuckles. They say all the knuckles have recently been cracked. Cannibalism may be involved, as police have found a rib cage that shows traces of barbecue sauce. More later.

Letter To a Friend

Dear Manny,

It was great to see you at the hospital last Sunday. You looked good and sounded very positive about yourself. Each time I visit, I can see how much you've improved. I will say, though, it was a lot more fun when you were really fucked up and couldn't remember anything.

Sincerely, Arlo

Krellingford's Restaurant:

Cooking Tips

Here are today's cooking tips from Krellingford's Family Restaurant: Hamburger meat that has become slightly hardened by sitting at room temperature for more than nine days can be perked up by soaking it in a mixture of gasoline and varnish remover. Soak the meat overnight and leave it in the sun for several days. Be sure to add a lot of extra-hot spices to offset the gasoline taste. Then try to put the meat to use immediately. By the way, food prepared this way should never be cooked over an open flame.

Here's another valuable cooking tip: You can prepare a delicious stew with just a volleyball, an old fatigue hat and six gallons of bathwater. Put the ingredients in a big pot and cook for thirty-six hours, or until the volleyball is tender. Serves twelve. Excellent with broccoli or corn. Try it over the holidays when the people you serve it to are people you don't see too often.

That's it, folks. Remember, these cooking tips are brought to you by Krellingford's, the home of the Ham and Cheese Caramel Corn Flake Surprise. Why not drop by and take a chance? No one lives forever.

Uncle d'Artagnan

Uncle d'Artagnan was known as a fancy dan, because he circumcised himself with pinking shears. His wife, Velveeta, the only woman ever to go down on Newt Gingrich, claimed that to the very end, d'Artagnan wore a golden tassel on his penis. He once told me that as a young man he caught the clap from one of the Doublemint twins and gave it to the other on the same night. He was a lot of fun. He could make his cat shit by pointing the TV remote at it and pressing the VOLUME button. His hobby was falling to the floor in hotel lobbies and pretending to have a stroke. Eventually, he was beaten to death with a cello by a classical musician he befriended at a juice bar.

Uncle Tonto

Uncle Tonto had a tough life; intercourse with a pelican is not an easy thing to live down. He drank excessively. One time he was so hungover he had to consult a cottage cheese carton to determine the approximate date. At parties, he was the designated drinker, his preference being crème de menthe, Sterno and goat droppings. When stopped and tested by police, he usually set the Breathalyzer on fire. Refusing to drive when he was sober, in the mornings he rode to work on an electric floor buffer, claiming the one drawback was the time he wasted traveling from side to side. He was sentenced to ten years for defecating in a cathedral, but was released immediately when the warden felt Tonto was lowering the prison's standards. After his release, he hitchhiked through Pennsylvania where he was beaten to death by a buggyload of Quakers.

Uncle Judas

Uncle Judas, a man smaller than life, never had a heyday. He peaked in third grade. Not only did opportunity fail to knock, it had deliberately thrown away his address. His existence was so boring he once proudly showed me his neighbor's parking space. In an effort to improve his life, he decided to sell his soul;

unfortunately, he sold it on eBay and was never paid. He didn't accomplish much; his autobiography was entitled *Whaddya Want from Me?* One thing he did take pride in: He was one of the few men who, at the age of eighty-five, could still remember the names of all his dentists. He died on the feast of St. Dismas, after mistakenly eating a bag of after-dinner mints before lunch.

Uncle Montezuma

Uncle Montezuma wasn't too bright; he thought Irving Berlin was the Jewish section of Germany. As a young man he wanted to be a gynecologist, but claimed he couldn't find an opening. He was proud of the fact that while serving a prison term for sodomizing a prairie dog, he learned to drink beer through his nose. For years, he managed a gay car wash but lost all his money investing in a roadside sausage museum. His last job was managing a Playboy club in Auschwitz. When he retired, he wasn't given a gold watch, but his former boss would call him once a week and tell him what time it was. Finally, after marrying a woman who had re-peatedly blown Strom Thurmond during a military funeral, he died from eating a batch of carelessly made hollandaise sauce.

Euphemisms: Hotel Lingo

There is no part of American life that hasn't been soiled by the new, softer, artificial language. It's everywhere. When you travel, you notice it in the hotel business, or as they prefer to think of themselves now, the *hospitality industry*. And by the way, hotels are one more place where you will run into job-title inflation.

There was a time in a hotel when you checked in with the *desk clerk;* now he's the *front-desk agent*. But when he answers the phone he becomes *guest services*. I guess it's only fair, everyone else in the hotel has been upgraded. The bellhop has somehow become a *luggage assistant,* and he claims to work in *luggage services*. The *maids* have been upgraded several times over the years: *cleaning woman, maid, housekeeper;* now they're *room attendants*.

And on the subject of rooms, depending on where you're staying, *room service* is likely to be called *in-room dining*. Or *private dining*. One brochure I read called it *your private dining experience*. Pretentiousness. Never underestimate the role pretension plays when it comes to creating euphemistic language. Here's another example of it:

At one hotel where I stayed, the restaurant was temporarily located on the lower level. I was told the reason was that they were undergoing *restaurant enhancement*. Okay? The concierge actually uttered that phrase. Not remodeling — restaurant enhancement. And he said it as if it were something people say all the time.

By the way, I shouldn't have to remind you that that *lower level* he referred to was once called the *basement*. I guess I don't really mind the phrase lower level; at least it's *descriptive*, although it is the comparative form and not an absolute. Lower than what? It also bothers me when they tell me the gym is located on *level three*. Level three is just plain old pretentiousness.

And I wish hotels would make up their minds on what to call the *gym*. It's been everything: *gym, fitness center, exercise room, health club. Spa*. God! Spa-a-a-ah! Used to be you had to go to Europe to find a spa. Now any place that has a sink and more than three towels is a fucking spa!

One more thing about hotels. A lot of them have replaced the DO NOT DISTURB signs with signs that say PRIVACY, PLEASE. It seems like a small thing, but there's a difference that's worth noting:

Do not disturb is assertive; it's strong. Do not disturb! It means GO AWAY! But *privacy, please* is weak; it sounds as if you're pleading with people: "Privacy . . . please?" Softness. To my mind, it's one more example of the feminization of language that has taken place in this country. And, more important, it represents a retreat from reality.

Put It Out, Fucko!

Here's another example of the same problem:

THANK YOU FOR NOT SMOKING. Now, speaking strictly for myself, I find nothing wrong with the phrase *no smoking*. It's simple, it's direct, it's firm. No smoking! Any questions? Fine.

But thank you for not smoking. First of all, it's weak. And second, for God's sake, why are you thanking them? It's as if you think they're doing you a favor by not giving you emphysema.

Personally, if I were trying to discourage people from smoking, my sign would be a little different. In fact, I might even go too far in the opposite direction. My sign would say something like, "Smoke if you wish. But if you do, be prepared for the following series of events: First, we will confiscate your cigarette and extinguish it somewhere on the surface of your skin. We will then run your nicotine-stained fingers through a paper shredder and throw them into the street, where wild dogs will swallow and then regurgitate them into the sewers, so that infected rats can further soil them before they're flushed out to sea with the rest of the city's filth. After such time, we will systematically seek out your friends and loved ones and destroy their lives."

Wouldn't you like to see a sign like that? I'll bet a lot of smokers would think twice about lighting up near a sign like that. You have to be direct. Thank you for not smoking is simply embarrassing.

Personally, I think all of this upgraded, feel-good language is a further sign of America's increasing uncertainty about itself.

Gimme a Burger

Have you noticed that many restaurants can't simply say "cheeseburger" on the menu. They have to get cute and over-descriptive? Well, why not go along with them? Why not use the menu's own language when you place your order? But if you do, you must do it right; no fair reading directly from the menu. Instead, you must memorize the exact description given of the item you've chosen, and then look the waiter directly in the eye as you say:

"I'll have the succulent, fresh-ground, government-inspected, choice, all-beef, eight-ounce, charbroiled sirloin patty, served on your own award-winning, lightly toasted sesame-seed bun, and topped with a generous slice of Wisconsin's finest golden cheddar cheese, made from pure, grade A, premium milk recently extracted from a big, fat, smelly cow infected with flesh-eating bacteria." See if that doesn't get you good service.

But before the waiter leaves your table, ask for a glass of water. Say, "Would you mind bringing me a clear, cylindrical, machine-crafted, moderate-capacity, drinking vessel filled with nature's own colorless, odorless, extra-wet, liquid water?" Pisses them off.

Roll 'Em

I'm never critical or judgmental about whether or not a movie is any good. The way I look at it, if several hundred people got together every day for a year or so — a number of them willing to put on heavy makeup, wear clothes that weren't their own and pretend to be people other than themselves — and their whole purpose for doing all this was to entertain me, then I'm not gonna start worrying about whether or not they did a good job. The effort alone was enough to make me happy.

Nothing Changes

Dear Political Activists,

All your chanting, marching, voting, picketing, boycotting and letter-writing will not change a thing; you will never right the wrongs of this world. The only thing your activity will accomplish is to make some of you feel better. Such activity makes powerless people feel useful, and provides them the illusion that they're making a difference. But it doesn't work. Nothing changes. The pow-

erful keep the power. That's why they're called the powerful.

This is similar to people's belief that love can overcome everything, that it has some special power. It doesn't. Except one on one. One on one, love is incredibly powerful. It is a beautiful thing. But if love had any power to change the world, it would have prevailed by now. Love can't change the world. It's nice. It's pleasant. It's better than hate. But it has no special power over things. It just feels good. Love yourself, find another person to love and feel good.

Love, George

Bits and Pieces

- Remember, drinking and driving don't mix. Safety experts suggest you do your drinking first and get it out of the way. Then go driving.

- When your toilet won't stop running, and you put your hand in the tank to fix the chain, don't you wonder, briefly, whether or not the water in the tank has already been in the toilet bowl?

- If you can't say something nice about a person, go ahead.

- I'm not taking sides here, but in listening to a discussion about the Middle East on C-SPAN the other night, I realized I would rather tongue-kiss Yasir Arafat than ass-fuck Ariel Sharon. It's got nothing to do with politics, it's just a feeling I had.

- "Is Bruno a sadist?"
  "Beats me."

- They say that rather than cursing the darkness, one should light a candle.

They don't mention anything about cursing a lack of candles.

- Beethoven was a pupil of Haydn, and Schubert lived near the two of them. Supposedly they all frequented the same little cafés. I wonder if they ever got together and gang-banged a lady piano player. Just a thought.

- If you're a criminal, the best way to be is "at large."

- We have classifications called "legally blind" and "legally dead." What about "legally tired"? I think a guy should be able to declare himself legally tired, so he could get out of doing things he didn't want to do.

- If I ever have a stroke, I hope it will be early in the morning, so I don't take my vitamins that day for no reason.

- The American Eye Association reminds you that sties are caused by watching young girls get undressed.

- You know what kind of guy you never see anymore? A fop.

- I typed the word *Google* into Google. Guess what came up? Everything.

TRUE FACT: The Professional Bowlers Association sanctions a tournament called the Odor Eaters Open. It's probably because of all those rented shoes.

- I wonder how many eventual homicides have resulted from wedding ceremonies performed at the Happy Wedding-Bell Chapel in Las Vegas.

- I'll never forget Spondo. Spondo wasn't able to sit around and talk about the good times, because in the sixty years he lived he'd had only one good time. And he would never tell anyone what it was, because he was afraid that if he talked about it, it wouldn't seem as good anymore.

- I notice Connie Chung has faded away again.

- Personal ad: "Hello, I am Henri. I am fifty-five years old, and I am looking for someone who will leave me alone. Please respond. And then leave me alone."

- Christians must be sick in the head. Only someone who hates himself could possibly think of the pleasures of masturbation as self-abuse.

- I believe the next trend in cosmetic surgery will be a procedure that leaves the person with a cryptic smile. Occasionally, of course, the surgeon's hand will slip, and the patient will wind up with a baffled look.

- Are you sick of crime? Well, some communities are doing something about it; they're putting people to death for no reason. Why not start a similar program in your town? Hang a few people in a public area and watch those crime statistics improve. You'll be amazed.

- Ignore these four words.

- There are some people who are so nondescript that if their identities were stolen it would be an improvement.

  TRUE FACT: It's against the law to mutilate grave remains. So apparently, it's not illegal to be in *possession* of grave remains, the trouble starts when you mutilate them. Nice distinction.

- I have an *im*personal trainer. We meet at the gym, we don't talk, he works out alone and I go home.

- Here's how money can buy happiness: Money gives you options, options give you breathing room, breathing room gives you control and control can offer you a measure of happiness. Maybe.

TRUE FACT: You can now buy vibrating panties. They're a kind of thong with a built-in vibrator. Just what we needed.

- If no one knows when a person is going to die, how can we say he died prematurely?

- I can't help it, I just have this gut feeling that the Mafia is controlled by organized crime. I don't know what it is, but something fishy is going on.

- I wonder if a classical music composer ever intentionally composed a piano piece that was physically impossible to play and then stuck it away in a trunk to be found years after his death, knowing it would forever drive perfectionist musicians crazy.

• Why don't these guys named Allen, Allan, Allyn and Alan get together and decide how the fuck to spell their name? I'm tired of guessing. The same with Sean, Shaun and Shawn. Stop with all these cute attempts to be different. If you wanna be different, call yourself Margaret Mary.

• All patriarchal societies are either preparing for war, at war, or recovering from war.

• Somebody said to me, "I can't believe Jerry Garcia is dead." And I thought, Doesn't this guy know? Everybody's dead. It's all a matter of degree.

• I can't wait for the sun to explode; it's gonna be great. Just three billion years. I'm so fuckin' impatient.

• If you have a legal problem, guess how you determine whether or not you need a lawyer. You see a lawyer. Isn't that weird?

- Middlebrow bumper sticker in California: IF YOU CAN DREAM IT, YOU CAN DO IT. Yeah, sure. Unless the thing you're dreaming is impossible. Then, chances are, you can't do it. But try to enjoy life anyway.

- "I collect rocks."
  "How many you got?"
  "One. I just started."

- Advice to kids: Get high on sports, not drugs. But if there are no sports in your neighborhood, go ahead and get high on drugs.

- If you had yourself cloned, who, exactly, would be your parents? Can you raise yourself? I guess so. And it might be fun. Just think, by the age of six you'd be driving yourself to school.

- Regarding creationists: Aren't these the same people who gave us alchemy and astrology, and who told us the earth, besides being flat, was at the center of the universe? Why don't we just kill these fuckin' people?

- Idle thought: Do you suppose a perverted priest has ever tried to stick a crucifix up a kid's ass? Just wondering.

- The wrong two Beatles died first.

- I wonder if anyone who was working in or near the World Trade Center that day took advantage of all the confusion to simply disappear. What a great way to get away from your family.

- Indoor electric illumination is often referred to as "artificial light." How can it be artificial? The way I look at it is this: If I can read by it, see myself in the mirror and recognize my friends, it's probably as real as I'm ever going to need it to be.

- You know what you never see anymore? A guy with a pencil behind his ear.

TRUE FACT: One of those clubs that feature nude dancers recently got in trouble with the government because it didn't have wheelchair ramps.

I Just Don't See It

Here's something I don't care about in a movie or a TV show: a blind girl. "This is the story of a blind girl who . . ." *CLICK!* You know what? As far as I'm concerned, there's nothing they can do with a blind girl . . . well, maybe a couple of things, but there's nothing they can tell me about a blind girl that's going to interest me. I don't care that she's blind; I don't care if she learns how to communicate with geese; I don't care if she can identify three hundred different flowers from their smell. I really don't care. Does she fuck? Now you're talkin'!

Fart Retrieval League

"Hello. I'm Fred Ponsaloney III, president of the Fart Retrieval League. We all know that millions of farts are released by Americans each day, but did you know not all of them are free to rejoin the atmosphere? It's true. A small but significant number of farts each day are hopelessly trapped in seat cushions, suspended forever in cotton padding or foam rubber. We're asking you to help rescue these forgotten farts by sending your donations to the Fart Retrieval League. We'll send you a booklet entitled *The Facts on Farts*. And next time you're in a hotel lobby, do your part: Jump up and down on a seat cushion for several minutes and liberate a few trapped farts."

As the Turd Whirls

The Noodleman Twins Television Network proudly presents America's longest-running daytime drama, *As the Turd Whirls*, a day-to-day chronicle of ordinary people desperately in need of professional intervention and perhaps even cranial surgery. Take a break in your day as once again we flush the toilet of life, and as blue water fills the bowl, we watch, fascinated. . . . *As the Turd Whirls*.

(Romantic violin music is heard as a well-built man approaches a beautiful woman in an upscale bar)

Vinny: Hi. You wanna play a game?

Nadia: What kind of game?

Vinny: It's called Count the Man's Balls.

Nadia: Die in a fire, bourgeois scum!

Vinny: We really should get together, I'm an interesting guy. I can take a live cock-a-roach and put it up my nose and pretend it's not there. I also like to do unusual things to small woodland mammals, but not until I pull out all their claws. Otherwise, look out! Lots of screaming from Vinny. I'll bet you never dated a guy like me. Believe me, I'm worth a try.

Nadia: I wouldn't go home with you if you had six dicks.

Vinny: Come on. I purposely didn't jerk off today just so I could take someone home. You wanna compare hard-ons?

Nadia: I'm a woman, trouser-stain!

Vinny: So? Lemme see your hard-on.

Nadia: Listen! I can't take the time to explain anatomy to you. I've been waiting all day just to get out of this tight underwear. I'm getting real moist in my groin area. I'd love to take off my clothes and have someone massage me, firmly but gently, all around my crotch. My female organs are warm and pulsating, and I can smell the sexual fluids and secretions flowing out of me and mingling with my sweat.

Vinny: Now you're talkin'. Let's go to my house.

Nadia: Okay, but no sex. Understand?

Vinny: Fine by me. But can I at least jerk off? I waited all day.

Join us again tomorrow on *As the Turd Whirls*, as Trent has to decide whether to blow the mailman in exchange for free stamps.

The Farming Racket

Farmers are on government welfare and you pay for it. Good year, bad year — doesn't matter. They still get money. In a bad year — drought or floods — the crop is poor, incomes drop, farmers can't make their payments and they need financial help; you pay for it. In a good year — favorable weather — there's a bumper crop, prices fall, income drops, farmers can't make their payments and they need financial help; you pay for it. Either way, farmers win, you lose. Oh well, I guess we should be grateful; at least there's plenty of tasteless food, all safely sprayed and filled with contaminants. You know, "Bless us, O Lord, and these, thy gifts . . ."

Cellular Chitchat

You know what I don't understand? People on the street having casual conversations on a cell phone. Casual stuff. Walking along, just visiting.

"So how's Ellen? Good. Tell her I said hello."

Too casual for me. You know what a cell-phone call oughta sound like?

"Hello, Tony? Listen, my pants are on fire. I'm goin' to the fire house. What? Take my pants off? Good idea. Thanks. Listen, say hello to Ellen, will ya? I gotta go, my bush is catching fire."

Now that's a fuckin' cell-phone call. Not this shit:

"So, what are you doin', Joey, watchin' TV? Really? I was only guessin'. What's on? Oh, I saw that. Try another channel. Yeah, go ahead, I'll wait."

Try to find a phone plan that provides more than just free minutes. See if any companies are offering free brains.

Is Anyone There?

(Phone rings)

Man: Hello. Philosophy Department.

Caller: Is Jack there?

Man: Well, what do we mean when we say, "Jack"? Is there really such an entity? Or is Jack simply a description? A label. There are countless people who call themselves Jack. Can they all be doing so accurately? And by the way, where is this "there" you speak of? As I listen to you, I experience your voice as a physical sensation within my head. Certainly Jack isn't in *there*. Wherever your entity called Jack is, it's probably safe to say that that is where he is. At least for the moment.

Caller: I just would like to speak with Jack.

Man: I'm sorry, Jack was killed this morning. Or was he? After all, here we are, talking about him. Is he truly gone? One way of looking at it would be —

(*Click!*)

It's No Bullshit!

AN ASTOUNDING COLLECTION OF AMAZING STORIES FROM THE SECRET FILES OF *BELIEVE IT OR ELSE* MAGAZINE. READ THESE ASTONISHING FACTS AND FEEL YOUR FUCKIN' BRAIN MELT.

The sun does not really give off light. It merely appears to give off light because everything around it is so dark.

The Belzini tribe of South American Indians will eventually be extinct, because they initiate their young by putting them to death at the age of three.

During her entire sixty-four-year reign, Queen Victoria never once went to the bathroom. She said she was holding it in for a more appropriate time. Her words were, "We don't have to go just now."

Indianapolis, the capital of Indiana, is actually located in Brazil. It only seems to be in Indiana when viewed on a map.

When the Alexander Farkington family

moved from Boston to San Diego, they had to leave their dog, Peckerhead, behind. Miraculously, two weeks later the dog showed up in Key West, Florida. Mistakenly, Peckerhead had taken Interstate 95 south instead of getting on the Massachusetts Turnpike.

Contrary to popular belief, Babe Ruth did not call his famous home-run shot. He was actually giving the finger to a hot-dog vendor who had cheated him out of twelve cents.

Incredibly, there was no Hitler. There is no record of any such person. It's true, there was a little German man with a small moustache who combed his hair to one side and started World War II. He also killed six million Jews. But he was not Hitler. He was, in fact, a shoemaker named Hank Fleck.

A cheetah is actually slower than an armadillo. It only appears to be faster, because the armadillo moves so slowly.

Unbelievably, a goldfish can kill a gorilla. However, it does require a substantial element of surprise.

It's now possible to travel completely around the world without money or credit cards. You must be prepared, however, to walk and swim extremely long distances.

A forty-two-year-old man from Ball-bender, Wyoming, drove a riding lawn mower backward from Vermont to Argentina. The trip put him under such stress that he is now incapable of thought.

The pyramids are not really old. They were built in 1943 as a joke by drunken Italian soldiers on leave in Egypt at the time. All photographs of the area taken before that time have been retouched.

The sky is not blue. It merely looks that way because blue is the name we have given that color.

Two times two is not four. It is nine. Actually, everything is nine except seventeen. Seventeen is actually six.

Placing a two-hundred-pound pile of cooked garlic, dogshit and chocolate chips on the doorstep of your newly purchased home will keep your enemies away. However, it will not prevent your new neighbors from considering you a family that bears watching.

The record for the greatest amount of Jell-O in one location belongs to Lemon Lime, Minnesota, where residents poured twenty thousand boxes of Jell-O into a lake and heated it, just to claim the title. Most of them are happy with the results. However, some local residents, diving in the shallow areas, claim to have hit their heads on small pieces of fruit cocktail.

BELIEVE IT OR ELSE, BUT IT'S NO BULLSHIT!

Buy This and Get One of These: Act Now

Here's one more thing you don't need that costs too much and won't last long. Even if you've never had credit before; even if you owe money; even if you're bankrupt; even if you don't intend to pay; we don't care. Thousands of customers come back to us year after year, and they all say the same thing: "Please, give us our money back!" Remember, it costs a little more, but it doesn't work as well. And, it's loaded with things you can't pronounce. Special prices for senior citizens — triple. Don't forget, we're big enough to give you a good screwing and small enough to smile while we're doing it.

Smart Shopper

Usually, when you go to someone's house they offer you coffee. They say, "You want some coffee?" I tell them, "No thanks, I have coffee at home. But I could use a little pancake mix." I try to get things I need. If I don't need coffee, I'm usually prepared with options:

"Do you have any of those Chef Boyardee SpaghettiOs? The ones with the little hunks of weenie in 'em? Good, I'll take a couple of cans of them. Large, if you have 'em. By any chance, you don't have any Hebrew alphabet soup, do you? No? Okay. I didn't think so. How do the wax beans look today? I see, the produce didn't come in yet. Well, I guess you better just give me a couple of rolls of toilet paper and some Glass Wax and I'll be on my way. I have to get over to

Farley's house and do my drugstore shopping. He's havin' a special on gauze pads." Be a smart shopper. And don't forget to bring your coupons.

Fruit-Flavored Teas

I would like to talk to you about fruit-flavored teas. These would be teas that are flavored like fruit. Fruit-flavored teas. You need to understand that. These are not fruits. They're teas.

But they taste like fruit. All right? They have names like strawberry kiwi, lemon berry, orange mango, wild cherry, blackberry and cranberry. They taste like fruit. And they sound like fruits, too, don't they? They're not. They're teas. Fruit-flavored teas. And frankly, I don't understand this.

Personally, I've always been of a mind that if you're looking for fruit flavor, if you're genuinely interested in something that tastes like fruit, and you find yourself in the tea section, you're probably in the wrong aisle.

My advice is, if it's fruit flavor you're after, play it safe, go ahead and get some fruit. I have found in my experience that fruit almost always turns out to be a reliable source of fruit flavor.

Another good place you may wish to look for fruit flavor would be in fruit juice. Fruit juice is made by squeezing the juice out of the fruit. Apparently, the juice that runs out of the fruit has a fruit flavor. Perhaps that's why they call it fruit juice. It doesn't taste like tea. For tea taste, you would need to get some tea.

So let's sum this up: If it's fruit flavor you want, you can't go wrong with fruit. Or, as I've pointed out, fruit juice. Don't be ordering tea. Tea has a tea flavor. It's not like fruit. It's more like tea. If you want tea, I say order tea. That's a different experience. It's known as "having tea."

Have you noticed, by the way, there are no tea-flavored fruits? Take a clue from nature.

Leave My Chocolate Alone

I don't understand why a chocolate dessert should include raspberries or strawberries. Intrusions of that type spoil the dessert. Leave the chocolate alone; it was doing fine by itself.

I mean, here I am, innocently sitting at my

table, waiting for a nice chocolate thing with lots of whipped cream and chocolate sauce to arrive, and I find that some asshole in the kitchen has decided to show off by throwing a bunch of strawberries around. Chef's ego! Strawberries belong in strawberry short-cake, not in chocolate desserts.

I wouldn't want a bunch of chocolate in my strawberry shortcake, would you? No. Ergo, I don't want strawberries hangin' around my chocolate cake. Chocolate cake is called chocolate cake for a reason — it's chocolate. Leave it alone. Put the strawber-ries in a nice sherbet if you must. Or put 'em in a bowl by themselves, over there near the raspberries. But please don't spoil my choc-olate.

Hey, chef! You want to exercise your ego? Weave the berries into fabric and make a strawberry chef's hat. Be as creative as you want, but stop fucking with my chocolate.

P.S. — People who dip sweetly tart stawberries into liquified chocolate, wait for it to cool, and then eat the whole thing ought to be placed in mental institutions. What you should do is this: Drink the choc-olate before it cools, then put the straw-berries on your kids' cereal.

And while we're at it folks, nuts have no business in ice cream. Ice cream should be creamy. Nuts interrupt the creamy idea. Chunks of nuts don't belong in ice cream. Put 'em in a little bowl by themselves; put 'em in a candy bar; stick 'em up your nose for all I care, but leave my ice cream alone. And, in general, please folks, stop fucking with my desserts!

Euphemisms: Food and Restaurants

Euphemisms and politically correct speech have also infiltrated the food and restaurant businesses. We may as well begin with the inflated job titles, since they seem to be showing up everywhere we visit.

In a truly absurd departure from reality, at some point *waiters* temporarily became *waitpersons,* as if *waiters* and *waitresses* were somehow sexist terms. For a while there, a few of them even became known as *waitrons* — until everyone involved simply refused to call them that. Now they seem to have settled on *servers*. These servers are said to be on the *waitstaff*. Waitstaff seems forced, doesn't it? And it goes without saying, no restaurant today would dare allow a *cook* to *cook* the *food;* instead, the *cuisine* must be *prepared* by a *chef.*

An important factor to keep in mind with all of this restaurant and food talk is yuppie pretentiousness. I was in a Yuppie joint last year where the cover of the noontime menu, instead of saying *menu,* actually had the words *lunch solutions.* There I sat, unaware that I even had problems, and those nice folks were ready to provide solutions. Once again, I feel the need to emphasize that I actually saw this. Every example I offer you on these euphemism topics has been personally observed.

And before we get to the food itself, I just want to remind you that you can usually determine a restaurant's price range by noticing how it advertises. If it uses the word *cuisine,* it will be expensive; if it mentions *food,* the prices will be moderate; however, if the word *eats* is employed, rest assured any savings you make on the food will be more than offset by high medical expenses.

Now, on the subject of food itself, I'm sure you know that certain foods have been altered. I don't mean genetically, I mean euphemistically. They tried to do it to prunes. The California Prune Board wanted to change the word *prunes* to *dried plums,* because research told them that women in their thirties reacted more favorably to the phrase dried plums. California women in their thirties — does that tell you enough?

And the poor prunes were not alone. A long time ago the same thing happened to *garbanzo beans.* Apparently, someone thought the word *garbanzos* sounded too much like a circus act, so they began using the older name, *chickpeas.* Also at about that time — again, for marketing purposes — *Chinese gooseberries* became *kiwifruit.* And since it was obvious feminists would never use an oil derived from *rapeseed,* we were all introduced to *canola oil.* And just to round out our meal, the reason *Chilean sea bass* became so trendy a few years ago was because it was no longer being called *Patagonian tooth fish.* That item needs no comment.

And let's not even mention *capellini,* which became *angel-hair pasta.* Jesus! Angel hair. And by the way, who was it that took the perfectly nice word *macaroni* and started calling it *pasta* in the first place? That sounds like more of that marketing bullshit. Never underestimate the relentlessness of the marketing people. Because long before we had yuppies, consumer goods had been getting image upgrades from the marketers.

For example, *seltzer water* has variously been known as *seltzer, carbonated water, soda water, club soda* and, finally — enter the yuppies — *sparkling water.* Sometimes these days, the label on the sparkling water says *lightly carbonated.* Of course, that means they had to find a name for water that wasn't carbonated, and since *noncarbonated* sounded far too ordinary, the trendier restaurants decided on *flat water.* There are even a few places that refer to it as *still water.* It's subtle, but it's clearly a decision that when it comes to beverages, flat may possibly be seen as negative.

Never overlook pretentiousness. Pretentiousness is the reason we don't *drink water* anymore; instead we *hydrate ourselves.* Hey, I'll hydrate myself to that.

Euphemisms: Buy This and Eat It

Food Lingo

Food-advertising language. You're familiar with the words. You hear them all the time: *Fresh, natural, hearty, old-fashioned, homemade* goodness. In a can. Well, if those are the words they want to use, let's take a look at them.

Old-fashioned

When they say old-fashioned, they want us to think about the old days, don't they? The old days. You know, before we had sanitation laws; before hygiene became popular; back when E. coli was still considered a condiment.

Homemade

Right next to old-fashioned in the warmth and nostalgia department is homemade. You see it on packages in the supermarket: *homemade flavor*. Folks, take my word for this, a food company operating out of a ninety-acre processing plant is functionally incapable of producing anything homemade. I don't care if the CEO is living in the basement, wearing an apron and cooking on a hot plate. It's not gonna happen.

Same with restaurants. *Homemade soup.* Once again, it doesn't matter how much the four-foot, amphetamine-laced waitress with the bright orange hair smoking the three Marlboros reminds you of your dear old mother, the soup is not homemade. Unless the chef and his family are sleeping in the kitchen. And if that's the case, I'm not hungry.

Homemade is a myth. You want to know some things that are homemade? Crystal meth. Crack cocaine. A pipe bomb full of nails. Now we're talkin' homemade. If you need further information, check the notes of Timothy McVeigh. Old Tim knew how to cook up little homemade goodies.

Home-style

Sometimes the advertising people realize that homemade sounds too full of shit, so they switch to *home-style*. They'll say something has *home-style flavor*. Well, whose home are we talking about? Jeffrey Dahmer's? Believe me, folks, there's nothing home-style about the boiled head of a Cambodian teenager. Even if you sprinkle parsley on the hair and serve it with oven-roasted potatoes.

Style

Style is another bullshit word you have to keep an eye on. Any time you see the word *style* added to another word, someone is pulling your prick. *New York–style deli.* You know why they call it that? Because it's not in New York. That's the only reason. It's probably in Bumfuk, Egypt, the owner is from Rwanda and the food tastes like something the Hutus would feed to the Tutsis.

Another bogus use of the word *style* is in *family-style restaurant.* What that means is that there's an argument going on at every table. And the eldest male is punching the women. You know, "family-style."

Gourmet

Here's another word the advertising sluts have completely wiped their asses with. Everything is gourmet now: *gourmet* cuisine in a can, *gourmet dining in a cup.* Folks, try not to be too fuckin' stupid, will ya? There's no such thing as *gourmet coffee, gourmet rolls* or *gourmet pizza.* Gourmet means one thing: "We're going to charge you more."

The same is true of the word *cuisine.* The difference between food and cuisine is sixty dollars. That's it. They're stealing from you. You want to know some real gourmet food? Toasted snail penises; candied filet of panda asshole; deep-dish duck dick. Now you're talkin' cuisine.

Hearty

This is a word only a bullshitter could love: *hearty*. Soups are hearty, breakfast is hearty. Folks, next time you see the word *hearty*, take a good look at the rest of the label. "Hmmm! Six hundred grams of saturated fat." You know, hearty. As in heart attack.

The *y* words

It's a good idea to be wary of any words ending in *y*, in particular such words as *butter-y*, *lemon-y* and *chocolate-y*. Any time marketers add a *y* to the name of a food, you can be sure they're yanking your schwantz. *Real chocolatey goodness.* Translation? No fuckin' chocolate!

And while we're at it, *zesty* and *tangy* are not real words that normal people use in conversation. Has anyone ever turned to you in a restaurant and said, "This pork is really zesty. And it's tangy, too"? My comment? "Hey, Zesty, I got somethin' tangy for ya!"

Flavored

Folks, watch out for the word *flavored*. *Lemon-flavored drink.* Oh yeah? Lemme know if you spot any trace of a goddamn lemon in there.

There's even a pet food that calls itself a *chicken-flavored treat*. Well, a dog doesn't know what chicken tastes like. He might like it if you give him some, but he's not gonna say, "Oh good, I was hoping we'd have something chicken-flavored again. One grows tired of beef."

Natural

The last one of these bullshit food words is *natural*. And these comments are directed at all you environmental jackoffs out there. The word *natural* is completely meaningless. Everything is natural. Nature includes everything. It's not just trees and flowers and the northern spotted owl. It's everything in the universe. Untreated raw sewage, polyester, toxic chemical waste, used bandages, monkey shit. It's all perfectly natural. It's just not real good food. But you know something? It is zesty. And it's tangy, too. Bon appétit, consumers.

Retail Blues

Let's Take the Gloves Off

When did they pass a law that says the people who make my sandwiches have to be wearing gloves? I'm not comfortable with this. I don't want glove residue all over my food; it's not sanitary. Who knows where these gloves have been? Let's get back to the practice of human hands making sandwiches for human beings.

And we have to stop this tipping-people-for-counter-service thing. No one should get a tip for standing erect, moving a few feet to one side and picking up a muffin. The sign on the pathetic little tip cup says TIPS WOULD BE APPRECIATED. Well, so would some fuckin' decent service. Let's be honest, folks, there's not a great deal of IQ floating around behind these counters.

Maybe in their homelands some of these people might pass for intelligent, but to me, if they live in this country and can't speak English, their IQ plunges about three hundred points. I shouldn't have to leave a tip in order to pay for someone's English lessons.

Don't Be a Phonee

Store clerks! You should not be on the phone when you're waiting on me. When I, the customer, walk up to the counter, the phone should be put down. And if it rings while you're waiting on me, let it ring. After ten rings, pick it up, and, without even saying hello, say, "I'm currently waiting on an actual, paying customer who has money and has had the courtesy to come into the store to transact business. I will get to you when the store is empty. Stay on the line if you wish, but I may not get to you till sundown." Then smile at me and say, "Where were we?" The in-store customer should always come first.

Movin' On Up

And where did this new rule come from that says the second person standing on line in a store has to hang back and leave about six feet of space between himself and the customer being waited on? You know, one person is already up at the counter and the next person is standing back five or six feet, leaving all this unused space. When did this shit start?

And I'm not talking about stores where there's an obvious central feeder-line — one line that feeds a number of counter positions. I'm talking about an individual line that feeds a single counter, and these dopey people hang back like they're afraid of offending someone. This has obviously grown out of some perverted, politically correct impulse. Move up, motherfucker! Take up the slack! You know what I do when I'm behind one of these timid jackoffs? I step right in front of him and take his place in line. If he doesn't like it, I say, "You should have moved up, twat-face. Don't you know space is at a premium? I gave you a full minute and you didn't move. Now *I'm* next!"

The Undecideds

I also get very unhappy with people in super-markets who stop their carts in the middle of the aisle and just stand there looking at the soup. They don't know what they want, so they're looking. Parked. Middle of the aisle. They're trying to decide. Why would you go to the supermarket if you didn't know what you wanted? You know how I shop? I enter the store with a list in my hand, and I move quickly through the aisles from item to item, and I'm in the parking lot before Hamlet has figured out if the cream of mushroom is a better bargain than the chicken with stars. I say, know what you want, get what you need, and get the fuck out of there. That's how ya shop.

Message From a Cockroach

"Hello there, I'm a cockroach. Listen, I'm gonna keep this to a minimum, because I gotta get back to the kitchen and eat a bunch of crumbs that I spotted on the table. Plus there's a little puddle of gravy on the left side of the sink near the drain that nobody noticed. Okay, here's my deal: Bug sprays. We don't like 'em, we don't need 'em, we don't want 'em. We say get rid of 'em. Okay? That's it. Otherwise, if you don't do what we want, we're gonna crawl all over your face while you're asleep. We'll even go up your nose. We don't care. Thanks. I'll see you later. And for chrissakes, turn out the lights, will ya?"

Fly the Friendly Skies

When I'm on a commercial flight, and I see a fly flying down the center of the airplane from back to front, I like to take him off to one side and ask him if he understands how fast he's moving. They never really know. So the first thing I do is briefly explain Newton's laws of motion, complete with a small diagram to make it a bit easier. But the only thing their little fly egos are interested in is how fast they're moving. So I tell them that in order to calculate their velocity relative to the ground, all they have to do is add their own flying speed to the speed of the airplane. I show them how it works and they can't believe it when they discover that they're actually traveling over five hundred miles an hour. The first thing most of them mention is that a frog's tongue wouldn't stand a chance against that kind of speed.

Please Don't Say That

Here is a small sampling of embarrassing societal clichés that I find tiresome and, in some cases, just plain ignorant.

If It Saves Just One Life

You often hear a new policy or procedure justified by the specious idea that "If it saves the life of just one (insert here 'child' or 'American soldier'), it will be worth it." Well, maybe not. Maybe a closer look would show that the cost in time, money or inconvenience would be much too high to justify merely saving one life. What's wrong with looking at it like that? Governments and corporations make those calculations all the time.

Every Child is Special

An empty and meaningless sentiment. What about every adult? Isn't every adult special? And if not, then at what age does a person go from being special to being not-so-special? And if every adult *is* also special, then that means all people are special and the idea has no meaning. This embarrassing sentiment is usually advanced to further some position that is either political or fund-raising in nature. It's similar to "children are our future." It's completely meaningless and is probably being used in some self-serving way.

He's Smiling Down

After the death of some person (even many years after) you will often hear someone refer to the deceased by saying, "I get the feeling he's up there now, smiling down on us. And I think he's pleased." I actually heard this when some dead coach's son was being inducted into the Football Hall of Fame.

First of all, it's extremely doubtful that there's any "up there" to smile down from. It's poetic, and I guess it's comforting. But it probably doesn't exist. Besides, if a person *did* somehow survive death in a non-physical form, he would be far too busy with other things to be smiling down on people.

And why is it we never hear that someone is "smiling up at us." I suppose it doesn't occur to people that a loved one might be in hell. And in that case the person in question probably wouldn't be smiling. More likely, he'd be screaming. "I get the feeling he's down there now, screaming up at us. And I think he's in pain." People just refuse to be realistic.

This Puts Everything in Perspective

This nonsense will often crop up after some unexpected sports death like that of Cardinals pitcher Darryl Kile. After one of these athletes' sudden death, one of his dopey teammates will say, "This really puts everything in perspective." And I say, listen, putz, if you need someone to die in order to put things in perspective, you've got problems. You ain't payin' enough attention.

America's Lost Innocence

I keep hearing that America lost its innocence on 9/11. I thought that happened when JFK was shot. Or was it Vietnam? Pearl Harbor? How many times can America lose its innocence? Maybe we keep finding it again. Doubtful. Because, actually, if you look at the record, you'll find that America has had very little innocence from the beginning.

Let the Healing Begin

This bothersome sentiment is usually heard following some large-scale killing or accident that's been overreported in the news. Like Columbine, Oklahoma City or the World Trade Center. It's often accompanied by another meaningless, overworked cliché, "closure." People can't seem to get it through their heads that there is never any healing or closure. Ever. There is only a short pause before the next "horrifying" event. People forget there is such a thing as memory, and that when a wound "heals" it leaves a permanent scar that never goes away, but merely fades a little. What really ought to be said after one of these so-called tragedies is, "Let the scarring begin." Just trying to be helpful here.

Consolidated International:

We Need You

We're Consolidated International, and we might be looking for you. Are you one of those submissive people who show up, punch in, put out, pitch in, punch out, clean up, head home, throw up, turn in, sack out and shut up? That's what we need, people we can keep in line. We just might have a place for you. Consolidated International: People making things, so people have things to do things to other people with.

The Fanatics Will Win

I hope you good, loyal Americans understand that in the long run the Islamist extremists are going to win. Because you can't beat numbers, and you can't beat fanaticism — the willingness to die for an idea.

A country like ours, preoccupied with Jet Skis, off-road vehicles, snow boards, Jacuzzis, microwave ovens, pornography, lap dances, massage parlors, escort services, panty liners, penis enhancement, tummy tucks, thongs and Odor Eaters doesn't have a prayer — not even a good, old-fashioned Christian prayer — against a billion fanatics who hate that country, detest its materialism and have nothing really to lose. Maybe fifty years ago, but not today when germs and chemicals and nuclear materials are for sale everywhere.

People who don't give a shit and have nothing to lose will always prevail over people who are fighting for some vague sentiment scrawled on a piece of parchment. Folks, they're gonna getcha; and it ain't gonna be pleasant.

We can't drop a five-thousand-pound bomb on every one of them. They will either run all over us or, in trying, they will turn us into even bigger monsters than we already are.

And don't get all excited about this goofy idea, "the spread of democracy." No matter who the United States puts in charge to bring peace and order in Iraq or Palestine or anywhere else, those people will be killed. It's that simple. Anyone who supports the United

States will be killed. Peace and order will not be tolerated. Start saving your cash for the black market, folks, you're gonna need it.

The Channel Seven Editorial Reply

Announcer: Channel seven recognizes its obligation to provide equal time to viewers who disagree with its editorial policy. Here, then, with an editorial reply, is Dr. Steven Wanker, a clinical psychologist. Dr. Wanker speaks as a private citizen.

Dr. Wanker: Thank you. Are these channel seven people kidding? Hah? What kind of crap are they trying to pull? Did you hear that shit they said last week about the budget? Jesus Christ! I couldn't believe it! What kind of assholes do they think we are?

And they're always acting so self-righteous, like they know what's good for us and we're too stupid to think. I'm gettin' tired of this shit. How about you? Hah? Fuck these people! Who do they think they are, with their goddamn three-piece suits and fancy eyeglasses?

And, by the way, do you know how long it takes to get one of these goddamn editorial replies on the air? Three fuckin' years! Three years ago I started asking to do this shit! They kept sayin', "Well, we're not sure you're stable enough to be allowed on the air." And I said, "Stable? What're you fuckin' people, crazy? I'm as stable as the next cocksucker!" I said to 'em, "Bend over and I'll give you somethin' stable!"

Fortunately, they were able to recognize the logic

of my argument and here I am. But you know what I found out these assholes can do? They can cut you off the air if they want to. For instance, if they don't like what you're saying, they can just fuckin' interru—

Announcer: That was Steven Wanker, a clinical psychologist. Tune in to channel seven tomorrow night for another editorial reply, as schoolteacher Howard Boudreaux delivers an opinion titled, "What's All This Phony Bullshit about Drunk Driving?" And, later in the week, don't miss Mayor Cosmo Drelling as he addresses another important issue: "What's So Bad about Slavery?" Thank you, ladies and gentlemen. We now join *Blowjobs of the Rich and Famous* in progress.

And later this evening, tune in *Doctor Jim* as he removes a wart from a lesbian.

Keep TV Family-Free

I'm always glad when some group of American hostages is released overseas, and they finally get to come home to their families. I'm not glad because I particularly care about them, but because I get sick of hearing about them on TV, and I get sick of listening to their families. Jesus, did I get tired of all those whining hostage-families during that bullshit in Iran in the 1970s. "My husband's a hostage! The government's not doing enough!"

Hey, lady, if you don't want your husband to be a hostage, tell him to stay the fuck out of Iran or places like it in the first place. It's a simple thing; you don't have to be a theoretical physicist to figure it out. If you stay out of these places, you've got a good chance of not becoming a hostage.

And the media always refers to them as "innocent Americans." Bullshit. There are no innocent Americans. And whatever they are, they're certainly not news. First thing you know, once they're back they start writing books, one by one, and you have to endure the whole thing all over again, seeing them on every talk show, regurgitating the whole fuckin' boring story again.

Here are some more families I'm not interested in: astronauts' families. Who cares about these people? Astronauts' wives and children. They're not news — keep 'em off TV. I don't even care about the astronauts themselves. Anal-retentive robots wasting money in space. And — not incidentally — spreading our foul, grotesquely distorted DNA beyond this biosphere.

I say, keep the infection local. God! Haven't we done enough damage on *this* planet? Now we're going to go somewhere else and leave our filth and garbage all over the universe? Jesus, what a pack of fuckin' idiots we are. Thank you.

Seems Like Old Times: A Dialogue

Kevin: Boy, a lot has changed in twenty years.

Ray: Yeah.

Kevin: Is Naughton still around?

Ray: Frankie?

Kevin: No, Jimmy.

Ray: Jimmy's dead. And Frankie died at the funeral. They're both dead.

Kevin: What about Bobby? How's he?

Ray: He's dead, too. A lot of 'em are dead.

Kevin: What was the other Naughton kid's name? Tommy? Is he dead?

Ray: No. Tommy's not dead.

Kevin: Thank God for that.

Ray: He's dying.

Kevin: Jeez! The mother must be heart-broken.

Ray: The mother was killed in a boiler explosion. Blown to pieces.

Kevin: Jeez. I'll never forget that house the Naughtons lived in. Kind of a cute little place with green shutters.

Ray: Hit by lightning fifteen years ago.

Burned to the ground. All the pets were killed.

Kevin: Jeez. That's too bad. I remember the Naughtons always liked that house because it was so close to the church.

Ray: Our Lady of Perpetual Suffering?

Kevin: Yeah.

Ray: The church is gone. Condemned by the city last year and demolished on Good Friday.

Kevin: So where do the neighborhood kids go to school?

Ray: Most of the neighborhood kids were killed a few years ago by a rapist who worked at the grocery store.

Kevin: Dorian's?

Ray: No, Babington's.

Kevin: I liked Dorian's. They always had good produce.

Ray: Dorian's collapsed ten years ago and killed nineteen customers. The entire Halloran family was decapitated at the butcher counter while they were pickin' out meat.

Kevin: Jeez. Times really change.

Ray: Well, life goes on.

Real Realism for Realists

Drink Up

I think the warning labels on alcoholic beverages are too bland. They should be more vivid. Here are a few I would suggest:

"Alcohol will turn you into the same asshole your father was."

"Drinking will significantly improve your chances of murdering a loved one."

"If you drink long enough, at some point you will vomit up the lining of your stomach."

"Use this product and you may wake up in Morocco wearing a cowboy suit and tongue-kissing a transmission salesman."

"Men: When emptying your pockets after a night of using this product, you may come across a human finger, a wad of Turkish money and a snapshot of a naked ex-convict named Dogmeat. The photo will be inscribed, 'To Dave, my new old lady.'"

"Women: Drink enough of this and you will spend the rest of your life raising malnourished children in a rusting trailer with a man who sleeps all day. Except for the rapes."

God Rest His Soul

Newspaper death notices could also be written more honestly. Have you seen the lies they print? "Cherished and beloved husband of Kathleen, devoted and esteemed father of Thomas; loving brother of Edward"? Bullshit. Let's be realistic:

"Ryan, James D.; jealous and abusive husband of Kate; lustful, wanton father of Maureen; controlling and manipulative father of Matthew; cruel, envious and conniving brother of Thomas, died yesterday to the great relief of the family. May he burn a long time in the worst parts of the deepest pits of the hottest precincts of hell. It is good to have him out of our lives.

"Funeral at the Church of the Holy Bleeding Wounds, burial in Crown of Thorns Cemetery. No flowers; donations should be made in cash directly to the family for purposes of celebration."

On Bended Knee

This idea could spread. It might even inspire young men to make more realistic marriage proposals: "Honey, let's get married. I realize I'm asking you to take a chance on a proven loser — I don't have any money or stuff like that — but maybe — hear me out — maybe we could find a cheap, unclean apartment in a dangerous neighborhood and have more kids than we can afford. If we're lucky, maybe a few of them won't be born sickly and disfigured, in spite of our genetic histories. Meanwhile, I could find a dehumanizing, low-paying, dead-end job with no benefits, while you stay home watching TV and gaining weight.

"And if things get bad — like if I get para-lyzed, and you get raped by Mexican sailors and lose your mind and start crying all the time — we can always move in with my par-ents. They love kids, and their incest coun-seling is almost complete. And I've noticed Dad's 'episodes' are starting to result in far less property damage than before. What do you say, honey? You want to give it a shot? Maybe our second set of HIV tests will turn up negative."

Early Boarding: Children

If I may renew a theme found elsewhere in the book, I have a bit more to say about early boarding on the airlines. It's not just favor-itism to the "disabled" that bothers me; that's unfair enough. But! Immediately after the various cripples, limpers and wheelchair jockeys have been unfairly allowed to board early, the airline then has the nerve to allow people with children to get on the plane. Once again, at the expense of the rest of us. I do not understand this policy at all.

Why should people board early simply be-cause they have children? What's so special about having kids? After all, a lot of kids are accidents; many people wind up with children simply because they're unlucky. Is that something we should be rewarding? I don't think being careless in bed should qualify someone for special treatment on an airplane.

And by the way, as with the devious methods of the cane-and-crutch crowd mentioned earlier, I think there are some couples who bring their kids along on a trip for the sole purpose of early boarding. What other reason would you have for including kids on a trip? Enjoyment? Hardly.

In fact — and this may seem extreme to some — it's my conviction that there are some couples who have intentionally gotten married and had families specifically for the purpose of getting on the plane early. I know it sounds unlikely to you, but don't forget, these are cold, pragmatic, striving yuppie-boomers; unsentimental people who largely regard children as props and commodities, anyway: "Honey, let's have a kid, so we can board planes early." "Great idea, Scott! You start making a list of good preschools, and I'll get the lubricating jelly." Believe me, it happens more than you may think.

So, during this preflight, pre-boarding fiasco, after the crippled and the maimed have been safely strapped in, the airline people tell us they will now "preboard passengers traveling with small children." Well, that's fine as far as it goes, but what about passengers traveling with large children? Suppose you have a six-month-old son with a growth-hormone disorder? One of those seven-foot infants with oversized heads that you see in the *National Enquirer*. Actually, with a kid like that I think you're better off checking him in at the curb, don't you? He'd probably enjoy it in the luggage compartment. It's dark in there, and I would imagine he's used to that.

But I digress. Forgive me for indulging my weakness for flights of colorful narration. Back to the real problem: people with children on airplanes. Here's how you solve this. You make the following announcement:

"Ladies and gentlemen, this is a preboarding announcement only. We would like to address those of you who, both today and in your lives generally, find yourselves burdened with needy and annoying children. We sympathize with you, but as long as you've decided to drag them along with you to Pittsburgh, we wish to minimize the inconvenience of their presence to the rest of us. Here is what is going to happen:

"First of all, you're getting on last — if there's room. Before that, we're going to board the full-grown humans and allow them to settle in, get comfortable and have a drink or two. You may be standing out here for an hour or more. Then, you and your children will be swiftly escorted onto the aircraft and placed in a special, soundproof, walled-off area in the rear of the plane. There will be standing room only. For safety purposes, you will be tethered to one another and secured to the wall with leashes and straps.

"More than likely, there will not be any food left for you, but your children will be allowed to scavenge the trays of those passengers who did not finish their meals. Aside from that food service, you will be left alone and expected to keep the children quiet.

"And now, we ask that you please gather your precious creatures around you, and, when you hear the whistle, see to it that they move smartly and swiftly onto the plane, remaining quiet and avoiding any eye contact with grown-ups. Thank you for flying the friendly skies of Sensible Airlines."

Traffic Accidents

Never Hang Around

I don't often write about my own experiences; it's not my style. But I had a recent incident in traffic that I'd like to tell you about. And before I begin, there are a couple of things you ought to know about me: I drive kind of recklessly, I take a lot of chances, I never maintain my vehicles and I don't believe in traffic laws. And so, because of these practices, I tend to have what a picky person would probably refer to as a lot of traffic accidents.

And wouldn't you know, last week I ran over a sheep.

Or, possibly, I ran over a small man wearing a sheepskin coat. I'm not sure, really, because I didn't stop. That's another rule of mine: I never stop when I have a traffic accident. Do you? No. You can't. Who has time? Not me.

If I hit something, or I run somebody over, I keep moving! Especially if I've injured someone. I refuse to involve myself in other people's injuries. I'm not a doctor, I've had no medical training; I'm just another guy, out, driving around looking for a little fun. And I can't be stopping for every-thing.

Listen, folks. Let's be logical about it. If you stop at the scene of the accident, all you do is add to the confusion. These people you ran over have enough troubles of their own without you stopping and making things worse. Think about it — they've just been involved in a major traffic accident! The last thing they need is for you to stop, get out of your car, go over to the wreckage and start bothering them with stupid ques-tions: "Are you hurt?"

Well, of course they're hurt. Look at all the blood! You just hit them with a ton and a half of steel — of course they're hurt. Leave these people alone. Haven't you done enough? For once in your life do the decent thing — don't get involved.

Look at it this way, it's none of your busi-ness in the first place; the whole thing took place *outside* of your car. Legally speaking, these people were not even on your property at the time you ran them over. They were standing in the street; that's city property. You are not responsible! If they don't like it, let 'em sue the mayor.

And besides, the whole thing is over now; it happened back *there, behind you!* For God's sake, stop living in the past. Do yourself a favor, count your blessings, be glad it wasn't you. As it is, there's probably a substantial dent in your fender. So be satisfied, my friend, you got off easy.

And I'll give you a truly practical reason not to stop. If you *do* stop, sooner or later the police are going to show up. Is that what you want? To waste even more of your time, standing around with a bunch of worthless civil servants, filling out forms, answering a lot of foolish questions . . . lying to the authorities?

And one more thing: Didn't anyone *else* see this accident? Are you the only one who can provide information? Surely the people you ran over caught a glimpse of it at the last moment. So, let *them* tell the police what happened. They certainly had a better view of it than you did.

There's just no sense in having two conflicting stories floating around about the same dumb-ass traffic accident. Things are bad enough: People are dead, families have been destroyed, it's time to *get moving!* Chances are you're late for dinner as it is.

Exception to the Rule

Now, folks. There are two sides to this. Helping people by leaving them alone when they're injured is one thing, that's my altruistic side; people need to be self-reliant, and I want to do what I can to foster that. But it's often hard for me to drive away from a nice fiery accident scene, because I have a self-indulgent side, and that needs to be honored too.

And so, on the other hand, if I'm out driving, enjoying a lovely day, and I *see* a traffic accident — one I'm not involved in — I stop immediately! I wanna get a good look at what's goin' on. I enjoy that sort of thing. If people are injured, I wanna take a look! I am Curious George.

Of course, the police don't like that. They say you're rubbernecking and blockin' traffic. I tell 'em, "Never mind that rubberneckin' shit, I wanna take a look!" My philosophy: I'm never too busy that I can't stop to enjoy someone else's suffering. I'm looking for a little entertainment. To me, traffic accidents are one more form of entertainment.

You want to hear my dream accident? Two buses and a chicken truck gettin' hit by a circus train in front of a flea market. Entertainment! I'm lookin' for an antique lamp stickin' out of a clown's ass. If I'm gonna take the time to stop, I expect a couple of fuckin' laughs.

And if the traffic situation is such that I can't quite see what's going on — can't get a good enough look — I'm not the least bit shy about asking the police to bring the bodies over a little closer to the car.

"Pardon me, Officer. Would you fellows mind dragging that twisted-looking chap over here a little closer to the car? My wife has never seen anyone shaped quite like that. Look at that, Sugarlips! Those are his testicles hanging from the rearview mirror. Thank you, Officer, that will be all now, you can throw him back on the pile. We'll be moving along."

And off we go, out onto the highway looking for a little fun. Perhaps a flatbed truck loaded with human cadavers will explode in front of a *Star Trek* reunion. One can only dream and hope.

A Cry for Help

Dear Friend:

Your name has been provided to us, because we have discovered that, in spite of America's recent economic problems, you may still have a few dollars tucked away that you are saving for a future financial emergency. Well, that emergency is here. We're hoping you will be sympathetic to our effort and express it with your generosity.

Stated quite simply, we're raising money to help the rich and powerful. These hard-driving people continue to require large amounts of money, and most of them are far too busy to attend to this sort of direct appeal for themselves. We are here to help.

The rich and powerful need your financial support in order to increase their wealth and power, so they can exercise even greater influence over national events, and, of course, over your lives. Remember, these people are small in number and, therefore, inadequately represented in our system of proportional government. They consequently lack influence and suffer the fate of many minorities, i.e., being ignored by the very government they have helped elect. It is for these reasons they have decided to band together to better present their ideas and especially to expand their influence with elected officials. But first they need your help. They need money.

In the first stage, your money is needed for basics: stationery, office supplies, postage, phones and rent (first month, last month, security deposit). The rich and powerful need to set up a headquarters so they can start really raising money in order to live properly. But once they reach that level that doesn't mean your job is done. Not at all.

In fact, once things are running smoothly there'll be a continuing and even greater need for more and more of your money in order to provide all of the expensive clothing, imported cars, fine jewelry, gourmet foods and exotic pets that these people require. That's when your dollars will really count, helping provide the lifestyle to which the rich and powerful are not only accustomed but entitled.

In addition to these considerable personal expenses, there will, of course, be a need for large amounts of money to persuade and influence the many politicians and government officials who, after all, have financial obligations of their own. Most of these dedicated public servants are underpaid and must find ways of supplementing their in-

come without taking time off from work. Your money, funneled through the rich and powerful, can go a long way toward solving their financial problems. And you will have the satisfaction of knowing you have helped advance the selfless agenda the rich and powerful have laid out in their effort to improve our country.

Can we count on you? Will you help? Will you give yourself the opportunity to say you helped the rich and powerful when they really needed it? Do it now. Do it for yourself and for your children. Sit down and write out a check for a substantial amount, maybe even more than you can afford. Make it payable to The Fund for the Rich and Powerful. You'll take satisfaction knowing you have done your part. And you'll be secure in the knowledge that whenever you have a problem, the rich and powerful will always be there to help.

Sincerely,
Esterbrook Winslow
Somewhere Offshore

P.S. Your canceled check is your receipt.

Bob Calling

Bob dials a number.
   Don: Hello?

Bob: Hi, is this Don?

Don: Yes.

Bob: Hi, Don, this is Bob.

Don: Oh. Hi, Bob.

Bob: Hi. Well, I guess I'll let you go now. Bye.

Don: Okay. Bye.

Bob dials again.

Carl: Hello?

Bob: Hi, is this Carl?

Carl: Yes.

Bob: This is Bob.

Carl: Oh. Hi, Bob.

Bob: Hi. Well, you're probably a busy guy. I'll let you go. Bye.

Carl: Bye.

Bob dials again.

Tom: Hello?

Bob: Hello, Tom?

Tom: Yes. Who's this?

Bob: Bob.

Tom: Hi, Bob. What's goin' on?

Bob: Not much, how about you?

Tom: Same old same old.

Bob: Great. Well, I gotta go. I've got a bunch of calls to make.

Tom: Okay. Bye.

Bob opens his phone book and makes a list of more people he wants to bond with. His phone rings.

Bob: Hello?

Voice: Hi, is this Bob?

Bob: Yes.

Voice: This is Steve.

Bob: Oh, hi, Steve. How are you?

Steve: Well, that's the reason I'm calling.

Bob: Oh?

Steve: Yes. I'm doing fine. So I thought I'd let you know that and maybe save you a call.

Bob: Well, that's mighty thoughtful of you. Thanks.

Steve: That's okay. Well, that's it. I guess we'll talk tomorrow.

Bob: You got a deal. Bye.

Steve: Bye.

Bob scratches Steve's name from his list

of calls and reaches for the receiver. So much still to do.

Bits and Pieces

- Remember, kids, Mr. Policeman is your friend. Always cooperate with him. Mr. Policeman wants to help you, so you must help Mr. Policeman. Don't forget, if you refuse to cooperate, Mr. Policeman will beat you to death. Especially if you're not white.

- I'm not a person who thinks he can have it all, but I certainly feel that with a bit of effort and guile I should be able to have more than my fair share.

- You know what would be fun? To have a set of twins, name them Dumbo and Goofy and then just sit back and see how their personalities develop. I'll bet they'd really enjoy going to school every day.

- I'd like to point out that during the twentieth century, white, God-fearing, predominately Christian Europe produced Lenin, Stalin, Franco, Hitler and Mussolini.

- Next time you're in an elevator, blow

your nose real loud into your bare hands and then ask if anyone has a Kleenex. Or blow your nose into a Kleenex, open it up and stare at the stuff and say, "Wow! Look at this. It's all green and yellow." Then show it to the other people. I guarantee you won't pass many floors before you have the elevator all to yourself.

- I've never seen a homeless guy with a bottle of Gatorade.

- One great thing about getting old is that you can get out of all kinds of social obligations simply by saying you're too tired.

- You know who you have to admire? A Catholic hit man who blesses himself just before he strangles someone.

- I've noticed that a Jew will sometimes use a little paper clip to hold on his yarmulke. Shouldn't that be God's responsibility? I mean, you did your part, you put the thing on. Shouldn't it be God's job to keep it there? Or why don't Jews just wear larger yarmulkes that grip the head better? Maybe with an elastic strap that could go under the chin. By the way,

I know a hip-hop Jew who wears his yarmulke backward. It's hard to detect, but I think it looks great.

- Suppose you tried to fuck a woman who had ten personalities, and nine of them said okay, but one of them resisted and tried to fight you off. Would that still be a rape?

- "Where do we go from here?"
"Who says we're here?"

- Because of mad cow disease, they're now going to leave certain cow parts out of hamburger meat, including the skull. Well, I don't know about you folks, but I can't imagine enjoying a hamburger that doesn't have at least a hint of cow skull in it.

- I was looking in the mirror the other day and I realized I haven't changed much since I was in my twenties. The only difference is I look a whole lot older now.

- Here's a safety tip from the Fire Department: Kitchen-grease fires can be quickly and safely extinguished by dousing them with a mixture of benzine and lighter fluid. Apply quickly and stand clear.

TRUE FACT: More children in the United States are molested each year than wear braces.

- I'd like to know the suicide rate among people who call in to radio psychologists and actually follow the advice they get.

- I have no regrets in life. Although I am kind of sorry I never got to beat a man to death while wearing a tuxedo.

- There's a message window that comes up on my computer screen whenever I type in a command the computer doesn't like. It says, "Fuck you, I don't do that."

- When people use the phrase *call it quits,* why do they use the plural? It would make more sense to say, "I'm going to call it quit."

- I recently witnessed something I'll never forget: an eclipse of the earth. But because it was an eclipse of the earth, there was no place to look. So I looked at the earth. And as I did, the earth got very dark. But the period of darkness was brief because of how close we are to the earth. Remember, kids, never look directly at an eclipse, always get someone else to tell you about it.

- The National Rifle Association reminds its members: Never fire a gun at your own body. Unless you're trying to seriously injure yourself.

- As a part of those displays that honor rock stars in the Rock and Roll Hall of Fame, I think they should show the amount of money each artist spent on drugs, year by year. Also, it wouldn't be a bad idea to list which drugs the artists were taking while recording particular songs and albums. Just so we'd all know.

TRUE FACT: In 1733, the Russian army had a treatment for soldiers who suffered severe homesickness. At the first sign of the condition, they buried the soldier alive. That's good. I like people who go right to the heart of a problem.

- Do you have any perfectly good possessions you don't need? Send them to Ill Will Industries, where our completely healthy and able-bodied employees earn money by breaking things and rendering them useless. Call Ill Will. Help those who are already doing fine.

- I'm in favor of anything that destabilizes the republic.

- Regarding the Menendez brothers, my opinion is that you can rarely get two kids to agree to kill their parents unless the parents really deserve it.

  TRUE FACT: Purina now has a cat food made especially for cats who live indoors. "Indoor cat food for indoor cats." Meanwhile, I'm sure you're aware that some human beings have no food at all.

- The worst thing about e-mail is that you can't interrupt the other person. You have to read the whole thing and then e-mail them back, pointing out all their mistakes and faulty assumptions. It's frustrating and it's time-consuming. God bless phone calls.

- I can't understand a grown man whose

nickname is Fuzzy and who actually allows people to call him that. Do these guys really introduce themselves that way? "Hi, I'm Fuzzy." If some guy said that to me, I would say to him, "Well, you don't look very fuzzy to me."

- If you vote once, you're considered a good citizen. If you vote twice, you face four years in jail.

- In this country, alcohol is hardly ever seen as a drug problem. Instead, we think of it as more of a driving problem.

- Life is simple: Your happiness will be based completely on luck and genetics. Everything comes down to luck and genetics. And when you think about it, even your genetics is luck.

- Seems as though I never get to do the fox-trot anymore.

- What's going on with these people who tell you to "have a safe trip"? I would never tell a person that. Because if they died it would feel really creepy.

- If I had been in charge of reorganizing

the government's security agencies into a homeland defense organization, I would have divided the responsibilities into two agencies: The Bureau of What the Fuck Was That? and The Department of What the Fuck Are We Gonna Do Now?

Read Only

Don't you get tired of this simpleminded Laura Bush nonsense about children reading, or reading to children, or teaching children to read, or reading to children about teaching, or whatever the fuck it is? What is it with these Bush women? His mother — the big silver douche bag — was into the same sort of nonsense. These women should not be encouraging children to read, they should be encouraging children to *question* what they read. Content is far more important than the mere act of sitting with your mother and dragging your eyes across text. By the way, I noticed that, apparently, the idea of teaching children to read didn't work when Barbara tried it on George.

Euphemisms: Political-Interest Groups

Not all the political manipulation of language is done by the big bad politicians. A lot of it comes from people who think of themselves as good and virtuous: the politically active.

Activists. As opposed, I guess, to "passivists." Who should not be confused with pacifists, who are, after all, quite often activists.

God Help Us

Let's start with *faith-based,* which was chosen by right-wing holy people to replace the word *religious* in political contexts. In other words, they've conceded that religion has a bad name. I guess they figured people worry about *religious fanatics,* but no one's ever heard of a *faith-based fanatic.*

And by the way, none of the Bush religious fanatics will admit this, but the destruction of the World Trade Center was a *faith-based initiative.* A fundamentalist-Moslem, faith-based initiative. Different faith, but hey, we're all about diversity here.

The use of faith-based is just one more way the Bush administration found to bypass the Constitution. They knew Americans would never approve of government-promoted religious initiatives, but faith-based? Hey, what's the problem?

The term faith-based is nothing more than an attempt to slip religion past you when you're not thinking; which is the way religion is always slipped past you. It deprives you of choice; *choice* being another word the political-speech manipulators find extremely useful.

Choosing Sides

School choice, and the more sophisticated version, *parental choice,* are code phrases that disguise the right wing's plan to use government money to finance religious education. If you hear the word *voucher,* watch out for the religious right. Again, though, be alert for the more sophisticated term for vouchers: *opportunity scholarships.*

It's impossible to mention the word *choice* without thinking of the language that has come out of the abortion wars. Back when those battles were first being joined, the religious fanatics realized that *antiabortion* sounded negative and lacked emotional power. So they decided to call themselves *pro-life.* Pro-life not only made them appear virtuous, it had the additional advantage of suggesting their opponents were *anti-life,* and, therefore, *pro-death.* They also came up with a lovely variation designed to get you all warm inside: *pro-family.*

Well, the left wing didn't want to be seen as either anti-life or pro-death, and they knew *pro-abortion* wasn't what they needed, so they decided on *pro-choice*. That completed the name game and gave the world the now classic struggle: pro-choice vs. pro-life. The interesting part is that the words *life* and *choice* are not even opposites. But there they are, hangin' out together, bigger than life.

And by the way, during this period of name-choosing, thanks to one more touch of left-wing magic, thousands of *abortionists' offices* were slowly and mysteriously turning into *family-planning clinics*.

And on the subject of those places, I think the left really ought to do something about this needlessly emotional phrase *back-alley abortions*. "We don't want to go back to the days of back-alley abortions." Please. It's over-descriptive; how many abortions ever took place in back alleys? Or, okay, in places where the entrance was through a back alley? Long before *Roe v. Wade*, when I was a young man, every abortion I ever paid for took place in an ordinary doctor's office, in a medical building. We came in through the front door and took the elevator. The three of us. Of course, as we were leaving, the elevator carried a lighter load.

A Bunny in the Oven?

Then there's the *fetus–unborn child* argument. Even leaving aside personal feelings, the semantics of this alone are fun to unravel. To my way of thinking, *whatever* it is, if it's unborn, it's not a child. A child has already been born; that's what makes it a child. A fetus is not a child, because it hasn't been born yet. That's why it's called a fetus. You can call it an unborn fetus if you want (it's redundant), but you can't call it an unborn child. Because — not to belabor this — to be a child, it has to be born. Remember? The word *unborn* may sound wonderful to certain people, but it doesn't tell you anything. You could say a Volkswagen is unborn. But what would it mean?

The fanatics have another name for fetuses. They call them the *pre-born*. Now we're getting creative. If you accept pre-born, I think you would have to say that, at the moment of birth, we go instantly from being pre-born to being pre-dead. Makes sense, doesn't it? Technically, we're all pre-dead. Although, if you think about it even harder, the word pre-dead probably would best be reserved for describing stillborn babies. The post-born pre-dead.

By the way, I think the reason conservatives want all these babies to be born is that they simply like the idea of birth. That's why so many of them have been *born again*. They can't get enough of it.

Tarzan Would be Mortified

Here's some more left-wing nonsense, this time from the environmentalists, the folks who gave us the *rain forest*. "Save the rain forest." They decided to call it that because they needed to raise money, and they knew no one would give them money to save a *jungle*. "Save the jungle" doesn't sound right. Same with *swamp*. "Save the swamp!" Not gonna work. Swamp became *wetland!* Nicer word. Sounds more fragile. "Save the wetlands." Send money.

But I think the environmentalists still have their work cut out for them when it comes to *global warming* and the *greenhouse effect*. As I see it, these terms are far too pleasant for people to get all worked up about. For one thing, global is too all-embracing for Americans; it's not selfish enough. "Isn't globalization that thing that's been stealing our jobs?" Global doesn't make it. And *warming* is such a nice word. Who wouldn't want a little warming?

Similarly, greenhouse effect will never do. A greenhouse is full of plants and flowers, full of life and growth. Green equals life, house equals shelter. The greenhouse effect sounds like something that gives you life and shelter and growth. You're never gonna turn something like that into a villain.

And the environmentalists have another language problem, this one concerning nuclear energy: *meltdowns*. They like to warn us about meltdowns. But a meltdown sounds like fun, doesn't it? It sounds like some kind of cheese sandwich. "Would you like some fries with that meltdown?"

Euphemisms: Political-Interest Groups

A Few Afterthoughts

Here is more of the distorted language of political persuasion:

- Conservatives oppose *gun control*. Liberals know *control* is a negative word, so they call it *gun safety*. That's about what you'd expect, but it's hard to find words to describe the following distortion: some of the pro-gun people are referring to gun control as *victim disarmament*. Isn't that stunning? Victim disarmament! It takes your breath away. Like a gun.

- Liberals call it *affirmative action;* conservatives are less positive. They refer to *government-mandated quotas, racial preferences* and *unfair set-asides*.

- Rich Republicans want to keep their money in the family, and so the Republican party began to call the *inheritance* tax (a pro-tax term) the *estate tax* (a neutral term), which they later changed to the *death tax* (an anti-tax term).

- When liberals talk about *spending,* they call it *investing* or *funding*. Funding means *spending money*. "We need to do more to fund education." On the other side of the ledger, when Republicans need to *raise taxes,* they call it *revenue enhancement*.

- The energy criminals now refer to *oil*

drilling as *oil exploration*. Instead of Mobil and Exxon, they'd rather you picture Lewis and Clark.

- When the original Enron story was developing, Bush's people referred to the crimes as *violations*. They said a *review* might be necessary, but not an *investigation*. So I guess if the other guys do it, it's a *crime* that should be *investigated*, but if your guys do it, it's a violation that should be reviewed.

- Liberals call it *global warming*, conservatives call it *climate change*.

- If you want the individual to sound shady and suspicious, you call him an Eye-racky. If you want to upgrade him a bit, he becomes an *Iraqi-American*. If you're trying to clean him up completely, you call him an *American citizen of Iraqi descent*.

- When people came to this country, primarily from Europe, they were called *immigrants* and *refugees*. As they began arriving from Latin America and the Caribbean, we started calling them *aliens*. Some of them are here illegally. Those in this country who sympathize with that group don't call them *illegal aliens,* they refer to them as *undocumented workers.* Or *guest workers.* Sometimes they're identified by the purely descriptive term the *newly arrived.*

- *Most-favored-nation* trade status was considered too positive a term for China, so it was decided instead to call it *normal trade relations.* Aside from the language, there is no difference between the two policies.

- The Nazis referred to the extermination of the Jews as *special action.* In their version, the Jews were not killed, they were *resettled, evacuated* or *transferred.* The dead were referred to as the *no longer relevant.*

- In Palestine, Arabs refer to the areas Jews have taken over as *occupied territories.* Jews call them *disputed areas.* The Israelis call their assassinations of Palestinian leaders *focused thwartings, pinpoint elimination* and *preventive measures.*

- At one time in Iraq Hussein called the hostages he was holding his *guests.*

- Countries we used to call *rogue nations* are now referred to as *nations of concern,* so we can talk with them without insulting them outright. But as a result of bad behavior, North Korea has been downgraded from a *state of concern* to a *rogue state.* Likewise, *failed nations* are now called *messy states. Underdeveloped countries* have also been upgraded. They're now *developing nations.*

And finally . . .

- During the election that defeated Manuel Noriega in Panama, there were groups of thugs that wandered around beating and killing people and looting stores. They called themselves *dignity battalions.*

How Goes It?

If you enjoyed my earlier description of my new system for wishing people a nice day, perhaps you'll be interested in the following, equally innovative method I employ in similar situations. The difference is that this attempt to relieve the tedium of short exchanges involves the replies I give, as opposed to the good wishes I offer.

As an example, when someone asks me how I am, I try to make my answer as specific as possible. I'm not the type to toss off a casual, "I'm fine." I take care to express my exact condition. And thanks to my creative flair, I can choose from a number of options:

If I'm in a self-protective mood, a simple "guardedly well" often does the job. I find also "tentatively keen" doesn't give too much away. Of course, if there is the least bit of doubt, I simply rely on my old standby, the ever-cautious, "I'm fairly well, comparatively speaking." That works nicely, especially if I feel I genuinely have something to hide.

If I wish to be a little more open, "I'm semi-dandy, thank you for inquiring" is effective, and has the added advantage of acknowledging the other person's contribution to the exchange.

By the way, should it be one of today's trendy kids, I'm quick to drop a hip and with-it "moderately neato," in order to show that I'm really a cool guy and not just some old fuddy-duddy. Once again, with "moderately neato" I reveal only a limited bit of information.

Take That!

But sometimes I'm having one of my really great days, and I'm in a jaunty and expansive mood. In these situations I tend to throw caution to the wind and express my full feelings. Innocently enough, the person will inquire, "How are you?" And he has no idea what's coming. So I give him both barrels.

I lean forward, look him squarely in the eye, and hit him with a quick and cheery "I'm good, well, fine, keen, dandy, swell and excellent! And, might I add, fabuloso!" Believe me, I've bowled over more than one unsuspecting inquirer with this sudden volley of positive energy.

Weekend Wishes

Just so you know, I'm prepared for other situations as well. If someone says, "Have a nice weekend," I never say, "You too." Because I never know if, perhaps, by the time the weekend rolls around, I will have other plans for that person. Come Friday, I may wish to have them slain.

Yuletide

Also, I never say, "A merry Christmas to you and yours." I don't like the possibilities suggested by that use of the possessive pronoun *yours*. One never knows when the other person may be a slave owner. I certainly wouldn't want to encourage that sort of behavior.

Closing Thoughts

One last thing: My stingingly clever remarks sometimes extend to retail encounters. When the supermarket checkout person asks, "Paper or plastic?" I often say, "Woven silk," just to keep him on his toes. "Rolled steel" is not a bad answer either.

I'm happy to pass along to you these methods of mine for making the world a better place. I hope you use them wisely, and, may I be so bold as to say, "Have an excellent immediate future."

Too Many Thank-Yous

Hosts & Guests

I find it bothersome that on radio and TV interview shows, once the host says, "Thank you for being here," the guest always thinks he has to say, "Thank you for having me." It's not necessary. All that's needed is a simple "You're welcome" or "Nice to be here." "Having people on" is what they do on interview shows; they're looking for guests all the time. There's no need to thank them.

The same is true of radio call-in shows. The people who call in say, "Thank you for taking my call." Why do they bother? Think about it. Taking calls is what these shows do. They're call-in shows; they take calls. That's their function. Why thank them for doing what they can't avoid? It bothers me that people even *think* they need to say these things. It's all very insincere.

Telephone Operators

And on the subject of insincerity, let's not forget the nonsense that telephone operators are ordered to say by their corporate-drone bosses. Keeping in mind, of course, that telephone operators are not operators anymore, they're *attendants*. *Telephone attendants*. Or *telephone representatives*. I've also heard them called *communications facilitators*, and *customer care professionals*.

Anyway, these operators used to say, "Who did you want to speak with?" Now it's, "How may I direct your call?" I don't like that. It sounds artificial. And it has a ring of self-importance. "How may I direct your call?" Jesus, everyone wants to direct; it's not just actors anymore. And when you tell them who you're trying to reach, they say, "Thank you, it's a pleasure to forward your call." Sounds polite, doesn't it? It's not. It's insincere.

Too Many Telephone Thank-Yous

And on the subject of telephone operators, another complaint I have about these people takes me back to my original point — the unnecessary overuse of thank you. These days, I think there are far too many thank-yous being thrown around on the telephone. "Thank you for this," "Thank you for that," "Thank you for something else." I find myself being thanked for everything I do, and then some.

I recently called a friend who was staying at the Marriott. He was staying at the Marriott. I called him there — at the Marriott. I intentionally dialed the number of the Marriott, because that's where I expected him to be. The connection went through. Guess what the operator said? Right. "Thank you for calling the Marriott." Well, what did she think I was going to do? Call the Hyatt? He was staying at the Marriott. It wouldn't do me much good to call the Hyatt. We all know what they would have said: "Thank you for calling the Hyatt."

They even thank you for doing things you can't avoid. Did you ever have an operator say, "Thank you for calling the operator?" I've had that happen. Well, who did she think I was gonna call, the night watchman? The chairman of the board? Jesus! Thank you, thank you, thank you. It's annoying.

One time, at a hotel, I wanted to get my car. Naturally, I needed to call valet parking. I noticed the little plastic card next to my telephone. It said "Press nine for valet parking." I was about to press nine, but then I noticed I didn't have to press nine, because right there on the phone one of the speed-dial buttons had a little picture of a car next to it, and it said "Valet parking." So I pushed that button. The one that said "Valet parking." The one with the picture of the car. Someone answered. You know what he said? Right. "Thank you for calling valet parking."

Well, fuck! Didn't he know that if a guest wants to retrieve his car, he more or less *has* to call valet parking? That's where the cars are! And doesn't he know the designers of hotel telephones have gone to a great deal of trouble to make it easy for people to get their cars? I had simply taken advantage of their skills; I had called valet parking by pressing a single button. A button marked with a little picture of a car.

And I can assure you, folks, if I had thought for even a split second that valet parking *didn't* have my car — for instance, if I'd thought the bartender had it — I would have called the cocktail lounge. I would have pressed the little button with the picture of the martini next to it. Which would, of course, have given the bartender a chance to say, "Thank you for calling the cocktail lounge."

One further complaint: These days, if I call a hotel from the outside, the telephone operators waste an awful lot of my time: "Hello. Thank you for calling the Lincoln Plaza Hotel-Resort and Conference Center, my name is Taneesha, have a nice day, and how may I direct your call?" And I say, "I'll have to get back to you. I forgot why I called." Sometimes, just to scare the operator, I'll sob, "It's too late. He just died."

Thank you, thank you, thank you. It's too much. Occasionally, a *recording* will thank me. "Thank you for using AT&T." How can this be? Isn't gratitude a personal feeling? Recording devices don't have personal feelings, do they? No. But I do. And I feel this showy, hyper-politeness must be stopped. Thank you for reading this far.

Further Thoughts on Exploding Heads

Wouldn't it be interesting if the only way you could die was that suddenly your head blew up? If there were no other causes of death? Everyone died the same way? Sooner or later, without warning, your head simply exploded? You know what I think? I think people would get used to it. I believe people can learn to take anything in stride if they think it's unavoidable.

Picture a bunch of guys singin' "Happy Birthday":

"Happy birthday to you, Happy birthday to you, Happy birthday, dear Charlie . . ." BOOM!! And Charlie's head blows up. But all the candles go out, so it's actually a form of good luck. And everyone applauds.

Of course, there'd be an occasional downside. "God, another head? That's two this week. I just had this suit cleaned." But we'd learn to deal with it.

Let's say you were sitting in a restaurant with your girlfriend, and the waiter was reciting the specials:

"Tonight we have the marinated bat nipples on a bed of lightly sautéed panda assholes . . ." BOOM!! The waiter's head explodes. I'll bet you wouldn't miss a beat.

"Honey, did he say *bat* nipples or *cat* nipples? We'd better get another waiter. And some fresh salsa. I'm not eating this stuff; he was holding it when he blew. So anyway, I'm allergic to bat nipples. I think I might go with the free-range penguin dick or the deep-dish moose balls. How about you? Wait, hold still. There's a little piece of eyebrow on your cheek. There, I got it. By the way, honey, what wine goes with brain?"

Just a Stone's Throw

When I watch news tapes of the Intifada from Palestine, and see the Arab kids throwing stones at Israeli tanks, I always have fun watching for the kids who are lefthanded, because lefthanders have kind of a natural curveball. It's really interesting. I can't wait till major league baseball comes to the Middle East. Incidentally, I also noticed that Arab kids usually throw in a high arc, whereas the Catholic kids in Northern Ireland throw more of a line drive. Either way is all right with me as long as they're accurate. Kids are great.

Bud's Medical Center: C'mon In!

"Hi. I'm Bud, president and head doctor of Bud's Medical Center. Come on in to Bud's. This weekend we're havin' a special on head injuries: any sort of head injury you got, from a black eye to a completely caved-in skull, just a dollar fifty this weekend at Bud's. We'll also give a free estimate to anyone who's bleedin'. So if you're sick, injured, diseased, hurt, maimed, disfigured or just plain don't feel good, come on in to Bud's Medical Center. Bud's: Where all the sick people go."

Buried Alive at 65

Wouldn't it be weird if they just buried you alive when you got to be sixty-five? If that was the deal for everyone? Right after your sixty-fifth birthday party they came and got you and dumped you in a big pit with a bunch of other people your age, threw in all your birthday presents and buried you all alive? Wouldn't that be weird? Jesus, I'm glad they don't do that. That would be weird.

But sooner or later we'll have to do something like that; we'll have to. We can't take care of old people as it is, and there are going to be millions more of them. Good, early medical care is a mixed blessing; it leads to too many old people. What are you going to do with them? No one wants to take care of them. Their children put them in homes. Even the people whose job it is to take care of them in the homes don't give a shit; they abuse them. No one cares. It's my belief that, sooner or later, we're going to have to start killing old people before they become a burden. One good thing, though: We'll save a lot of money on Social Security and maybe the country won't go broke.

There's always a bright side.

Moment of Silence

The custom of observing a moment of silence before an athletic event to honor dead people strikes me as meaningless. And arbitrary. Because, if you'll notice, only certain people get this special treatment. It's highly selective. Therefore I've decided that someday, when the time comes that every single person in the world who dies receives a moment of silence, I will begin paying attention. Until then, count me out. It's ridiculous. Here's what I mean.

Let's say you live in Cleveland, and you decide to go to the Browns game. There you are in the football stadium, with a hot dog and a beer, ready to enjoy the action, and a somber-sounding public-address announcer interrupts the festivities, intoning darkly:

"And now, ladies and gentlemen, we ask that you remove your hats and join us in observing a moment of silence for the forty-three unattractive, mentally retarded, overweight Bolivian dance instructors who lost their lives this morning in a roller coaster accident at an amusement park near La Paz. Apparently, they all stood up on a sharp turn and went flying off, willy-nilly, into the cool, crisp, morning La Paz air. And, being heavier than air, crashed through the roof of the funhouse, landing on several clowns, killing them all and crushing their red noses beyond recognition."

Snickering is heard in the crowd. The American announcer continues:

"And, ladies and gentlemen, lest you think this amusing, lest you think this a time for laughter, I ask you please — please — to put yourself in the place of a bereaved Bolivian who may be seated near you this afternoon. Try reversing places. Imagine yourself visiting Bolivia and taking in a soccer game. Imagine yourself seated in the stadium with a burrito and a cerveza, ready to enjoy the action, and a somber-sounding, Spanish public-address announcer interrupts the festivities, intoning darkly:

" 'Señors y señoritas, we ask that you remove your sombreros and join us in observing un momento de silencio for the forty-three mentally retarded, overweight, unattractive American meat inspectors who lost their lives this morning in a Ferris wheel accident at a carnival near Ashtabula, Ohio.'

"The Spanish announcer continues:

" 'Apparently, the huge wheel flew out of control, spinning madly, flinging the poor meat inspectors off, willy-nilly, into the hot, humid, Midwestern air. And, being heavier than air, they crashed through the roof of the carnival freak show, crushing the dog-faced boy, and destroying many of his chew-toys.'

"And let's say, as you sit there in La Paz listening to this, you find yourself seated next to some Bolivian smart-ass who's giggling and poking his friend in the ribs. May I suggest you'd be highly pissed at this lack of respect for Americans? And, might I add, rightly so."

The American announcer continues his plea:

"And so, ladies and gentlemen, considering the many grieving Bolivians who may be seated among you today, and trying to keep in check that normal human impulse to laugh heartily when another person dies, let us try again — really hard this time — to observe a moment of silence for the forty-three unattractive, mentally retarded, overweight Bolivian dance instructors who went flying, willy-nilly, off the roller coaster in La Paz. Not to mention the poor, unsuspecting clowns who at the time were innocently filling their water pistols."

You can see the problem either announcer would face; the fans would simply not be able to get into it. But I understand that; I can empathize with the fans. Because, frankly, I don't know what to do during a moment of silence, either. Do you? What are you supposed to do? What do they expect? Do they want us to pray? They don't say that. If they want me to pray, they should ask. I'll pray, but at least have the courtesy to make a formal request.

But no. They offer no guidance, no instruction at all. I honestly don't know what to do. Sometimes I resort to evil thoughts: I wish my seatmates ill fortune in days to come; I fantasize about standing naked in front of the Lincoln Memorial and becoming sexually aroused; I picture thousands of penguins being hacked to death by boatloads of graduate students. More often, though, I wind up bored silly, searching for something to occupy my thoughts.

One time I inventoried the pimples on the neck of the man in front of me, hoping to find one with a hair growing through it, so I could quietly pluck it out during the confusion of halftime. On a happier occasion, I once found myself staring at the huge but perfectly formed breasts of the woman to my left, her fleshy mounds rising and falling softly in the late October sun. And my thoughts turned tenderly romantic:

"Holy shit! Look at the fuckin' knobs on her! Great fuckin' knobs! I think I'm gonna go to the refreshment stand, buy myself a weenie and hide it in my pants. Then, during halftime, I'm gonna whip out the weenie and force her to watch while I eat the bun and stuff the weenie up my . . . naaah! She's probably one of those uptight chicks who'd think I'm weird. She doesn't know the problem is I'm shy."

Those are my thoughts, and I can't help it. During a moment of silence my imagination runs away with me. I don't know what to do. And why is it silence they're looking for? What good is silence? The ones being remembered are already dead, they're not going to wake up now. Why not a moment of screaming? Wouldn't that be more appropriate for dead people? Wouldn't you like to hear 60,000 fans screaming, "Aaaaaiiiiiieeeeeaaagghh!!" It sure would put me in the mood for football.

And one more criticism. Why honor only

the dead? Why this favoritism? Why not the injured, as well? There are always more injured than there are dead in any decent tragedy. What about them? And what about those who aren't dead or injured, but are simply "treated and released"? How about, if not silence, at least a moment of muffled conversation for those who were treated and released? It's an honorable condition. Personally, I've always wanted to be treated and released. Usually, I'm treated and detained. Perhaps it's for the best.

Terrorism Misnomers:

Domestic Terrorism

When they talk about domestic terrorism, they often cite the Oklahoma City bombing. But that wasn't terrorism. Terrorism involves a series of acts intended to put a civilian population in a state of panic, fear and uncertainty, in order to achieve some political goal. Oklahoma City wasn't terrorism, it was payback. Revenge. Timothy McVeigh wanted to punish the federal government for what it did at Waco and Ruby Ridge. Revenge, not terrorism.

Terrorism Expert

Television news channels will often present some guest they identify as a *terrorism expert*. But you can take one look at him and see that he's clearly not a terrorism expert. He's a guy in a suit who obviously works in an office. And I say he's not a terrorism expert.

You wanna know who's a terrorism expert? Osama bin Laden. Ayman al-Zawahiri. The people they hang around with. Those are the terrorism experts. Has this guy in the suit ever blown anyone up? No. So why is he a terrorism expert?

I'm sure the TV people would say, "Well, because he's made a study of terrorism." Oh, I see. So really, he's an expert in the study of terrorism, the subject of terrorism. But can he make a suicide vest? Fuck, no. And if he can, he should make one, put it on and press the button. Then he'll be a real terrorism expert. Like those people he now only reads about.

Suicide Bomber

No. Sorry to disagree; it's anything *but* suicide. A person who commits suicide is someone who places no value on his life: "My life is worthless, I'm going to end it." These so-called suicide bombers don't feel that way. They feel their lives are worth something, and that by giving them up they make a statement to the world, furthering a cause they believe in deeply. In their eyes, their lives (when sacrificed) have value. And, by the way, the "suicide bombers" themselves don't call it that. In a stunning example of euphemism, they call it a *sacred explosion.* Holy smoke!

"Homicide Bombers"

And in spite of what Bush has been ordered to say, they're not *homicide bombers,* either. All bombings are intended to kill people, to produce homicides. Anyone who packs a bomb with nails and bits of steel, and sets it off in a public place, is hoping to commit homicide. This is true of any bomb, whether you drop it out of an airplane or leave it on a doorstep; you're hoping to kill people. That's the purpose. Killing people. In the case of these so-called suicide bombs, what's different is that the people setting them off are intentionally ending their own lives in the process. That's why we confuse the act with suicide.

Human Shields

During bombing raids in Iraq, the media liked to say that Saddam Hussein used people as *human shields*. That's not accurate. Although it's true they were used as shields, the fact is they were humans already. So if these humans were used as shields, they *were* human shields. They weren't *being used as* human shields.

Got that?

Cowards

Bush calls the al Qaeda people cowards, and says, "They like to hide." Well, isn't that what the American Continental Army did during the American Revolution? Our beloved patriots? They hid. They hid behind trees. Then they came out, killed some British soldiers, and ran away. Just like al Qaeda. That's what you do when you're outnumbered and have less firepower than the enemy. It's called "trying to win." It's not cowardly.

Bill Maher may have stretched the point a bit when he said that air force pilots who release their bombs from hundreds of miles away are cowards; flying combat jets doesn't attract many cowards. But it's not nearly as courageous an act as deliberately strapping a bomb to your chest and heading for the disco with no intention of dancing.

I will say this. Getting out of the Vietnam war through Daddy's connections and then not living up to your end of the bargain is probably a form of cowardice.

"Heroes" Who "Died for Their Country"

The Port Authority of New York and New Jersey said that changing the name of Newark Airport to Liberty International Airport would be a way of honoring "the more than 3,000 heroes who died for their country in the World Trade Center." Pardon me for pointing this out, folks, but stock traders, clerks, receptionists, cooks, waiters and building maintenance people in the World Trade Center didn't *die for their country*. They died because they went to work. Not one of them would have shown up for work that day if you had told them they would die as a result. Try to get your heroes straight.

Not everyone who died in 9/11 was a *hero*. Hero is a very special word, that's why we reserve it for certain special people. Not every fireman and policeman who was on duty that day was a hero. The ones who risked or lost their lives trying to rescue people were heroes. They acted heroically. The others probably did a good job and were very helpful, but heroes?

If everyone's a hero, then the word doesn't mean much anymore. And sooner or later we'll have to give the real heroes (the heroic ones) a new name, to distinguish them from the rest of the pack. Too bad "superheroes" is already taken; it would have been perfect. But relax, folks, if I know us, "megahero" can't be too far over the horizon. Although to be honest, I kind of like the alliteration in "hyperhero." Let's shoot for that.

War, God, Stuff Like That

These anti-war demonstrators are really unimpressive people. They're against war? How groundbreaking; what a courageous stand. Listen, angry asshole, pick something difficult. Like religion. Why don't you get out on the street and start marching around against religion — something that's really harmful to mankind. War is simply nature's way of doing things; of keeping down the count. Religion is the problem. Get rid of religion and you've done the planet a favor. So how about getting out there next weekend and marching around with a sign that says HO HO HO! RELIGION MUST GO!? Come on, protesters, show some balls.

. . . And the Horse You Rode In On

I can't understand what it is people like about John Wayne movies; I think they suck. I find him inauthentic. Sometimes, when I'm clicking around the channels, looking for the least objectionable program, I come across a movie scene in progress. It's in black and white, it's clearly a Western, and it looks old enough that it could actually be fun to watch. I see guys like John Ireland, Barton MacLane, Ward Bond, Anthony Quinn, Charles Bronson, Dan Duryea, Thomas Mitchell, Lee Van Cleef and Brian Donlevy shooting each other, drinking and playing cards, and I get this great nostalgic feeling. Then John Wayne rides up. And I have to reach for the remote. It's a fuckin' shame. He spoils war movies in the same way. By the way, I feel the same about Jimmy Stewart. These people should not have been allowed to spoil so many perfectly good movies.

Don't Ask the Doctor

Announcer: Good afternoon, folks. This is Pedro Fleming. Welcome to *Don't Ask the Doctor*, America's only medical advice program based on questions that are not pertinent to the field of medicine. Here is our medical expert, Dr. Ned Gittles. How are you today, Doctor?

Doctor: Not bad, Pedro, considering all the sick people I see. How about you?

Pedro: Well, I have a malignant tumor inside my nose.

Doctor: Don't ignore that. Take some pills. Do you have any pills at home?

Pedro: Sure, lots of different kinds.

Doctor: Good, take some of them. That's my advice.

Pedro: And good advice it is. Well, let's get started. Here's a question from Elaine Trickler in Frog Balls, Tennessee. She writes, "Doctor, my car seems to hesitate a little when I accelerate from a red light, and I'm afraid it will stall. What should I do?"

Doctor: Don't ask me.

Pedro: That's right. Don't ask the doctor. How would he know? That's obviously a question for a mechanic.

Doctor: Righty-ho!

Pedro: For having her question used on *Don't Ask the Doctor*, Elaine Trickler will receive a free rectal thermometer by Recto-Swell, the last word in rectal thermometers. See the new Recto-Swell line of monogrammed thermometers at leading rectal equipment dealers in your area. Try Orifice Max or Brown's Personal Items for Inside the Rectum.

Doctor: Recto-Swell is a good one, Pedro. Sometimes I use mine when I'm cooking a turkey.

Pedro: Great idea, Doctor. Well, folks, that's it for today. Tune in again tomorrow when Dr. Ned Gittles will answer the question, "How can I increase my soybean yield?" on America's favorite medical advice program, *Don't Ask the Doctor*.
Stay tuned for *Video Magazine*, as beauty expert Mavis Davis shows a young albino girl how to keep her hair from turning prematurely brown. You're tuned to Elaine and Joe's Radio Network.

It's No Use

Usage-Use

I object to the use of *usage* when it's used in place of *use*. There's nothing wrong with using *use;* it's been in use a long time and I'm used to it. It isn't that *usage* isn't useful; I simply have no use for its current usage. The use of *usage* should be consistent with good usage: I'd prefer to say, "My use of the Internet" rather than "my usage." If I meant it collectively, I might say, "American usage of the Internet." But so far I haven't meant that.

And, as I'm using space on *usage,* I'll use some more on *utilize.* Using *utilize* instead of utilizing *use* is one of those attempts to make things sound more important than they really are. Sports announcers do that all the time; they misapply big words: "He's not utilizing all his skills." They don't understand that an athlete doesn't utilize his skills, he uses them. The coach utilizes his players, but the players use their skills. Don't use *utilize* when you should be *utilizing* use.

Making a Difference

Another sports-announcer crime is the use of the word *differential* when they mean *difference*. "There was a twelve-point differential at halftime." No. Sorry. There was a twelve-point *difference*. Differential is a mechanical or mathematical term. And by mathematical I don't mean Knicks 55, Pacers 43. *Difference* and *differential* are different. Go Knicks!

On the Links

It also annoys me that people sometimes claim to see a *linkage* when they actually see a *link*. I think link is fine. *Linkage* reminds me of my car's transmission. In fact, I think my car's linkage is located somewhere near the differential.

Stoppage

Stoppage is another ungainly word. The most frequently heard euphemism for a labor strike is *work stoppage*. Apparently, *labor strike* sounded too Marxist for loyal Americans. But stoppage sounds like an obstructed bowel. And *stoppage* is much too close to *sewage* for my comfort.

Outage

Usage, linkage and *stoppage* remind me of *outage.* This is a word I simply dislike. It's an awkward, ugly word. *Outage.* It sounds like something that's done when a gay person's identity is revealed. But actually its most frequent use is in describing a loss of electricity: *power outage.* We used to say *power failure,* but I guess Americans don't like to admit failure — even when it's manifest. Regardless, we ought to find a better way to answer the question, "What happened to the lights?"*

*I recently heard the following sentence on CNN: "Because of high winds, about 250,000 people in New England are without power." I thought, "Gee, when you think about it, about 275 million people in the United States are without power. They just aren't aware of it."

Uncalled-For Editorial Comments:

Who's Responsible for This?

When reporting a bombing by some radical group, the news media will often inform us that *"No one has claimed responsibility."* Why is this wording used instead of *"No one has taken credit"*? To save the feelings of the dead people's relatives? The people who did the bombing surely see it as credit. Let them have their moment in the sun. Look at all the trouble they went to.

Unfortunately, They All Got Out Alive

Here's another gratuitous editorial appendage often heard on the TV-news coverage of a fire or an accident: "Luckily, no one was hurt" or "The good news is no one was injured." I consider those to be editorial comments. After all, I may not think it's such good news that no one was hurt. I'm entitled to decide for myself whether or not injuries to strangers are good or bad news. I may prefer hearing, "It's a shame no one was hurt." It's entirely possible. Please save the commentary for the editorial page.

Put On a Happy Face

And I could also do without these grim, mock-serious facial expressions and sad voices the television-news people affect when reporting these so-called tragedies. Diane Sawyer is one of the worst offenders. She lowers her voice dramatically and puts on this really sad face and tells you all about the baby who died in a washing machine. If you weren't listening carefully, you'd think the goddamn "tragedy" happened to her. Is that good? I don't think so. Just let me have the news, please; I'll get Meryl Streep to handle the sad faces.

Thoughts On "Thoughts"

Another empty sentiment concerning the death of people; you hear it on the news, and you hear it in real life: *"Our thoughts are with the family."* What exactly does that mean? Sympathies I can understand; prayers, as ineffective as they are, I can understand. But thoughts? Why thoughts? What kind of thoughts? Just thoughts? Like, "Gee, he's dead"? How does that help?

When first reporting on Michael J. Fox's Parkinson's disease, one newslady announced that *"Everyone's thoughts are with Michael."* Well, I'm by no means happy that he's sick, and he happens to be one of the few celebrities I genuinely like. But to be perfectly honest with you, for most of the day my thoughts were definitely not with Michael. I wish him well, and I admire the way he copes. But at any given moment, my thoughts are probably on pussy.

The Explicit TV Channel

The satellite service I get has this great channel, Explicit TV. It's not nearly as limited in content as the standard channels you see. Here are a few excerpts from their program guide:

Daytime Drama

Harper Darrow and Mary Jane Crotchjockey star in the continuing story of hardship, sorrow, fear, pain, disillusionment, guilt and suicide in a blue-collar family living in a rundown neighborhood. Don't miss the acclaimed daytime drama *Fuck This Shit*. In tomorrow's episode, Velma is given a cesarean section by Nick and Artie, two neighbors who are handy with tools, only to discover that she wasn't really pregnant. (Partial nudity, heavy drinking, spousal abuse, despair, home-improvement tips)

Public Service Program

Every evening at seven-thirty, citizens and consumers get a chance to sound off and air their complaints. Don't miss *Blow It Out Your Ass!*, with consumer ombudsman Susan Dorkalot. If you have a complaint to register, be sure you call in, talk to Susan, explain your grievances and complaints and then listen carefully as she bellows, "Blow It Out Your Ass!" (Con games, larceny, gullibility, anger, hostility)

Financial News

Every evening at six o'clock, catch the Wall Street buzz on *Money Talks, Shit Walks*. Tonight, Ron Insana interviews Windfall Profitz III, one more worthless cocksucker who makes his living on Wall Street. Don't be left behind in the fast-changing world of business and finance. Keep up-to-date by watching *Money Talks, Shit Walks*, brought to you by Pennington-Craymore: Wall Street scumbags since 1869. (Greed, envy, arrogance, predatory males)

Old-Time Comedy Favorites

Comedy rules the house on Wednesday night with four of your all-time favorites in a row. First, on *Mork and Mindy*, Mork is caught performing cunnilingus on a gumball machine. The fun begins and the gumballs fly when Mindy tries to work Mork's tongue loose, gets sexually aroused and has her first quintuple orgasm. (Gum-chewing, moaning, Lord's name taken in vain)

Then, on *All in the Family*, Archie Bunker kills a nigger, blames it on a spic and two chinks and hires a yid lawyer to bribe the judge. Don't miss the laughs as two guineas beat the shit out of Archie just for the fun of it. Meanwhile, police arrest Michael for pimping out Gloria to Louise Jefferson for a mixed-race, dyke gangbang in the back of George's dry cleaners. (Racism, bigotry, vaginal bruising)

After that, on *I Love Lucy*, Ricky pays Ethel twenty dollars for a quick hand job in the broom closet, but things get really hilarious when Fred is caught placing a kosher knockwurst in Lucy's asshole. Things get worse when Ricky's nightclub show is canceled as twelve members of the band come down with anal warts and have to play standing up. (Nudity, sex, sphincter jokes, bogus Latin music)

Our quartet of madcap sitcoms concludes with *Leave it to Beaver*, as Beaver and Wally fall out of a maple tree while masturbating each other. Imagine everyone's surprise when they land smack on top of a flustered June Cleaver, who is giving Eddie Haskell a blow job under the tree. (Pee-pee jokes)

Frontier Nostalgia

Next week, back to back on *Nostalgia Theater*, you'll see two of America's favorite episodes of *Little House on the Prairie*. First, the 1975 Christmas show, "A Douche Bag for Clara." Little Clara comes of age and asks Santa for her own douche bag. At first it looks like a disaster when, out of inexperience, she sticks it in the wrong hole. But Luke, the disturbed neighbor boy, saves the day when he distracts everyone by removing his dog's vital organs with a stick. Clara later learns to douche properly after several long sessions with old Doc Flathammer.

Then, you'll see just about everyone's favorite *Little House on the Prairie*, the hilarious "Missy Takes a Dump in the Woods," as our young heroine answers nature's call while wearing high heels and a long dress. Watch her as she tries to maneuver through bramble bushes and poison sumac. Then, too late, she finds out there's no toilet paper and has to wipe herself with several pine cones. The fun (and the screaming) begins when she unknowingly pulls the cones in the wrong direction. (Partial nudity, douche lessons, unpleasant language)

Dueling Talk Shows

Since last month Oprah had a special show, "Women Who Fake Orgasms," this month, not to be outdone, Jerry Springer is presenting a nighttime special, "Men Who Fake Bowel Movements." (Graphic video, foul odors)

Dr. Phil

In a special program, Dr. Phil welcomes famed psychic medium John Edwards to the show and they try to contact dead whores. Then, in a special pre-taped segment, Dr. Phil cures a woman's fear of flying by throwing her out of an airplane. (Limited intellects)

Even More Talk

Two fascinating glimpses into the medical world as Montel Williams investigates "Doctors Who Intentionally Give Patients the Siff" and Maury Povich interviews "Twins Who Eat Each Other's Feces." (Indigestion)

Documentary

Award-winning documentary maker Ken Burns continues his penetrating look at America's history as he takes on a three-part study, *The Great Cabbage-Fart Panic of 1860.* The disaster, which lasted an entire summer, took the lives of thirty-five hundred people, mostly from lung diseases. The special sound effects heard required the services of over three-hundred Milwaukee men who were fed only beer and cabbage for seven weeks. Fourteen stuntmen died during the re-creations.

Music Special

Then, Friday at midnight, don't miss Willie Nelson's pay-per-view concert, *Wankin' with Willie.* Willie kicks off the festivities in great fashion as he gets right into one of his all-time best sellers, "Too Drunk to Jerk Off."

Then he introduces his guest star, Loretta Lynn, who sings her big hit "Your Love Ran Down My Leg and Now You're Gone." Willie then joins her onstage and they warble a pair of romantic love songs: "Kiss Me I'm Coming" and "You Blew My Mind,

Now Blow Me." The pair's tandem segment concludes as Willie serenades Loretta with his special new arrangement of "We Kissed and My Balls Exploded."

Willie then takes the solo spotlight again with his familiar country lament, "I Shoulda Fucked Old What's-Her-Name."

And what would a Willie Nelson show be without a good ol' cowboy song? This time he honors the late Roy Rogers and does an authentic western ballad written by Roy called "It's Midnight in Montana and I Can't Get My Dick Outta This Cow." Home-movie footage of the original incident, taken by Roy's beloved wife, Dale Evans, adds to the song's authenticity. His faithful horse Trigger is seen off to the side brandishing a huge hard-on.

The whole shebang then ends with more vintage video, this time from Willie's first special. Two of Willie's great buddies, Johnny Cash and Waylon Jennings, both now gone to that big corral in the sky, are seen with Willie as they all deliver a rousing version of that definitive honky-tonk anthem, "Drinkin' Beer, Takin' a Shit, and Passin' Out."

As the closing credits roll and his band plays "God Bless America," Willie is seen smoking a big joint rolled in American flag paper.

Concerned Parents

Dad: How was Debbie's checkup?

Mom: The dentist was very pleased. Only six extractions this time.

Dad: Great.

Mom: Plus she needs a jawbone graft and twelve implants.

Dad: Must be that new gel toothpaste we've been using.

Mom: Yes! Patented new Choppersheen! Removes unwanted pulp, enamel and bone.

Dad: Choppersheen. Now in refreshing mint!

Memo to Self

Here's a piece of graffiti I saw scrawled in black marking pen on one of those newspaper dispensers you see on New York sidewalks. It said, "Rosie O'Donnell sleeps with her head between a woman's legs." I couldn't help wondering who had written it, and under what circumstances.

I wondered, had someone simply awakened that morning and decided the time had come to share this little tidbit he'd been thinking about for a long time? And had he gone out that day determined to find a good place to write it? And this seemed like the best spot? Was it that simple?

Or was the person just out walking around and had this sudden burst of inspiration — something he didn't want to forget — but didn't have a piece of paper handy? And why didn't he take the newspaper dispenser home with him to refer to later?

And I also wondered, if that was it, what kind of person was walking around with one of those thick, felt-tip marking pens in his pocket in the first place? This wasn't no Sharpie, folks, this was one of those serious, thick, chisel-tip pens that gets you high if you leave it open too long.

It's thoughts of this sort that seriously limit the size of my circle of friends.

Answer This, You Prick

(Drum roll)

Announcer: Good evening, ladies and gentlemen, this is your announcer, Dondelayo Prell. Join us now as we play America's favorite game, *Answer This, You Prick!* The show where folks just like you, although, perhaps, less attractive, have a chance to win fabulous prizes. And now here's America's favorite prick, Anthony Boff.

(Applause, cymbal crash)

Boff: Hi, folks. I'm your genial host, Anthony Boff. Our jackpot today is one hundred and eleven dollars, plus a trip up north. Let's meet our first two contestants, Clark Fark and Dolly Drelman. What do you do, Clark?

Fark: I pretty much just sit around, Anthony.

Boff: Swell. What about you, Dolly?

307

Dolly: No sitting around for me, Mr. Boff. I stand near the window.

Boff: All day?

Dolly: Except for meals. Unless I'm fasting.

Boff: Well, you sound like interesting people. Let's get right to our game. Just before airtime, a short backstage shoving match determined that Clark would get the first question. So here it is. Are you ready, Clark?

Fark: Ready as a bastard, Mr. Boff.

Boff: Okay. Remember, the category is "People." Now then, Clark Fark, as America watches, please . . . answer this, you prick!

(Sound of a clock ticking)

Damon and Sylvia Prongster live in Thighmaster, Maine, on the corner of Watkins and Schermerhorn. Last Tuesday, at six in the evening, a brown Chevrolet drove past their house. What was the name of the last mechanic to change the oil on that car, and what was the name of his grandfather's first-grade teacher? You have three seconds.

(Music and ticking)

Fark: Jason Warburton and Mrs. Amelia Day Higgins.

Boff: Oh, I'm awfully sorry, Clark. Your answer is incorrect. The correct answer is Dudley Manoosh and Clara Wheatley.

Fark: Well, I just took a wild guess.

Dolly: I knew that answer.

Boff: Not fuckin' likely, Dolly.

Fark: I agree, Mr. Boff. I think she's full of shit.

Boff: Clark, I'm awfully sorry you did such a poor job. I see your family in our audience and they look ashamed. But you do win a roll of quarters and the home version of teacher-approved *Answer This, You Prick!* Play it with your kids. And we'll add a dollar to our jackpot, bringing our total to one hundred and twelve dollars. It's too late for us to get to Dolly Drelman, but that's just too bad for her.

Don't forget to join us again in June or May to play *Answer This, You Prick!* when one of our main questions will be "Who was the first person to strangle someone he had known for more than six years?" Goodnight, everybody.

Announcer: Guests on *Answer This, You Prick!* receive a framed picture of Henry Kissinger and stay at the luxurious Hotel for the Malformed in downtown Watsonville. Watsonville: the last place you wanna be.

(Music, applause up and out)

Three Short Conversations

Bless Me, Father

Penitent: Bless me, Father, for I have sinned. Yesterday, I killed my third priest in a month. The first time it scared me. The second time I had no feelings at all. The third time . . . I actually began to like it.

Priest: I'm not really a priest, son. I'm just cleaning the confessional.

Thanksgiving, in the Kitchen

Bart: You look great in that dress, Marian. Really sexy. I was thinkin', if, God forbid, something ever happened to Joe and Estelle, I'd sure like to spend some time with you.

Marian: I feel the same way about you, Bart.

Bart: Really? Look, maybe we wouldn't have to wait for something to happen to Joe and Estelle. Whaddya think?

Walk/Don't Walk

Joey: I heard Phil Hanley died. What happened?

Sid: It's the strangest thing. He was
walkin' down Fifth Avenue on his
way to Times Square. He took a
right at Forty-second Street and
headed over to Broadway. He was
just strollin' along, mindin' his own
business, when suddenly a big chunk
of concrete fell on him and crushed
him to death.

Joey: Jesus! What a way to go!

Sid: I know. I woulda taken a right at Fif-
tieth Street, gone over to Broadway
and then headed down to Times
Square.

Uncle Lochinvar

Uncle Lochinvar, although a moral vegetarian who only ate meat if the animal had died in its sleep, once punched out his twin daughters because they wouldn't lend him fifteen cents. He could speak seven languages, but unfortunately, he was disliked in all those countries. His hobby was visiting cemeteries in poor areas and guessing which people had the worst lives. He fell in love with a fish dentist named Chiquita, and a week later she died from using infected toilet paper while watching a TV show called *Progress in Medicine.* Inconsolable, Lochinvar, after composing his own epitaph, "Believe me, I wasn't a schmuck," died as part of a group-enema suicide pact.

Uncle Sherlock

Uncle Sherlock was a proctologist's mate in the navy who fought in Korea and the Philippines. Unfortunately, it was just last year and he was jailed in both countries. He was the only man ever brought before the World Court for unpaid parking tickets. His personal checks did not depict nature scenes, they showed animal euthanasia and the Allied fire-bombing of Dresden. During a bungee jump, he fell in love with a Dutch courtroom artist and they were married in a windmill the next day, during a relative calm. They drifted apart when he realized that all she wanted to do was sit for hours and listen to skiing on the radio. Later he moved to Milan and was killed when a riot broke out at the La Scala candy counter during the second act of *Rigoletto*.

Uncle Dagwood

Uncle Dagwood was a fun guy. He once claimed the most difficult thing he ever did was to take a shit in a phone booth without removing his overcoat. He met his wife, Spatula, at a UFO convention where she was conducting a basketball clinic for abductees. The instant they met, Dagwood knew she was his kind of woman: She had peach preserves in her hair and brown gravy caked on her neck. Spatula worked for years as an unregistered nurse and eventually ran off with an ironmonger. She and her new lover, Rolf, died in a blimp fire over Newfoundland, and

Dagwood was killed in a Barcalounger, having rough sex with a Norwegian fisherman.

Uncle Lucifer

Uncle Lucifer was my most interesting uncle. He was an elk hunter, but he wouldn't kill the elk. Instead, he would chase it down, knock it to the ground and suck all the gristle out of its neck through a Donald Duck straw. He was fun to be with; he could eat a whole bowl of alphabet soup and then vomit up the vowels and consonants separately. His hobby was attending reunions of groups he never belonged to and pretending to be people who were long dead. Till the end of his days, Lucifer remained bitter that when he was a boy there had been no seedless red grapes. He died in an Indiana furniture outlet when he was torn to pieces by a pack of Cape hunting dogs.

Child Care Tip

Never use a hammer to smooth out the lumps on a newborn baby's head. Instead, wrap a soft, clean cloth around a ten-inch length of wood and pound each lump repeatedly until the larger ones are gone and the area is smooth. Follow up by rubbing vigorously with a wire brush. Remember, never use a hammer on a child of any age, especially an infant.

News Report: the Death of Humpty Dumpty

Anchorman: From the Nursery Newsroom, this is Keith Blanchgetter. A mystery on the West Side today with the apparent death of the beloved Humpty Dumpty. We begin our *Action Central News* team coverage tonight with Joanie Wong at the scene of the tragedy.

Wong: Thank you, Dan. Well, it's true, Humpty Dumpty is dead. The cause of death was apparently a great fall from this wall behind me.

Anchorman: Joanie, what's the scene like out there right now?

Wong: Well, as you can see, police have taped off the area and are treating it as a crime scene, and no one seems to know why. According to one eyewitness, all the king's horses and all the king's men tried to put Humpty Dumpty back together again, but were unable to do so. We have with us now one of the king's men. What is your name, sir?

King's Man: Dooley. Kevin Dooley.

Wong: And you're one of the king's men?

King's Man: That's right. I've been one of the king's men for seventeen years.

Wong: And were you the first on the scene?

King's Man: That is correct. My partner and I responded to a 10–43. That's an egg-on-a-wall.

Wong: Egg on a wall?

King's Man: Right. It's a routine call, we get them all the time. Usually, by the time we arrive the egg is gone. Or else we arrive and the egg is intoxicated and we have to remove him.

Wong: And what was different this time?

King's Man: Well, this time we've got a dead egg on our hands. He either fell or jumped. There's a chance he was pushed; we can't rule it out.

Wong: Is that why you're treating it as a crime scene?

King's Man: That is correct. Crime-scene people are checking the area for trace evidence. Hair and fibers, stuff like that.

Wong: We've been told that all the king's horses and all the king's men tried to put Humpty Dumpty back together again.

King's Man: That's not completely true.

Some of the king's horses and a few of the king's men. But not all. The king has a lot of horses and men. They're needed for parades.

Wong: So they weren't able to put him back together again?

King's Man: No. He never had a chance. His yolk was broken. Once the yolk is gone on these eggs, it's all over.

Wong: Do the police have any theories?

King's Man: We're developing leads at this time, questioning some other eggs who were seen with him earlier today. Apparently, there was some drinking going on at a picnic. All in all, we're told there were about a dozen eggs out there, and I guess it got pretty rowdy. They were singing dirty songs and harassing females.

Wong: Can the public help?

King's Man: We're asking people who may have information to call our tip-line, 800-429-EGGS. All calls will be held in strict confidence.

Wong: Thank you for talking with us, Officer Dooley. Well, that's it from the scene, Keith. Humpty Dumpty dead, at the bottom of a wall. Now let's send it over to Marcia Lopez at the Dumpty family residence. Marcia?

Lopez: Thank you, Joanie. I'm standing here with Humpty's best friend, Vinny Omeletta. Vinny, what kind of an egg was he?

Omeletta: Easygoing. Nice guy. One time, when some kids were teasing him about bein' fat, he bought 'em all an ice cream.

Lopez: What do you think happened?

Omeletta: I don't know. I saw him just yesterday, he was fine. I told him to stay off that wall. It's not safe, some of those bricks are loose. But he was headstrong; he never listened.

Lopez: Thank you, Vinny. We're going to talk now with his widow, Arlene Dumpty. Mrs. Dumpty, thanks for taking a moment with us. This must be a very difficult time for you.

Mrs. Dumpty: Yes. I'm still in shock. My thoughts are all scrambled.

Lopez: How did you feel when you found out he was dead?

Mrs. Dumpty: It was no fun, I can tell you that. He was a good egg.

Lopez: What do you suppose he was doing on the wall?

Mrs. Dumpty: He went up there all the time. He would just sit there and think. He was very deep. For an egg.

Lopez: What are your plans for services? Will there be services?

Mrs. Dumpty: Well, he was very conservative, so we'll probably stick with a traditional egg funeral.

Lopez: What is that?

Mrs. Dumpty: You know, skillet, a little butter, salt and pepper. Maybe some peppers and onions.

Lopez: Will you have an open casket?

Mrs. Dumpty: I'm not sure. A lot of him has already soaked into the ground. But we'll Krazy Glue the shell together as best we can, and go from there.

Lopez: How can people express their condolences?

Mrs. Dumpty: We're asking people just to send bacon. Or ham, if they like. And maybe some home fries, but not too greasy. Or they can just make a contribution to the Humpty Dumpty Foundation for Research on Safer Egg Salad.

Lopez: Thank you so much, Mrs. Dumpty.

Mrs. Dumpty: No sweat, my pleasure. I'm sure he's smiling down on us from wherever it is eggs go. Although he *was* an egg-nogstic. Ha ha, he would've liked that.

Lopez: Well, that's it. Humpty Dumpty is dead and no one knows why. A story we'll undoubtedly hear more about. From the scene, this is Marcia Lopez — now back to our studio.

Goodnight, Timmy

Here's a good way to provide some entertainment for your four-year-old when you tuck him in at night, and at the same time, stimulate his imagination.

"I came up to say goodnight and tuck you in, Timmy. You had a big day, so make sure you get a good night's sleep. And don't forget to watch out for the Boogie Man. Remember what Daddy and I told you about the Boogie Man? How he kills little boys? What do you think, Timmy? Is the Boogie Man here in your room, hiding somewhere? Is he in the closet? Is he going to jump out and kill you when I leave the room? He might; you never know.

"Maybe he's under the bed. He likes to hide there, too. He might claw his way through the mattress and kill you. Don't let him kill you, Timmy. You know what he does? He sticks a sharp metal tube up your nose and sucks the fluid out of your brain. It really hurts a lot.

"I'm going to turn out the light now and leave you alone in the dark. All by yourself. And I don't want to hear a peep out of you. If I hear any noise coming out of this room, I'm going to come up here and beat you. Try to get a good night's sleep. By the way, Daddy saw a monster walking up and down the hall last night. The monster had a piece of paper in his hand with your name on it. Night-night."

Bits and Pieces

- Here's a surefire way to stimulate the economy and increase productivity at the same time: From now on, when someone asks what time it is, it costs a dollar; that would stimulate the economy. Then, if they don't want to pay, they have to go find out for themselves; that would increase productivity. Some of my ideas may not be perfect, but they're always worth considering.

- The best thing about visiting a hospital is that you see a lot of people who are much sicker than you, and it kind of makes you feel good.

  TRUE FACT: I read that there's a rich couple in the Hamptons on Long Island who have palm trees on their property, and in the winter they fly the trees to Palm Beach to get them out of the cold weather. I can't help wondering how they treat their servants.

- You know how sometimes you have a song going through your head over and over all day long, maybe even two or three days? And it's driving you crazy because you can't get it out of your mind? Well, I know how to fix that. It's extreme, but it works every time. You kill yourself.

- They're always talking about what separates the men from the boys. Well, I'm gonna tell you what separates the men from the boys. The sodomy laws.

- Regarding a wild-goose chase, why are these wild geese supposed to be so hard to find? They're right up there in the sky. I see them flying over in big flocks all the time in the spring and fall. They don't seem to be hiding. So why do we make such a big deal out of this?

- Live every day as if it's your last and eventually it will be. You'll be fully prepared.

- I hope I meet Senator Dole someday. I plan to grab his bad right arm and shake it like crazy. By the way, I'm glad he didn't get to be President. I prefer a guy who can push the nuclear button with either hand.

- The feminists have this thing, "Take Our Daughters to Work Day." Why don't the men have "Take Our Sons to the Cat-House Night"?

- At the beginning of the Iraq war I saw a red, white and blue bumper sticker that said UNITED WE STAND. What is that supposed to mean? During the Revolutionary War it referred to the American colonies. What does it mean now? That we should all think alike and there should be no dissenting opinions? As far as I'm concerned, United We're Fucked.

- O.J. Simpson has already received the ultimate punishment: For the rest of his life he has to associate with golfers.

- I don't believe in road rage; I prefer the gentle rebuke. If I don't like the way someone is driving, I pull up alongside the other car and say, "I hope your children turn out poorly." Only once have I lost my cool. That was the time I said to a woman, "I hope you get a blister on your cunt." But I said it with a smile.

TRUE FACT: A headline said "Peacekeeper killed in safe haven." Good. That'll show him.

- A lot of gay men stay in the closet because they're interested in fashion.

- I wonder if a person who comes out of a coma feels refreshed and well rested.

- One day it dawned on me that Hitler had a mom and dad. The phrase "Hitler's mom and dad" has an odd ring to it, doesn't it? It's kind of like when CNN used to talk about the city of Tikrit in Iraq being "Saddam Hussein's hometown." The two ideas don't seem to go together.

- You know what's good about being in your sixties? Your children are in their forties, so you don't have to worry about child molesters anymore. Unless, of course, one of your forty-year-old children is a child molester.

- I drove past a school with a sign that said WE'RE DRUG-FREE AND GUN-FREE. Later that day I drove past another school that didn't have a sign like that. What am I supposed to infer from this about the second school?

- REASONS FOR GIVING UP HOPE: Nothing works, nothing counts, nothing fits, no one cares, no one listens, standards have fallen, everyone's fatter, lines are longer, traffic's worse, kids are dumber and the air is dirty. I'll be back later with more reasons for giving up hope. In the meantime, try to come up with a few of your own.

• Here's a thought: If you have a perfectly DNA-matched identical twin, technically, it's possible to go fuck yourself.

• Sometimes you hear people say, "What kind of message does that send to our children?" And I think, What messages are these people talking about? When I was a kid, I never got any messages. Maybe an aunt would send me a birthday card or something; or once in a while my mother would get a Western Union telegram. But at our house, that was about it.

• Good news for senior citizens: Death is near!

• During one of those patriotic orgies of self-congratulation that followed the first Gulf War, as General Schwarzkopf was bragging about dropping fire on women and babies, a protester interrupted his speech. The man who had killed a few hundred thousand civilians continued to speak. The protester was charged with disturbing the peace.

- In New York State, there's a town called Eastchester. It's in a county called Westchester.

- I think we need some new Christmas carols with a more modern approach. Of course, I wouldn't abandon the religious theme completely. How about "Holy Christ, the Christmas Tree's on Fire"? Or "Jesus, can you Believe It's Christmas Again?" This ought to get the ball rolling; I'm hoping you people will take it from here.

TRUE FACT: In 2002, in the U.S. Supreme Court, the surviving heirs of the famous film comedy trio were awarded "the intellectual rights to the Three Stooges."

- I don't know about you, but years ago, when Evel Knievel was jumping across the Snake River, I was rooting for the river.

- In the news from Israel, I keep hearing about the "cycle of violence." It reminded me that when I was a kid I had one of them, too. After school, I used to pedal it around the neighborhood, hitting other kids over the head with a big steel pipe.

- They always say the vice president is just a heartbeat away from the presidency. Don't they mean the *lack* of a heartbeat?

- I always feel good when I visit a sickroom supply store and see all the things I don't need.

- The last thing a young girl needs is a hands-on father.

- I feel really good. I wish I felt even more like this.

Dear Mom,

How are you? I am fine. I tried to donate my liver to science but they wouldn't take it. Next time I'm going to add some sautéed onions and a light sauce. I'll let you know how it goes.

Love, Neil

There's nothing wrong with a man who enjoys a good blow job.

— Anonymous

- I read an article that cautioned people against shaken-baby syndrome. Do people really need to be told this sort of thing? And if some people do need to be told, are these the kind of people who are very likely to heed the advice? Personally, I never shake a baby. Unless the recipe calls for it.

- Imagine how creepy it would be to be sexually abused by your great-great-grandparents.

- Do you know why it is that when a rancher fucks a sheep he does it at the edge of a cliff? It's so the sheep will push back.

  TRUE FACT: A guy somewhere in the Midwest was sued for having too many Christmas lights on his house. Happy holidays.

- I think Western Union should have a service where women with big tits come to your house and sing "Happy Birthday."

They could call it a mammogram.

- Whenever I hear about someone who "died for the flag," I always wonder about his real motives. And then I remember, Oh yeah, they shoot deserters.

- A lot of the people who worry about the safety of nuclear plants don't bother using their seat belts.

- HERE'S SOME FUN: Just keep calling telephone numbers at random and yelling, "Get off the line."

- This is National Disabled Month. Do your part. Cripple someone today.

- Two soldiers get into a fight. Two other soldiers pull them apart and tell them not to fight. Then they all pick up their guns and go kill people.

- "Which came first, the chicken or the egg?"
  "The chicken."
  "What about the egg?"
  "Okay, the egg."

- Using technology to clean up the mess

made by technology doesn't seem too intelligent.

- At one time, if you had had a telephone in a restaurant it would have been a novelty and attracted more attention than the food. Now if you have a telephone in a restaurant it's considered a nuisance.

- Why don't they just let these gay Boy Scouts join the Girl Scouts? What the fuck, you've got two groups. Use them both.

- There's a whole different now now.

- When you drive into California from Las Vegas they have an agricultural inspection station where they ask you if you have any fruits or vegetables with you. And then they just believe whatever you tell them. What's the point of that? You know what I do? On every trip I put a yam in the glove compartment, just to be sure I'm breaking the law.

- We ought to have a name for the day before yesterday. Dayforeday? Yesterforday? Why don't you people just come up with something and get back to me.

- I don't own any stocks or bonds. All my money is tied up in debt.

- A good motto to live by: "Always try not to get killed."

- If Marilyn Monroe were alive today she would be seventy-five, and I'll bet there would still be guys lining up for a chance to fuck her.

- Why not join the army? Join up and die. How do you expect to keep America free if you won't die? I'm dead; I died in Vietnam. I'm dead, and all my old army buddies are dead. Can you say that? No. What's wrong with you?

Euphemisms: It's Gettin' Old

Perhaps you've noticed, we no longer have *old people* in this country; they're all gone, replaced by *senior citizens*. Somehow we wound up with millions of these unfortunate creatures known as *golden-agers* and *mature adults*. These are cold, lifeless, antiseptic terms. Typically American. All ways of sidestepping the fear of aging.

And it's not difficult to understand the fear of aging. It's natural. And it's universal; no one wants to get old. No one wants to die. But we do. We die. And we don't like that, so we shade the truth. I started doing it when I reached my forties. I'd look in the mirror at that time and think, "Well, I guess I'm getting . . . *older!*" That sounded a little better than *old*. It sounded like it might even last a bit longer.

But people forget that older is comparative, and they use it as an absolute: "She's an *older woman*."

"Oh, really? Older than what? Than she used to be? Well, yeah, so?"

People think *getting* old is bad, because they think *being* old is bad. But you know something? Being old is just fine; in fact, it can be terrific. And anyway, it's one of those things you don't get to choose. It's not optional.

But that insufferable group among us known as baby boomers (ages forty-two through fifty-nine, as of 2005) are beginning to get old, and they're having trouble dealing with that. Remember, these baby boomers are the ones who gave us this soft, politically correct language in the first place.

So rather than admit they're getting old, the baby boomers have come up with a new term to describe themselves as they approach the grave. They don't care for *middle-aged,* so instead — get this, folks — instead, they claim to be *pre-elderly.* Don't you love that? Pre-elderly. It's a real word. You don't hear it a lot, but it's out there. The boomers claim that if you're between fifty and sixty-five, you're pre-elderly.

But I'd be willing to bet that in 2011, when they begin turning sixty-five, they will not be calling themselves *elderly.* I have a hunch they'll come up with some new way of avoiding reality, and I have a suggestion for them. They should call themselves the *pre-dead.* It's a perfect term, because, for them, it's accurate and it's highly descriptive.

By the way, those ever-clever boomers have also come up with a word to describe the jobs they feel are most suitable for retired people who wish to keep working. They call these jobs *elder-friendly*. Isn't that sad? God, that's just really, really sad.

And so, to sum up, we have these senior citizens. And, whether I like that phrase or not, unfortunately, I got used to it, and I no longer react too violently when I hear it. But there is still one description for old people that I will never accept. That's when I hear someone describe an old guy as being, for instance, *eighty years young*. Even though I know it's tongue-in-cheek, it makes my skin crawl. It's overly cute and precious, and it's an evasion. It's junk language.

More: On CBS's *60 Minutes*, Leslie Stahl, God help her, actually referred to some old man as being a *ninety-something*. Please. Leslie. I need a small, personal break here.

One last, pathetic example in this category: On the radio, I heard Matt Drudge actually refer to *people of age*. And he wasn't being sarcastic. He said, "The West Nile virus is a particular threat to people of age." Poor Matt. Apparently, he's more fucked up than he seems.

Now, going to an adjacent subject: One unfortunate fact of life for many of these eighty- or ninety-somethings is that they're forced to live in places where they'd rather not be. Old-people's homes. So what name should we use for these places where we hide our old people? When I was a little boy, there was a building in my neighborhood called the *home for the aged*. It had a copper sign on the gate: HOME FOR THE AGED. It always looked deserted; I never saw anyone go in. Naturally, I never saw anyone come out, either.

Later, I noticed people started calling those places *nursing homes* and *rest homes*. Apparently, it was decided that some of these old people needed nurses, while others just needed a little rest. What you hear them called now is *retirement homes* or *long-term-care facilities*. There's another one of those truly bloodless terms: long-term-care facility.

But actually, it makes sense to give it a name like that, because if you do, you make it a lot easier for the person you're putting in there to acquiesce and cooperate with you. I remember old people used to tell their families, "Whatever you do, don't put me in a home. Please don't put me in a home." But it's hard to imagine one of them saying, "Whatever you do, don't put me in a long-term-care facility." So calling it that is really a trick. "C'mon, Grandpa, it's not a home. It's long-term care!"

By the way, while we're on the subject of the language of getting old, I want to tell you something that happened to me in New York on a recent evening. I was standing in line at the Carnegie Deli to pay my check, and there was a guy ahead of me who looked like he was in his sixties. He gave the cashier a ten-dollar bill, but apparently, it wasn't enough. When the cashier mentioned it to him in a nice way, he said, "Oh, I'm sorry. I guess I had a *senior moment*." And I thought how sad that was. To blame a simple mistake on the fact that you're in your sixties, even if you're just sort of joking. As if anyone would think a twenty-year-old couldn't make the same mistake. I only mention this because it's an example of how people can brainwash themselves by adopting popular language.

I wanted to pull him aside and say, "Listen, I just heard you refer to yourself as a senior. And I wanted to ask, were you by any chance a junior last year? Because if you weren't a junior last year, then you're not a senior *this* year." I wanted to say it, but I figured, why would he listen to me? After all, I'm only a freshman.

Eye Safety Tip

Here's a safety tip from the American Eye Association: Never jab a knitting needle directly into your eye and repeatedly thrust it in and out. You could be inviting vision problems. If you should suffer an eye injury, rinse the eye immediately with a caustic solution of Clorox and ammonia, and rub the surface of the eye vigorously for about ten minutes with #3 sandpaper. The American Eye Association reminds you: Don't fuck around with your eyes. They're the key to vision.

Body of Work: Part 1

(Not for the queasy.)

Don't Gimme No Lip

Do you ever get lip crud? That sticky film that sometimes forms on your lips? Especially the lower lip? It's a kind of gooey crud that builds up, and when it dries it turns into a gummy, crusty coating? Thicker at the corners of the mouth, but thinning out as it works its way down toward the center of the lip? And when it's really bad, the corners of your mouth look like parentheses? Do you ever get that? Lip crud?

Well, here's how you get rid of it. It's a simple, low-tech operation, and it requires just a single tool: the thumbnail. That's all you need. You scrape the crud off with your thumbnail. You just scrape, scrape, scrape it on down, scrape it on down, and you keep on scrapin' — don't worry about those people watchin' from the bus stop; if they knew anything they wouldn't be ridin' the bus. You scrape it on down, you scrape it on down, and finally, when it's all off, you take it and roll it up into a little ball, and then you *save that son of a bitch!* That's my practice, folks. I save it. Personally, I'm a lip-crud buff.

It Pays to Save

In fact, I save everything I remove from my body. Don't you? At least for a little while? Don't you look at things when they first come off you? Study them? Aren't you curious? Don't you spend a few minutes lookin' at somethin', trying to figure out what it is and what it's doin' on you in the first place? Sure you do. You don't just pull some growth off your neck and throw it in the trash. You study it. You wanna know what it is.

Besides, you never know when you're gonna need parts. Isn't that true? Have you ever seen these guys on TV, they're in the hospital? One guy's waitin' for a kidney, another guy's waitin' for a lung. I say, "Fuck that shit, I've got parts at home! I have a freezer full of viable organs. Two of everything, ready to go. Whaddya need? A spleen? An esophagus? How about a nice used ballbag? Hah? Come on. Caucasian ballbag, one owner, good condition. He only scratched it on Sundays. Come on, folks, take a chance. I've got everything you need."

The Thrill of Discovery

But regardless of your need for parts, the larger point is true: Most people study the things they pick off their bodies before they throw them away. Because you want to know what somethin' is. You don't want to spend fifteen minutes peeling a malignant tumor off your forehead, just to toss it out the window, sight unseen, into the neighbor's swimming pool. No! You want to take a good, long look at it. You may even want to share the experience:

"Holy shit, Honey! Looka this thing! Holy jump-in' fuck-in' Jesus! Looka this! Hey! Honey? Come in here, will ya, goddammit! Fuck the Rice-A-Roni! Get your ass in here! (Displaying item proudly) Look at this thing. Ain't it somethin'? Guess where I got it? A minute or two ago it was a part of my head. Not anymore. I pried the bastard off with paint thinner and a Phillips-head screwdriver.

"But look at it, Honey! Look at the colors! It's green, blue, yellow, orange, brown, tan, khaki, beige, bronze, olive, neutral, black, off-black, champagne gold, Navajo white, turquoise . . . and Band-Aid color! Plus — get this — it's exactly the same shape as Iraq. That is, if you leave out that northern section where the Kurds live. I'm not throwin' this bastard away, it might become a collectible! Dial up those dickheads on eBay. We can make some fuckin' money on this thing."

Strap It On and Pump Me Up

It annoys me when people complain about athletes taking steroids to improve athletic performance. It's a phony argument, because over the years every single piece of sports equipment used by athletes has been improved many times over. Golf balls and clubs; tennis balls, racquets; baseball gloves and bats; football pads and helmets and so on through every sport. Each time technology has found a way to improve equipment it has done so. So why shouldn't a person treat his body the same way? In the context of sports, the body is nothing more than one more piece of equipment, anyway. So why not improve it with new technology? Athletes use weights, why shouldn't they use chemicals?

Consider the Greek Phidippides, a professional runner who, in 490 B.C., ran from Athens to Sparta and back (280 miles) to ask the Spartans for help against the Persians in an impending battle that threatened Athens. Don't you think his generals would have been happy to give him amphetamines if they had been available? And a nice pair of New Balance high-performance running shoes while they were at it? Grow up, purists. The body is not a sacred vessel, it's a tool.

It's Not Polite to Point

I don't care for athletes who point to the sky after they've accomplished something on the field. Even worse are the ones who kneel down, bow their heads and make a big show of being "believers." You know something? God doesn't like that shit. He's not impressed with spiritual grandstanding; it embarrasses him. He says, "Get up, you phony, showoff bullshit artist and pay attention to the fuckin' game. I took the points!" Imagine the conceit of these people who think God is helping them and is looking for their acknowledgment. I say, play now, pray later.

Attitude Check

Let's straighten out this whole "attitude" thing. Someone on TV said the sports anchor guys on ESPN have a lot of attitude. Let me tell you something, what these guys have is not attitude.

Here's attitude: One day, when I was about eighteen, I was standing at the bar in the Moylan Tavern with a couple of guys from my New York neighborhood. The

Moylan had big windows, so if you were standing at the bar, you could easily see the people walking by on Broadway.

One of the guys in our group was a little older than the rest of us — an ex-convict named John Cooney. All of a sudden, in the middle of the conversation, he looked out the window and saw someone walking past. He reached behind the bar for the baseball bat — the one the bartenders used for settling sports and political arguments — and he went outside, walked up to the guy on the sidewalk and just started smashing him with the baseball bat. The guy fell down, John walked back into the bar and put the bat away. He said, "The guy owes me money." That's attitude.

The guys on ESPN don't have that. What they have is a kind of smart-mouth, white-boy, college mentality. They're snotty, superficial white guys. Even the black anchors on ESPN are nothing more than snotty white guys. Snotty is not attitude. Snotty is just bad manners. And it's boring.

John Cooney knew attitude. He also knew more about how to swing a bat than any one of these blow-dried, never-were-athletes sitting safely behind their fruity little desks.

Good Cheer

Twenty-five years ago, two lovely girls in San Carlos, California, were kind enough to perform this football cheer for me, and in 1984 I used it on an HBO show. I'm passing it along now and would like to point out that it's actually quite useful at sporting events of any kind. In fact, I've found it to be a big crowd pleaser at weddings, baptisms and first communions, as well. Here it is. Chant it in good health:

Rat shit! Bat shit!
Dirty ol' twat!
Sixty-nine assholes
Tied in a knot!
Hooray!
Lizard shit!
Fuck!

Let's go over that again, this time with a few comments:

Rat shit! Bat shit!
   (How nice to begin with a reference to nature.)
Dirty ol' twat!
   (A perfectly normal sports reference, as far as I'm concerned.)

Sixty-nine assholes
Tied in a knot!
 (No, I don't know what that means, ei-
ther.)
Hooray!
 (There's the cheer part.)
Lizard shit!
 (Back to nature once again.)
Fuck!
 (And we end on an uplifting note.)

Now here's the happy postscript: About
ten years later, I met a guy named Michael
who gave me the second verse to the cheer. I
hope those San Carlos girls will see this and
accept it as my way of saying thanks:

Eat, bite, fuck, suck!
Nibble, gobble, chew!
Finger fuck! Hair pie!
Dick, cunt, screw!
Hooray!
Bat fuck!
Blow me!

Let's go over that again:

Eat, bite, fuck, suck!
 (Once again, off to an excellent start.)
Nibble, gobble, chew!

(I notice verbs are more prominent this time.)

Finger fuck! Hair pie!

Dick, cunt, screw!

(More good sports references.)

Hooray!

(Can't have a cheer without it.)

Bat fuck!

(Truly an interesting thought.)

Blow me!

(Once again, ending on an uplifting note.)

Cheers!

One at a Time, Please

Never buy two different garments of the same type at the same time, such as two sport shirts. Inevitably, you will like one better than the other and you will choose to wear it every time. The second one will always remain second choice and it will stay in the closet, coming out only occasionally, when you hold it in front of you at arm's length and decide not to wear it. Here's how you handle this problem: Exercise a little discipline at the store and buy just one shirt. Then, if you like it, wait a month and buy another. That's it. Next, I'm gonna work on nuclear proliferation.

Keepin' It Real in the Ring

Another area of speech that could benefit from a bit more realism would be those announcements that are made just before a boxing match:

"Ladies and gentlemen, the main event of the evening: twelve rounds of heavyweight boxing. In this corner, from Cornhole, Mississippi, weighing two hundred pounds and wearing soiled white trunks, an utter and complete loser who is wanted in six states for crimes against the animal kingdom. Considered a complete scumbag by his family, he once fucked his sister at a church picnic and forced her to walk home alone. Also, on at least four occasions he has taken out his dick at the circus and waved it at the trapeze lady. Here is, He-e-e-n-r-y-y Gonz-a-a-a-lez!

"In the other corner, wearing a pair of lame, out-of-style zebra-skin shorts that he found on the street, from Sweatband, Arkansas, an unattractive and disturbed young man who, by court order, is not permitted to be alone for more than two minutes at a time. In and out of sixteen mental institutions over the years, he is a dangerous sociopath who once killed a nun for blocking his view. He has been legally barred from more than fifteen hundred bars in the New York City area, and recently, while visiting a supermarket, he forced a fat woman to blow him in the meat section. Here he is, Ma-a-a-tty Mu-u-u-urphy-y-y!"

The fighters move out to the center of the ring to have the boxing rules recited to them.

"All right, boys, you know the rules: No biting, scratching, clawing or tripping. No yanking dicks. No grabbing the other guy's testicles and snapping them up and down. No using a small screwdriver to punch holes in the other guy's neck during clinches. And if you're gonna call the other guy's mother a diseased, two-dollar whore, please, in the interest of accuracy, use her full name."

Well-Wishing

When taking leave of one another, we often say, "Be well." Perhaps we should be more precise and a bit more practical. Reasonably, we can't expect everyone to be healthy all the time. Good wishes should be more realistic: "I hope you remain reasonably healthy during the next eighteen months or so, and if you have a stroke, I hope it only paralyzes you on one side, leaving you free to take phone calls." I think people would appreciate such thoughtfulness and precision.

Prepositional Phrases

We Americans love our prepositional phrases.

Out of sight, off the charts, in the groove, on the ball; up the creek, down the tubes, in the dumper, out the yin-yang; off the wall, 'round the bend, below the belt, under the weather.

And of course . . . *under the table.*

Table Talk

But rather than <u>under</u> the table, let us begin <u>on</u> the table. That's a phrase you hear a lot in the news, especially from Washington. In negotiations of any kind, certain things are said to be *on the table*. Implying that other things are *off the table*. And sometimes, regardless of what's on the table, a settlement is reached *under the table*.

The table seems important. If a person is highly qualified, we say he brings a lot *to the table*. Unfortunately, those who bring a lot *to the table* often have too much *on their plates*. Still, they're guaranteed a seat *at the table*, because they think *outside the box*, which puts them *ahead of the curve*.

Now, if the negotiators agree on what's on the table, then they're *on the same page*. Personally, I don't like people on my page. If someone says to me, "We're on the same page," I say, "Do me a favor, please, turn the page; I'd rather not be on that page. In fact, I'd rather be in a completely different book." But that's *beside the point;* I've wandered *off the track*.

Returning to negotiations, if the sides are getting close, we're told they're *in the ballpark*. This often comes from people *in the know,* speaking *off the record*. And in Washington, many in the know are also *in the loop* because, after all, they work *inside the beltway*.

Now, there are other government people, <u>outside</u> the beltway, who, nonetheless, remain in the know and in the loop. They function in foreign countries and we say they're *on the ground*. If they're CIA, they're *under the radar* and paid *off the books*. Much of what they learn is picked up *on the street*. But they don't always need to be on the street, because a lot of information comes in *over the transom*.

House Parties

Putting aside government for the moment, I wonder if you're aware that a completely different group of people has recently emerged in America. They're not on the ground and they're not on the street. You know where they are? They're *in the house!* Apparently, they never went out! And there must be a lot of them, because you hear it all the time: "He's in the house!"

And, if I may broach a delicate subject here, some of these people who are in the house are also *in the closet*. Fortunately for them, if they somehow manage to get out of the closet, they'll still be in the house. That is, they will be until they've . . . *left the building!* How often these days we hear that someone has left the building.

Leave Me Tender

And I'm sure you've noticed it's mostly show business people who leave buildings — the accepted belief being that Elvis was the first to master this maneuver, although you can also find Beatles fans who will argue that the Fab Four were known to have left several buildings, as well, thereby accomplishing what would have been the first multi-star building-departures. Unfortunately, at the time, no one realized the significance of what the Beatles were doing.

Now, there are no doubt those among you who are seething because *has left the building* is not a prepositional phrase. I grant that, but you'd have to agree that nonetheless, it fits here very nicely. Because, after all, only people who are in the house can leave the building. But, alas, it's impossible to leave the building if you're still in the closet. In fact, you can't even get to the front door.

Coming Out

However, let's say everything breaks your way, and somehow you manage to leave the building; guess where you'll be? Right! Back on the street. With the CIA. So you'd better be *on your toes.* Because the CIA will get *on your case,* and they'll be *in your face.* Who knows? They might even go *upside your head.*

I'm sorry, folks, this is really getting *off the wall,* so let's return to where this whole thing began: under the table — where those shady deals are made. And isn't it interesting that under the table is similar to *under the counter,* where illegal products are sold? Under the counter, as opposed, of course, to *over the counter,* which describes a drug that does not require a prescription.

Counterpoint

But when you think about it, even drugs that require a prescription are sold over the counter. I mean, the pharmacist doesn't somehow give them to you <u>underneath</u> the counter; you don't get them by going around <u>behind</u> the counter. What happens is, you stand <u>at</u> the counter, pay the man, and he hands them to you <u>across</u> the counter. Or he sets them down <u>on</u> the counter, and you pick them up <u>off</u> the counter. Or, if you want, you can completely eliminate the counter by having the drugs delivered to your home. Provided, of course, that, at the time, you're *in the house.*

Well, folks, it turns out that one of the phrases I used at the beginning of this piece was more appropriate than I suspected at the time. It's clear to me now that *in the dumper* is exactly where this piece has wound up.

So that's it. I'm *out the door.*

Pass Me a Damp Towel

Here are some interesting sex facts from Thailand, accurate as of fifteen years ago. And I apologize for the dated quality of this information, but I find it fascinating, and since it's accurate, I wish to include it here. In 1990 alone, 5 million "sex tourists" — mostly affluent men from Japan — spent $4.5 billion on sex in Thailand. The country at that time had 800,000 child prostitutes under the age of sixteen, prostitution being the major occupation for children between ten and sixteen. The girls earn twenty to eighty cents a week, and their recruitment begins at six years of age.

Additionally, at that time there were

200,000 Thai prostitutes working in Europe. In 1993, there were 600,000 Thais infected with AIDS, with 1,200 new cases occurring every day. I have only one question: Doesn't anyone in Asia jerk off anymore?

P.S. I can't get newer statistics because, apparently, everyone in Thailand is too busy getting undressed.

Putting the Cat Out

It was nearly eleven-thirty, and I had just put the cat out. But it hadn't been easy. He had burned more fiercely than I anticipated.

The poor thing had caught fire earlier in the evening when, in an effort to test his reflexes, I had thrown his favorite toy mouse into the fireplace, and instinctively he raced in after it.

"WHOOOOOOOOM!!!" you might say.

At first, I let him burn awhile just to teach him a lesson, and to peel off a couple of layers of the mud, mange and matted hair which seemed lately, sadly, to have robbed him of a step or two. But I must admit I was also quite fascinated by the many spectacular colors he began to glow with. Colors, no doubt, owed in part to the countless hours he spent killing time in the toxic dump next door. It was quite a show. In fact, I saw several pyrotechnic effects I dare say have not been witnessed since the Grucci home exploded during the Bicentennial.

Then, as the feline conflagration began to burn itself out and I could see the clear, stark outline of his hairless body, he began to emit a dense cloud of smoke, along with some other gaseous substance which I can only describe as "cat steam." Acting quickly, I covered him with several cheap sweaters that no longer fit and pounded him gently, although not without anger, for just over an hour, or until the smoke died down and he stopped his by then bothersome screeching.

At that point, energized, apparently, by a sudden burst of pain and fear, he leapt several feet into the air, went stiff and spread-eagled and began to spin violently, giving off an ominous low-frequency hum and circling the ceiling fan in an elliptical orbit. He circled for the better part of an hour. Finally, exhausted, or, I thought, maybe dead, he went suddenly limp, his orbit decayed and he smashed into an eighteenth-century breakfront, landing heavily on the floor. For three days he lay motionless.

When finally he awoke, I opened a can of Bits O' Kidney and fed him by hand.

I can tell you this: Although he looked quite unusual, and he smelled god-awful, I was glad I could be there for him when he needed me.

Body of Work: Part 2

Toenail Clippings

Saving the little things we remove from our bodies comes from our natural curiosity. We all have it. We're curious about ourselves, we're curious about our bodies, so we're curious about the little parts that we clip, snip, pluck, pull or pick off of ourselves. Toenail clippings are a good example.

I'll set the scene for you: You're sittin' on the bed at home one night, and somethin' really shitty comes on TV. Like a regularly scheduled, prime-time network program. And you think, "Well, I'm not gonna watch *Raymond Blows the Milkman*. I'm gonna clip my fuckin' toenails."

So you start to clip your toenails. And every time you clip one of them, the little clipped part flies several feet away. You notice that? These things fly all over the bed. So when you're finished clipping, you have to gather them all back into a little pile. You can't leave them all over the bed, they make dents in your legs. You don't need that. You have to gather them back into a pile. And did you ever notice this? The bigger the pile gets, the more pride you have in the pile.

"Look at this, Honey. The biggest pile of toenail clippings we've had in this house since the day the Big Bopper died. Get the fuckin' camcorder! Call the Museum of Natural History! Tell them we have a good idea for one of those diorama things."

And then you search the bed for the largest clipping of all, the biggest one you can find, usually from the big toe, and you bend it for a while. Don't you? Yes! You do! You bend it, you squeeze it, you play with it. You have to. Why? Because you *can!* Because it's still lively and viable; it just came off your body, there's still moisture in it. *It's almost alive!!*

And sometimes I save my toenail clippings overnight. Do you ever do that. You put 'em in an ashtray and try to save them till the morning? It's no use. They're no good in the morning; they're too dry. You can't bend them. I say, fuck 'em, throw 'em away. Who needs unbendable toenails? Not me. I'm not that sick. I don't need parts that badly. No sir.

Pick of the Litter

Little things, folks. Little things you pick off your body — and your curiosity about them. Especially if it's something you can't really see before you pick it off.

For instance, you know how sometimes you're picking your ass? You know what I mean, just standing out in the driveway, idly picking your ass? And as you're picking and probing, you come across something that seems to be . . . a small object! And let's be real, here, folks. After you manage to pull it free, don't you smell it? Just a little bit? Sure you do. You have to, it's only natural. And you get excited!

"Honey, c'mere! Look! (He sniffs) You want a couple of hits off this thing? While it's still fresh? Remind me, baby. Did we eat at Fatburger this week? We did? (Sniffs again) Well, I don't remember orderin' anything that smelled like this. I believe this is a Shitburger. You know, tastes like a burger, smells like shit. Actually, it smells more like Ethel Merman. Call that Andrew Lloyd

Webber fella. Tell him we have a great idea for one of those fine shows he's always puttin' on Broadway. Then gimme the scrapbook, baby. This son of a bitch is goin' right next to that Lithuanian toe-jam we found at the Olympics."

It's an exciting moment the whole family can enjoy.

The Birthday Party

(Two bachelors at a neighborhood bar.)

Chester: Tomorrow's my fortieth birthday. I gotta go get candles and pick up my cake.

Lester: You're buyin' your own birthday cake?

Chester: No, I ain't buyin' my own birthday cake. My mother's buyin' it, I'm just pickin' it up. She's givin' me a surprise party but she don't feel good, so she can't pick up the cake.

Lester: It's a surprise party, and you're pickin' up the cake?

Chester: I ain't gonna *look* at it, okay? It's already wrapped. I'm just gonna pick it up.

Lester: But how can it be a surprise party if you're pickin' up the cake and you know the party is comin'?

Chester: I don't know *when* it's comin', do I? It could be eight in the morning, it could be midnight.

Lester: Eight in the morning? How can you have a birthday party at eight in the morning? Who the fuck is gonna come, the milkman?

Chester: Don't laugh, my mother would do it. One year, on my birthday, I got drunk and didn't come home. She threw the party without me.

Lester: What'd she sing? "Happy Birthday to Him"?

Chester: You're a fuckin' riot, ya know that?

Lester: How many candles ya gonna get?

Chester: Well, we already got sixteen from my kid's birthday last year, and twenty-four is how many come in a box. I'm forty, so I only gotta get one box. I guess I could go ahead and get two boxes and leave my kid's candles alone, but two boxes would be forty-eight candles, and what am I gonna do with the eight extras?

Lester: Save 'em?

Chester: Don't laugh. At my house we do save 'em. In fact, we don't even light 'em up.

Lester: Why not?

Chester: Well, if you light 'em up, they look crappy the next time you wanna use 'em — believe me, we don't waste nothin' at my house. In fact, listen to this: A couple of years ago, my grandfather turned ninety-six. Ninety-six is four boxes, right? Four times twenty-four?

Lester: Right.

Chester: Well, we only had sixty candles on hand, 'cause that's all we ever need for my mother — she's one of them people, when she turned sixty she decided to "stop havin' birthdays." So sixty is all we need. Two and a half boxes. So we bought three boxes. But that's seventy-two, givin' us twelve left over. Right?

Lester: I'm takin' your word for it.

Chester: Trust me, okay? So, we got twelve extra candles, and we decided to give them to my niece. She was just turnin' thirty-six, and she already had a brand-new box of twenty-four of her own. She's a widow with no kids, so she don't need too many candles. I think maybe on her cat's birthday or somethin' she sticks one on a cupcake. So with her, a box lasts a long time.

Lester: Keep goin'.

Chester: Anyway, like I say, it's my grand father's ninety-sixth birthday and we only had sixty candles. That means we need thirty-six more, a box and a half. So we borrow thirty-six from my brother. He had two full boxes, because in about six months it's his forty-eighth birthday. But that's still a ways off, so we borrow thirty-six from him, which leaves him with twelve, and that works out nice, because his kid is gonna be twelve next week, so we're covered all the way around.

Lester: You got an interesting family.

Chester: Anyways, we put the ninety-six candles on my grandfather's cake, and we start to light them up, okay? But there's so many of them, that by the time we get the last one lit, half of them are just little holes in the frosting with smoke comin' out. But if you looked down into the holes, you could still see the flames. So, my grandfather blew out all ninety-six candles, but he had to do 'em one at the time because he had to blow down each individual hole.

Plus he's short-winded. You know the good part?

Lester: I can't imagine.

Chester: He got ninety-six different wishes.

Lester: Did any of 'em come true?

Chester: I think three.

Lester: You believe in wishes? I mean, you believe they come true?

Chester: Nah. I believe in wishes, but I don't believe they come true. Not unless it's a real easy wish, like "I wish I was at a birthday party." But you gotta blow out all the candles, or else the wish don't come true. If one candle stays lit, you don't get your wish.

Lester: Well, suppose you wished one candle would stay lit.

Chester: Whaddya mean?

Lester: I mean suppose you wished

that one candle would stay lit, and then you blew them all out. What would happen?

Chester: Well, it couldn't happen. Unless you blew them all out.

Lester: But if you blew them all out, then one candle wouldn't have stayed lit, so your wish wouldn't have come true.

Chester: Don't give me that college shit, will ya? Jesus! Herbie, y'ever notice this guy? As soon as you start talkin' about somethin' intelligent, he has to throw in that college shit. He says, "If you wish for one candle to stay lit, it won't happen unless you blow all the candles out." That's the kind of shit they teach in college now.

Lester: That's right. It just so happens my major was Comparative Birthday Cakes, with a minor in Frosting.

Chester: It wouldn't surprise me.

Lester: Ya gonna have hats? It ain't a party without hats.

Chester: Naaah. No hats.

Lester: How come?

Chester: They come fifty in a box. What am I gonna do with forty-eight extra hats?

Lester: In your family it might work out.

Chester: I know. That's why I ain't gonna do it. See ya next week.

Lester: Okay, so long. Have a happy birthday!

Chester: I'll do my best.

Merry Christmas, Lil

One Christmas, when I was little, my aunt Lil gave me a book about railroads. It was just the kind of gift I hated. A book. I wanted a toy. Preferably a little car or truck, or maybe a few soldiers; I didn't ask much. Just some kind of toy a boy could play with every day and not get tired of. No. A boring fucking book about railroads with pictures of fucking trains.

My mother forced me to tell Aunt Lil that I really liked the book; she made me lie and say "thank you" and all that other drivel-shit parents are constantly trying to push into your head. She didn't want to hurt Lil's feelings. (Actually, she didn't want to look bad in Lil's eyes.)

Well, I made the mistake — common in childhood — of listening to my mother and following her advice. I thanked Lil. Guess the result. Right! Every Christmas and every birthday from then on, I got a fucking boring book from my fucking boring aunt fucking boring Lil. First buses, then airplanes, then trucks and then cars. And on and on through the years, until she ran out of conveyances and had to switch to buildings. I weep when I think of all the soldiers I could have had. Probably a battalion or two. Ah, well.

I realize the problem now: I was too young to have learned the following sentence: "Hey Lil! Take your fucking railroad book and stick it up your ass. And get me some goddamn soldiers!" That would have nipped the whole thing in the bud.

Turn Down the Radio!

Does anybody really listen to that shitty music they play on the radio? FM radio music? What's it called? Adult contemporary? Classic rock? Urban rhythm and blues? You know what the official business name for that shit is? "Corporate standardized programming." Just what an art form needs: corporate standardized programming. Derived from "scientific" surveys conducted by soulless businessmen.

Here's how bad it is: One nationwide chain that owns over a thousand radio stations conducts weekly telephone polls, asking listeners their opinions on twenty-five to thirty song "hooks" they play over the phone; hooks that the radio people have already selected. (Hooks are the short, repeated parts of pop songs that people remember easily.) Depending on these polls, the radio chain decides which songs to place on their stations' playlists.

Weeks later, they record the hooks of all the songs they're currently playing on their stations across the country, label them by title and artist and sell that information to record companies to help create more of the same bad music. They also sell the information to competing radio stations that want to play what the big chain is playing. All of this is done to prevent the possibility of original thinking somehow creeping into the system.

Lemme tell you something: In the first place, listening to music that someone else has picked out is not my idea of a good time. Second, and more important, the fact that a lot of people in America actually like the music automatically means it sucks. Especially since the people who like it have been told in advance by businessmen what it is they're supposed to like. Please. Save me from people who've been told what to like and then like it.

In my opinion, if you're over six years of age, and you're still getting your music from the radio, something is desperately wrong with you. I can only hope that somehow MP3 players and file sharing will destroy FM radio the way they're destroying record companies. Then, even though the air will probably never be safe to breathe again, maybe it will be safer to listen to.

Oh Say, Can You Hear?

What is the purpose of having a person "sign" "The Star-Spangled Banner"? Don't deaf people know the words by now? Besides, signing can't possibly convey the exact, personalized musical rendition the singer may be offering. How could a signer ever convey to a deaf person the elaborate, note-bending vocal gymnastics that black female singers put that anthem through? Especially those last few lines; the ones from "O'er the land . . ." all the way through ". . . of the brave," which sometimes can take more than six or seven minutes to complete. Why, I should think a signer would break an arm trying to get that stuff across.

Besides, what does the national anthem have to do with sports in the first place? I never understood that. Play Ball!

Practice, Practice, Practice

During the Middle Ages, it seems as though every castle had a group of trumpet players who stood in a line and played loud, intricate fanfares whenever something important happened. And it occurred to me that occasionally those guys must have needed to practice. You know, "Fanfare practice, three o'clock, near the moat." There could be any number of reasons: new guys in the group, new fanfares, the brand-new trumpets came in.

So I'm wondering, when these guys did hold practice — and they kept playing the fanfares over and over — were the people working around the castle required to constantly keep snapping to attention? Did maybe some of them do it anyway, out of force of habit? Or did everyone pretty much ignore the fanfares since they knew it was really only practice?

And, if so, at a time like that, when everyone had been lulled into a false sense of security, what if the king decided to walk across the yard to visit his sister in the dungeon? And they blew a fanfare for him? Half the people would probably just keep on working. Would that piss him off, or would he understand?

And what about coming-to-attention practice? Seems like fanfare practice would be a perfect time to hold it. You know, kill two birds . . . Ah well, fuck it. These are the sort of thoughts that hold me back in life.

Jump, Don't Scream

Here's why I'm opposed to singing. Singing strikes me as an indicator of limited language skills. My feeling is that if someone has a valid thought, deserving of expression, but somehow that thought can't be communicated without the assistance of a banjo or a tambourine, then maybe it's a thought the rest of us don't need to hear.

People will argue, "Singing has more to do with expressing emotion than it does with expressing thought." Well, fine. But from my point of view, when it comes to expressing emotion, singing is not nearly as effective a tool as screaming. Let's face it, if you want to express emotion, screaming is where it's at.

And to be fair, the more I think about it, the more I realize that singing itself is nothing more than a modified form of screaming. It's actually just carefully organized, socially acceptable screaming. And, folks, I think we have enough screaming in the world as it is.

Now, dancing, on the other hand, I can understand. Dancing is a highly developed form of jumping around, and there's certainly nothing wrong with jumping around.

Jumping around is fine in my book. In fact, I feel it's essential. So, please, feel free to jump around all you want. But if you fall and break a leg, don't come screaming to me. Write a song.

Can You Hear Me Now?

Have you noticed that whenever someone at a large gathering tries to get the attention of the crowd on a public address system, they always yell into the microphone? "ATTENTION!! ATTENTION PLEASE!! LADIES AND GENTLEMEN!! YOUR ATTENTION PLEASE!!" Don't these people understand that the whole purpose of a voice-amplifying system is to amplify the voice? I think the idea is that when you speak into it, it makes your voice sound louder. Maybe I'm way off on this, but it seems to me that if there is a device that makes your voice sound louder, there's probably no reason to yell into it. I don't know, maybe I'm just wrong on this. I'm willing to listen. But hold it down, will ya?

Cars as Personal Billboards

Never Mind the Biography

I'm tired of people using their cars as biographical information centers, informing the world of their sad-sack lives and boring interests. Keep that shit to yourself. I don't want to know what college you went to, who you intend to vote for or what your plan is for world peace. I don't care if you visited the Grand Canyon, Mount Rushmore or the birthplace of Wink Martindale. And I'm not interested in what radio station you listen to or what bands you like. In fact, I'm not interested in you in any way, except to see you in my rearview mirror.

Furthermore, I can do without your profession of faith in God, Allah, Jehova, Yahweh, Peter Cottontail or whoever the fuck it is you've turned your life over to; please keep your superstitions private. I can't tell you how happy it would make me to someday drive up to a flaming auto wreck and see smoke curling up around one of those little fish symbols with *Jesus* written inside it. And as far as I'm concerned, you can include the Darwin/fish-with-feet evolution symbol too. Far too cute for my taste.

So keep the personal and autobiograph-
ical messages to yourself. Here's an idea:
Maybe you could paste them up inside
your car, where you can see them and I
can't.

Proud Parents of Another Drone

Here's another segment of the bumper-
sticker population that ought to be locked
into portable toilets and set on fire. The ones
who want us to know how well their kids are
doing in school. Doing well, that is, according to today's lowered standards:

"We are the proud parents of an honors
student at the Franklin School." Or the
Midvale Academy. Or whatever other inno-
cent-sounding name has been assigned to
the indoctrination center where their child
has been sent to be stripped of his individuality and turned into an obedient, soul-
dead, conformist member of the American
consumer culture.

What kind of empty people need to vali-
date themselves through the achievements
of a child? How would you like to live with a

couple of these blockheads? "Say, Justin. How's that science project coming along?" "Fuck you, Dad, you simpleminded prick! Mind your own business and pass the Froot Loops. Fucking cunt dork."

Here are a few parental bumper stickers I'd like to see:

"We are the proud parents of a child whose self-esteem is sufficient that he doesn't need us promoting his minor scholastic achievements on the back of our car." That would be refreshing.

"We are the proud parents of a child who has resisted his teacher's attempts to break his spirit and bend him to the will of his corporate masters." A little Marxist, but what's wrong with that?

Here's something realistic: "We have a daughter in public school who hasn't been knocked up yet." And, for the boy: "We have a son in public school who hasn't shot any of his classmates yet. But he does sell drugs to your honors student. Plus, he knocked up your daughter."

And what about those parents who aren't too proud of their children? "We are the embarrassed parents of a cross-eyed, drooling little nitwit, who, at the age of ten, not only continues to wet the bed, but also shits on the school bus." Something like that on the back of the car might give the child a little more incentive. Get him to try a little harder next semester.

Plate Tectonics

My car complaints include personalized license plates, which in California have reached really bothersome levels. Among my least favorites are the ones where the guy tells me what kind of car it is, in case I'm fucking blind: BEAMER, BENZ, PORSH. How helpful. Then there are those very special guys who not only tell me what kind of car it is, but also who owns it: GARY'S Z, DON'S JAG, BOB'S BMW. What's wrong with these cretins? Have they never owned a car before?

And what's with these pinheads who feel compelled to announce their occupations? LAWYUR, SKINDOC, PLMBR, SHRYNK, POOLMAN. Why this pressing need to reveal one's profession? Drumming up business? Job insecurity? Identity crisis? Or is it just the usual American disease: being a jackoff.

And since these things are called "vanity plates" (they should be called "ego tags"), it comes as no surprise that the show-business professions abound with this nonsense. Among the worst offenders are writers. If you drive the streets and freeways of Los Angeles long enough, sooner or later you will see every variation of license plate these allegedly creative people have managed to come up with.

Here are the best of the lot: WRITTIR, WRYTRE, WRYTR, WRYYTRR, WRYTAR, RITER RITEUR, WRYTER, RYTER, TV RTR. God help them. Isn't a scriptwriting credit recognition enough? Or carrying a Writers Guild card? What are they looking for? Do they expect to be nominated for an Emmy at a red light? If these hacks spent half the time working on their scripts they spend thinking up license plates, entertainment in America would be vastly improved.

But writers aren't alone. It seems that any job in television demands an acknowledgment: TVGUY, TVMAN, TVHOST1, TVNUZE, TVVDEO, TVSOWND, TVBIZ, TVBIZZ, TVBIZZZ, TV SHOW. I suppose the idea is, "Why be involved in television at all if I can't tell the world?" After all, everyone knows what an outstanding field it is to be proud of.

One last item. To me, the biggest mystery of all is why a good-looking woman would get a license plate that says HOT BABE, PARTYGAL, HOTLIPS or BABE4U? Isn't she just asking for some crazy fuck with a hard-on to follow her home so he can find out if she's as hot she says she is? Maybe that's the point; to pick up horny freaks at random. Sounds dumb. I wonder how many of these women have been raped and killed by guys whose license plates said BIG-DICK, HOTROD, KILLGAL or RAPE-DUDE?

Body of Work: Part 3

Scab Labor

Here's another item you can't see while it's still on you: a scab on the top of your head. Did y'ever have that? Sure you have. A little scab on the top of your head? Not a big, red, juicy blood scab, like you get when someone at work hits you in the head with a Stilson wrench. Just a little scaly, scabby, dry spot. You find it one day by accident, when you're scratchin' your head. You come across it as if by good luck.

"Dum-dee-dee-da . . . Da-dum-da . . . Whooooaaa! What's this? A scab! Hot shit, a scab! I love fuckin' scabs. This is gonna be a lot of fun. I can't wait to pick off my scab and look at it. Oh boy, oh boy! I can't wait to pick off my scab and place it down on a contrasting material such as a black velvet tablecloth in order to see it in greater relief. Oh boy, oh boy, I can't wait to pick off my scab, this is gonna be a lot of fun.

"Wait! Wait! Wait! (Picking at scalp) Wait just a minute. It's not ready to come off yet! It's immature, it's still not ripe. It's not ready for plucking. I'll save this for Thursday! Thursday will be a good day. I only have half a day of work on Thursday. I'll come home early, masturbate in the kitchen, wash the floor and then I'll watch *The Montel Williams Show*. And while I do, I'll pick off my scab. Oh boy, oh boy! I can't wait to pick off my scab, this is gonna be a lot of fun."

The Waiting Game

So you wait. And you wait. And you wait, and you wait, and you wait. And you try not to knock it off by accident with the little plastic comb you bought in the vending machine at the Easy Livin' Motel when you hooked up with the two skanky-lookin' chicks who gave you the clap that night.

And now, finally, Thursday arrives. It's harvest time! Harvest time on the top of your head. So you come home early, and you masturbate, but you do it in your sister's bedroom just to give it a little extra thrill. Know what I mean? Then you shampoo the rug, and you watch *The Montel Williams Show*. Pretty interesting topic: "Women Who Take It up the Ass for Fifty Cents." Not the best show he's ever done, but you know somethin'? Not bad, either!

And now it's time. Time to go get this little scab. But you want to proceed carefully. You want to pry this thing off slowly and evenly, around the perimeter of the scab, so that it lifts off all in one piece. You don't want it to break into pieces. Who needs a fragmented scab? Not me. I don't need parts that badly, I'm not that disturbed.

What you really want; what you really need; what you really must have is a complete, whole scab you can set down, study, make notes on and perhaps write a series of penetrating articles on for *Scab Aficionado Magazine*. Who knows? You might rise to the top of the scab world in a big hurry. It's a small community and they need people at the top.

And so you proceed. With a single finger-nail extended — always choosing your best peeling and scraping nail — you find your way through the thicket of hair and locate the target. You make a careful, initial probe, and surprisingly, the prey yields easily, coming off all in one piece. And you lift it off carefully, through the hair, and position it on the tip of your picking finger.

And you look at the little thing, so pathetic there on your finger. Isolated, alone, out of its environment. And your heart begins to melt. So you take your new friend carefully between thumb and forefinger, and gently place it back on your head, setting it loose in the wild. And you feel the better man. You're in harmony with your body.

Think of it as catch and release.

Euphemisms: Broke, Nuts and on the Street

I Got No Money

While we in America have been busy creating politically correct euphemisms for old people

— thereby making their lives infinitely easier — we've also been working on our poor-people language problem. And we now have language that takes all the pain out of being poor. Having no money these days is easier than ever.

I can remember, when I was young, that *poor people lived in slums.* Not anymore. These days, the *economically disadvantaged occupy substandard housing in the inner cities.* It's so much nicer for them. And yet they're still considered *socially marginal.*

But as it turns out, many of these socially marginal people receive *public assistance* — once known as *welfare.* Before that it was called *being on relief,* or *being on the dole.* And at that time, being on the dole was the worst thing you could say about a family: "They're on the dole." People were ashamed. It was tough to get a date if you were on the dole.

But public assistance! That sounds good. Who of us hasn't benefited from some form of public assistance? Even huge businesses and agricultural interests receive public assistance. Ditto all the wealthiest taxpayers. So apparently, there is no shame attached to being on the dole after all.

I Got No Home

In this country, about the only thing worse than having no money is having no place to live. And over the years, those with no place to live have had many different names: *vagrants, tramps, hoboes, drifters* and *transients* come to mind. Which name applied to a person sometimes depended on his, his — God, this is difficult to say — *lifestyle*. There, it's out.

But can having no place to live actually be a lifestyle? Well, it seems to me that if you're going to use a questionable word like *lifestyle* at all, you should be forced to use it across the board. After all, if there's a *gay lifestyle* — which I doubt — and a *suburban lifestyle* — which seems more arguable — it stands to reason there must be a *homeless lifestyle*. And even, one would assume, a *prison lifestyle*.

Indeed, is it possible that those doomed souls in places like Buchenwald were actually enjoying a *concentration-camp lifestyle?* If they were, don't tell their families; you'll be misunderstood. And, taking this unfortunate word to its ultimate, logical extreme, I will not be surprised to someday see one of those spiritual mediums doing a TV show called *Lifestyles of the Dead*. (Incidentally, shouldn't a group of mediums be called *media?* Just asking.)

Back to the subject: vagrants, tramps, hoboes, drifters and transients. Without using a dictionary (which in many cases is no help at all), here are the distinctions I picked up in years past by listening to how people used these words. The sense I got was: Vagrants simply had no money; tramps and hoboes had no money, but they moved around; drifters moved around, but occasionally worked for a while and then drifted on, whereas tramps and hoboes didn't work at all. We'll get to transients in a moment.

There's one other distinction between tramps and hoboes that's worth mentioning. The word *tramp* might also have been used to describe the young woman your son brought home. Rarely did anyone's son bring home a hobo. Unless, of course, he was into the *gay hobo lifestyle.* Actually, there weren't too many gay hoboes. That's because if a hobo didn't have a home, he certainly didn't have a closet either to be in or to come out of. (Sudden thought: hobo rhymes with homo. Sorry.)

Another way to categorize this class of people was to call them transients. Sometimes, on skid row, where they had a lot of *bums* and *winos* (we'll get to them in a minute), you'd see a cheap hotel with a sign that said TRANSIENTS WELCOME.

Transients were like drifters, except transients seemed to stay in cities, whereas drifters moved through small towns and rural areas. You *had* to move through those places, because they weren't as tolerant as cities; they didn't have signs that said DRIFTERS WELCOME. It was usually just the opposite. Ask Clint Eastwood. By the way, isn't a hotel that says it welcomes transients a little like a restaurant that says it prefers people with stomachs? Just asking.

First cousin to a *transient hotel* was a *flophouse,* a magnificently descriptive piece of language that has all but disappeared. (Just for the record, these days transient hotels are called *limited service lodgings.*) Several cuts above all these places were *furnished rooms,* these days known by the phrase *SROs,* short for *single room occupancy.*

So, staying on track here, we began this section with people who have no place to live, which brings us to today's hot designation, *the homeless,* also known as *street people.* When I was a boy, we never heard those words; a dirty, drunk man on the street who wanted money was normally called a bum. Simple word, three letters, one syllable: *bum.* And a bum was usually also a wino.

You know, a *substance abuser*. He had a *chemical dependency*. Little did we know.

By the way, it should be pointed out that bum might also have been used to describe the young man your daughter brought home. Many's the bum who didn't pass muster with Dad. I wonder how many of those bums the daughters brought home wound up marrying the tramps the sons brought home? That might explain all those *homeless children*.

But the word *homeless* is useless. It's messy, it's inaccurate, it's not descriptive. It attempts to cover too many things: poverty, alcoholism, drug addiction, schizophrenia, no place to live and begging on the street.

Homeless should mean only one thing: no home. No place to live. Many of these people who beg on the street actually have places to live. I had one guy tell me he needed money to buy tires for his van. I gave him a dollar; I considered him both honest and enterprising.

The first word I remember for these people was *bag ladies*. I don't know why men were left out of this; I never heard anyone say *bag men*. I guess that's because a bag man is a different thing. A bag man is someone who delivers bribes or illegal gambling money. Probably, in today's evasive, dishonest, politically correct language, they'd be called *bag persons*. In my opinion, the closest we're ever going to get to a good descriptive name for these lovable grimy folks is street people.

And by the way, isn't it ironic that shopping bags (and shopping carts) — symbols of plenty — should be the objects most preferred by people who have nothing at all? I guess if you have nothing, you need something to carry it around in. Especially if you're crazy.

Wild and Crazy Guys

That's what a lot of these street people are, you know. They're crazy. I avoid terms like *mentally disturbed* and *emotionally impaired*. You can't let the politically correct language police dictate the way you express yourself. I prefer plain language: crazy, insane, nuts. "The whole world is crazy, and many of its inhabitants are insane. Or am I just nuts?" And for the most part, we humans do enjoy being colorful and creative when describing the condition of someone who's crazy. Here are a few descriptions of craziness that I enjoy:

- *One wheel in the sand.*
- *Seat back not in the full, upright position.*
- *Not playing with a full bag of jacks.*
- *Doesn't have both feet in the end zone.*
- *Lives out where the buses don't run.*
- *The cheese fell off his cracker a long time ago.*
- *His factory's still open, but it's makin' something else.*

Here's an odd one: *His squeegee doesn't go all the way to the bottom of the pail.* I think you have to have some serious time-management problems to be sitting around thinking up stuff like that. But there you are. This next one sounds really good, but I confess I don't quite understand it: *He belongs in a cotton box.* For some reason it sounds exactly right, though, doesn't it?

And if you're going to be irreverent about describing crazy people, you can't get soft when it comes to describing the places we keep them. Or used to keep them. In the 1980s, Ronald Reagan decided the best place to keep them was on the streets, which actually makes a lot of sense, because the streets are nothing more than a slightly larger, open-air asylum, anyway.

But around the turn of the nineteenth century, many states had places called *insti-*

tutions for the feebleminded. That name seemed too long for some people, so instead they referred to them as *madhouses.* "They took him to the madhouse. Boy, was he mad." Then these places became *insane asylums, mental homes, mental institutions* and, finally, *psychiatric facilities.*

I have three personal favorites. I always liked the *hoo-hoo hotel.* To me, that says it all. Here's another one that's not bad: *the puzzle factory.* It has a certain class to it, doesn't it? But if you prefer a gentler approach, you really can't beat *the enchanted kingdom.* "They took him away to the enchanted kingdom." And guess how they took him there? The *twinkymobile.* Now that's descriptive language.

A Toast to the Classics

When I see a symphony orchestra, a hundred or so people playing some incredibly difficult piece of music in complete and perfect unison as if they were a single organism, I remind myself that each one of them started the day in a different kitchen. A hundred different musicians in a hundred different kitchens, scattered across the city. And sometimes I find myself wondering how many of them had eggs that morning and how many chose cereal. I try to guess whether the percentage of muffin eaters is greater among the strings or the brass section. I ponder whether or not the percussionists drink a lot of coffee, whereas, perhaps, the piccolo players lean more toward flavored teas. I don't know why these thoughts come to me. But they sure fill the time between scherzos.

Fuck You, Father, for You Have Sinned

Catholic kids are stupid; they don't know how to handle a pedophile priest. Here's what you do: First of all, you don't get all scared and do whatever he tells you. Who wants to get sucked off by a forty-three-year-old clergyman with beard stubble? Not me. Instead, what you do is kick him in the nuts. You kick him squarely in the nuts, and you get the fuck out of there as fast as you can, and you go tell somebody right away; you tell as many grown-up people as you can — one of them is bound to believe you.

That's what you do. You don't wait thirty

years. You kick the priest in the nuts and say, "Fuck you, Father, I don't do that shit. Try Jimmy Fogarty, I heard he blew the choirmaster." And you're out the door. And don't forget to take your rosary. On second thought, leave the rosary. A lot of good it did you in the first place.

Three Short Stories

The Velvet Hat

She wore a velvet hat. She walked down the steps slowly, as if each one were a significant achievement. Her arm, bent severely at the elbow, pinned her purse close to her side. The surface of the last few steps was cracked and uneven, and so she extended her tiny arm to grip the railing. At that moment a man ran up and jammed an entire box of peppermints into her mouth.

Not Martha Stewart

Vinny had just squeezed off three really vicious, warm, partially liquid farts and was now trying with all his might to suck down from the back of his nose a huge gob of hardened snot that felt as big as a human embryo. Ignoring the dog shit encrusted under his fingernails from several weeks earlier, he reached deep into his throat, pulled loose some partially digested food, swallowed it again and continued to make hamburger patties for the kids.

Garnish

The man in the tweed hat stood by a tree, rolling a half-dried snot between his thumb and forefinger. Moments later, the snot now completely dry, he strolled casually past a sidewalk café and gently flicked it into a young lady's lemonade.

. . . Finish Your Sentences?

Stan: Why do you always . . .

Dan: . . . finish your sentences?

Stan: Yes, it's something that's . . .

Dan: . . . been bothering you for a long time?

Stan: Yes.

Dan: Well, it's a habit that started in grade school. When the teacher called on another kid, sometimes the kid would start to answer and then get stuck. So I would supply the rest of the answer.

Stan: And this habit has stayed with you . . .

Dan: . . . ever since that time.

Stan: But there must be something you can . . .

Dan: . . . do about it? The only thing I could do about it would be to find some person who might be willing to . . .

Stan: . . . finish *your* sentences?

Dan: Yes, if I could just find someone to finish *my* sentences . . .

Stan: . . . it would put a little balance in your life?

Dan: Right.

Stan: But why does it have to be someone *else?* Why couldn't it be . . .

Dan: . . . the same person? Why couldn't the same person whose sentences I finish . . .

Stan: . . . be the same person who finishes your sentences?

Dan: I don't know. Let's ask this . . .

Man: . . . man over here. What can I do for you fellows?

A Person I Know Day

The American Retail Association reminds you that next Sunday is A Person I Know Day. It's a lot like Mother's Day or Father's Day, but instead of honoring your parents, you take the time to honor some other person you know. It can be anyone at all: mailman, delivery boy, gas station attendant, drugstore clerk, even that interesting fellow who stands on the corner all day displaying his penis. Any person you know is eligible; in fact, *every* person you know is eligible. So why not honor them all? Go out today and buy gifts for all the people you know. It's the perfect way of showing your love and saying, "Hi, I'm sure glad I know you."

And when you think about it, you'll probably be in store for some nice gifts yourself on A Person I Know Day. In fact, the more people you know, the more gifts you'll receive. So go for a long walk today and introduce yourself to every person you see. Just walk up and say, "Don't I know you? If not, I'd sure like to." Then give them your address and tell them to send you a gift. You'll make lots and lots of new friends. And you'll be helping the economy.

If It Ain't Dirty, Why Clean It?

I've never seen anyone cleaning a church. I've seen many things, but never a cleaning crew working in a church; vacuuming, mopping, dusting the statues and scrubbing the altar. You know why? I figured it out: Churches don't need to be cleaned; God does it. It's one of those miracles. That's how they know it's a church in the first place.

Here's how it works: After a church has been built, the owners wait six months and then look inside. If it's clean, they know it's a church. So they get ready for the grand opening. And from that day on, they never have to clean it. No matter what kind of crud, grime or muck the sinners track in, the place remains spotless. But just between you and me, a little Windex on the stained glass wouldn't hurt once in a while. It would help bring out all those bright, pretty colors they use to show the torture and the bleeding of the saints.

Our Lady of the TV

"Hi. I'm Our Lady of the TV. I'm here to say hello, and to make sure everyone prays real hard for peace. Also, the last time I was here I forgot my sunglasses. Has anyone seen my sunglasses?"

(Stagehand hands her the glasses.)

"Thank you. Hold my purse, would you?"

(She hands him her purse and puts on the sunglasses.)

"I know that many of you lead a pointless existence. You have dead-end jobs, bad marriages and children who hate you because you've ruined their lives. I also know you look to symbols like me to provide solace and hope. Well, here's the deal: I have no solace to offer, and, frankly, there is no hope. I'm just an illusion; an illusion that means nothing. So work it out for yourselves; if you ask me, you're not trying hard enough. Thank you. I'll be back in a few years. And please stop bothering my son with stupid requests like winning the lottery."

(To the stagehand) "Gimme the purse."

Letter to a Friend

Dear Trevor,

The reason I'm writing is because I've lost your address and have no way of getting in touch with you. For that reason, chances are you won't receive this, in which case you should not feel obligated to reply. If, however, this letter does reach you and you wish to answer, please enclose your current address so I will know where to send this. By the way, you can ignore the return address on this envelope, as I am moving next week and, although I don't yet have my new address, I will be sending it along as soon as I hear from you.

Should you have any trouble locating me, please be assured I will contact you as soon as I have my new phone, so, by all means, give me a call and let me have your number. If it turns out I'm unable to reach you, please don't hesitate to get in touch, as I always mention it to my friends whenever neither of us hears from the other. Should you encounter any trouble reaching _me_, please let me know, and I will get back to you at once.

Then again, if you are unable to reach me, perhaps it would be better not to get in touch, because I will most likely be trying to get hold of you. And, of course, if I do reach you please let me know immediately. Conversely, if I don't reach you, you will probably hear from me right away.

Well, evening is rolling around, and, as they say in Portugal, "It's time to say goodbye." I hope you receive this before you mail your letter. *It's so good to communicate this way.*

Sincerely,
Sperla Vaughn

P.S. Should this letter be lost in transit, please disregard.

Bits and Pieces

TRUE FACT: I saw a guy on the street wearing a T-shirt that said "Couples for Christ." But he was all alone. And I wondered, What would Jesus think?

- What's the difference between a drop and a droplet? After all, if you divide a drop into smaller parts, all you really get is smaller drops. Big or little, a drop is a drop. Same thing with a crumb. But the odd thing about a crumb is that if you cut a crumb in half, you don't get two half-crumbs, you get two crumbs. To me, that sounds like magic. I gotta ask David Copperfield how they do that.

- When it comes to God's existence, I'm not an atheist and I'm not an agnostic. I'm an acrostic. The whole thing puzzles me.

- I saw a homeless guy sitting on the sidewalk, yammering to himself and repeatedly punctuating his remarks with, "You know what I'm sayin'? You know what I'm sayin'?" And I thought, For God's sake, the man is talking to himself! If *he* doesn't know what he's saying, who would?

TRUE FACT: On June 8, 1995, Glacier National Park was closed because of too much snow.

- Colin Powell spent his entire adult life as a soldier, trying to devise the most efficient ways of killing foreigners for his country. Then he became a diplomat, trying to devise the most efficient ways of getting foreigners to cooperate with his country. Tough sell.

- Whenever I hear about parents who have nine or ten children, the only thing I wonder is how they survive the birthday parties.

- I recently learned there are three people still alive who can do the minuet. Unfortunately, only one of them is able to move without a wheelchair.

- I think they should have a hotline that never answers, for people who don't follow advice in the first place.

- I finally figured out what e-mail is for. It's for communicating with people you'd rather not talk to.

- You know what I like most about the NCAA Basketball Tournament? Sixty-three losers.

- The United States most closely resembles a huge, poorly-thought-out sick joke.

- Health tip from the American Medical Association: Never pour corrosive chemicals on your testicles.

- A female teacher seduced a fourteen-year old boy and he turned her in to the police. What was this kid thinking? Was he fuckin' crazy? Or gay? I would have kept that kind of thing real quiet. At least until I graduated.

- Cigarette companies market heavily to young people. They need young customers because their product kills the older ones. It is the only product that, if used as intended, kills the consumer.

- More people write poetry than read it.

- I wish the ecology people would save one species that would make a dramatic comeback and then wipe us all out.

TRUE FACT: There is actually an erotic wrestler.

- When I'm in someone's house and I see something I want that's small and easy to conceal, I steal it. It's my belief that property belongs to the person who wants it most.

- Whatever became of alpha-carotene?

- I wonder what kind of masturbation fantasies Stephen King has.

- I also wonder if anyone has ever masturbated while fantasizing about having sex with a live chicken. Usually, I wonder about these things while I'm masturbating.

- Isaiah said, "They shall beat their swords into ploughshares and their spears into pruning hooks . . ." Let me ask you something. When was the last time you heard of someone who made a fortune selling ploughshares and pruning hooks?

- You're probably thinking to yourselves right now, "I wonder what he thinks I'm thinking right now." Or, you may be thinking, "I wonder when he's going to say, 'You're probably thinking to yourselves right now, I wonder what he thinks I'm thinking right now.'" Or you could be thinking, "I wonder when he's going to wonder when I . . ." Well, maybe not.

- Hey, guys, did you ever get your balls caught in the toaster when it was turned all the way up to dark brown, and your wife was trying to rub butter on your balls, and your pit bull was in the kitchen and he really loves butter? It's an awful feeling.

- When I'm writing, I always like to have the TV playing in the background. I usually try to find a program that's interesting enough to leave on, but stupid enough to ignore.

- I think sometimes the word *overseas* is pluralized unnecessarily. The way I look at it, New York to London is "oversea." After all, there's only one sea in between them.

- This statement is untrue.

- **Regarding astrology:** An obstetrician or a maternity nurse who weighs between one hundred and two hundred pounds actually exerts a greater gravitational force on a baby at the time of its birth than do any of the distant planets that are said to influence a person's personality and destiny. Why aren't these bulky, proximate objects factored into the astrological charts that are so carefully laid out?

- There are caregivers and there are caretakers, and yet the two words are not opposites. Why is this?

- Whenever I hear that someone lives in a gated community I think of places like Auschwitz.

  TRUE FACT: There is actually such a thing as the Paralyzed Veterans of America. And I wonder, Who answers the phone?

- Until you're a certain age, you don't have anything to "put behind you." That's what life seems to be: a process of

411

doing things that eventually you just
want to put behind you.

- There are now murderous turf-wars
going on in which people are being brutally killed over the right to sell a substance called ecstasy.

- You know something you don't see anymore? The sacking of a city. Rome and
Constantinople were good examples.
Next time we win a war, we ought to
sack the capital of the country we defeat. "U.S. TROOPS SACK BAGHDAD."
Wouldn't that be good? I guess we do
our sacking in subtler ways. Through
the business community.

- I think they ought to have really fast es-
calators that you have to jump on and
off, and if you get hurt, too bad.

- When I notice a dead fly on the
windowsill — one that wasn't there the
day before — I always wonder how he
died. I wonder if he had a stroke, or
maybe a little fly heart attack. Then I
think maybe he's just pretending to be
dead so I won't swat him. So I swat
him.

- Here's a tip from the power and light company on saving energy: If you have elderly people living with you, cut back on their heat and light. Old people often exaggerate how cold they feel.

No Child Left Behind

I was thinking the other day that one kid who's really gonna have emotional problems when she grows up is that Jon Benet Ramsey. You know, because of all the media attention, her parents being under suspicion, the speculations about sexual abuse. Jesus, that kind of thing would fuck any kid up. And then I remembered, hey, she was the one who got killed. And I thought, it's a good thing she's dead; at least she won't have to suffer.

Tell Pierre I Said Hello

Hank: I'm going up to San Francisco this weekend.

Frank: Oh. Well, tell Pierre I said hello.

Hank: Actually, I knew you would say that, so I took the liberty of calling him and telling him you said hello. He said in that case to tell you he also says hello. So, "Hello" from Pierre. And he said to add, "How's it goin'?"

Frank: Oh, that's great. Well tell him everything's going just fine. And don't forget to say, "How are you?"

Hank: Well, he and I knew you would ask that, and so Pierre has authorized me to say that he's glad you're fine, but that he hasn't been feeling too well lately.

Frank: Oh. Well, tell him I'm sorry to hear that and I hope it isn't serious.

Hank: He says he knew you would be sorry to hear that, but he thinks it will blow over.

Frank: Well, tell him if it doesn't I have a great doctor in San Francisco. Ginny and I met him in Hawaii when we were there last year.

Hank: Pierre says he knew you had a great doctor, but he wasn't aware he was located in San Francisco. He also says he didn't know you and Ginny had gone to Hawaii. He thought it was Cancún. And he also says, "How's Ginny?"

415

Frank: Tell him Ginny is dead.

Hank: Well, I'm sure he didn't know, but I'm going to go out on a limb here and say that he's real sorry to hear about that, and I'm willing to bet anything he offers his condolences. And, most likely, he'll also say that if there's anything he can do — anything — please don't hesitate to ask.

Frank: Excuse me, Hank. I'd love to keep talking, but I have to go buy underwear.

Hank: Oh. Well, Pierre says there's a sale at The Gap.

Frank: Get fucked, Hank.

Guys Will Be Guys

I don't know why people got all excited about that guy Jeffrey Dahmer. Because he broke a few laws? So what? There's nothing wrong with killing twelve people, having sex with their corpses, masturbating on them, eating their flesh and then saving the heads in the refrigerator. What's wrong with that? Nothing. So far, nobody has been able to explain to me what it was Jeffrey Dahmer did that was so wrong.

First of all, let's remember, *wrong* is a relative term. Who's to say what's wrong? Who are we to judge? Put yourself in the other man's shoes. Who among you, under certain circumstances, might not kill twelve people, have sex with their corpses, masturbate on them, eat their flesh and then save the heads in the refrigerator? Not one of you, I suspect. So cut the guy a little slack. Always remember, there, but for the grace of God . . .

You're Not Funny

Here are some things you should not say if you encounter a comedian. First: If you're with another person at the time, don't say to your friend, "You better watch out, he'll put you in one of his skits." We don't like that. It's not funny. And, by the way, we don't do skits. Second: If you meet him while you're at your job, do not say, "You oughtta work here, you'd get a lot of material." It's not true. Just because you work with a bunch of simpletons, doesn't mean it translates into comedy. Third: If you work at a store and we're shopping there, and some small mix-up occurs that needs to be sorted out, don't say to a co-worker, "He's gonna put this in one of his routines." He's not. One more thing we don't like: When you tell us something that you think is funny and then you say, "You can use that if you want." We don't want to use it. Believe me.

Pow! Smack! Bam!

True: I stopped behind a small, beat-up camper at a red light, and noticed three bumper stickers: DARE TO RESIST DRUGS AND VIOLENCE, THERE'S NO EXCUSE FOR DOMESTIC ABUSE, and STOP SENIOR ABUSE. And I thought, I'm really glad I don't live with those folks. I'd bet anything they were on their way to the hospital emergency room or perhaps intensive psychiatric counseling. If I'd caught up and looked inside the vehicle, I'm sure it would have resembled a Johnson & Johnson showroom.

Count to a Billion

Announcer: And now, ladies and gentlemen, direct from Dover, Delaware, Big Earl Stemplemeyer's Television Network presents *Count to a Billion*.

(Applause, lively organ music)

Yes, it's *Count to a Billion*, the show where ordinary people of limited intelligence can win big money by simply counting to a billion. As we like to say, "If you can count at all, and have a reasonable amount of time on your hands, chances are you can count to a billion." So now, here's your host, a man you can count on, that burly guy who's one in a billion, Basil Danderfleck.

(Applause, lively organ music)

Basil: Thank you, Wynonie Flench. And now, folks, let's meet our two players, Tillie Lipfinder and Zippy

Brillnipper, alias Skeezix Pendleton.

(Applause, lively organ music)

Basil: How about it, folks? Are you two ready to count to a billion?

Tillie: Yes sir.

Zippy: You bet your ass!

(Applause, lively organ music)

Basil: All right, let's get started. As you know, we have only one rule: No skipping any numbers. Ready, set, go!

(Loud bell, lively organ music, applause, yelps, cheers)

Tillie: (Incredibly rapid pace) 1, 2, 3, 4, 5, 6, 7, 8, 9, 10, 11, 12, 13, 14, 15, 16, 17, 18, 19, 20, 21, 22, 23, 24, 25, 26, 27, 28, 29, 30, 31, 32, 33 . . .

Zippy: (Extremely slowly) 1 . . . 2 . . . 3 . . . 4 . . .

Basil: Tillie appears to have jumped off to

an early lead, but as we know, slow and steady wins the race, so don't count Zippy out yet. By the way, tonight's winner will receive two free meals at Shorty and Bud's Restaurant for the Unclean, featuring their world-famous Chicken in a Shoe. As Shorty and Bud say, "Wouldn't You Like to Eat a Nice Hot Meal Out of Someone Else's Used Footwear?" Well, let's check back in with our two contestants.

Tillie: (Incredibly rapid pace) 10,366,793, 10,366,794, 10,366,795, 10,366,796 . . .

Zippy: (Extremely slowly) 25,853,264 . . . 25,853,265 . . . 25,853,266 . . . 25,853,267 . . . 25,853,268 . . . 25,853,269 . . .

Basil: Wow! Amazing! In no time at all, Zippy has caught up and pulled ahead. But he'd better not get overconfident, he still has 974 million to go.

We'll check back in a moment, but first, a reminder that tonight's runner-up will receive a handsome set of matching luggage from America's luggage leader, Packwell and Goforth, now featuring the newest innovation in luggage . . . portable suitcases! That's right, folks, these novel suitcases have actual handles built right into them, so now you can take your luggage with you anywhere you go. Take it on a plane, take it on a boat, you can even put it in your car. No more leaving your bags at home because they're "hard to carry." Take them with you and travel in style! Packwell and Goforth: ahead of their time since 1357.

Let's check in again with Zippy and Tillie.

Tillie: 536,895,241,   536,895,242, 536,895,243, 536,895,244 . . .

Zippy: 67,667,776 . . . 67,667,777 . . . 67,667,778 . . . 67,667,779 . . .

Well, Tillie has come back and taken a big lead, because, unfortunately, Zippy's severe lisp has slowed him down considerably here in this section which includes tho many thicktheth and theventh. I'm sorry . . . so many sixes and sevens. This does not look good for Zippy. But we're about out of time for now . . .

(Groans, hisses, boos, lively organ music)

. . . but join us again next week, as we watch the conclusion of this thrilling match on tape and meet two new contestants, as once again we play America's favorite counting game . . . *Count to a Billion!*

(Cheers, boos, applause, hisses, shouts, threats, curses, audience advancing menacingly toward stage, lively organ music)

Announcer: (over music and crowd noise) Tonight's guests will stay at the fabulous Fireproof Motel, located between Long John Silver's and the Rub It and Yank It massage parlor, just outside Dover, Delaware. Dover: "The City That Just Missed the Mark." Don't forget, the Fireproof Motel features superb drinks and finger food in the intimate cocktail lounge, Rita's Box. Drop in and ask Rita for some finger food.

Stay tuned now for a full-length movie on America's favorite new date show, *Dinner, Movie and a Hump.* Tonight, your hosts, Dagwood Parkhaven and Candace Nooch, cook up a delicious whale chowder and breast of hyena on a bed of diced badger as they present an award-winning film about an amnesia victim, *Who the Fuck Am I?*, starring Esther Sylvester, Kermit McDermott, Chi Chi Ameche and Skeeter Van Meter. And introducing Keith Bunghole as the queer.

After the movie and the food, Dagwood and Candace will tear off a lengthy piece of ass on the kitchen table, taking turns being on top, and demonstrating several interesting, new sexual positions, including the Baghdad Twirl and the Bosnian Dick-knot.

Good night everyone, and God bless America!

(Lively organ music, lustful throaty moans and maniacal screaming)

Euphemisms: Death and Dying

Some of our best work with euphemisms involves the subject that makes us the most uncomfortable: death.

Our most common euphemism for death is to say the person *passed away*. Or *passed on*. If you believe in an afterlife, you may prefer *crossed over;* or *crossed over to the other side*. Whenever I hear that someone has crossed over to the other side, I always picture Fifth Avenue.

Then there's the official term for dying, the doctor term. In this case the person simply *expires*. Like a magazine subscription. One month he just doesn't show up. Unfortunately, he can't renew. Or so they say. Better check with the Hindus on that.

Now, continuing. In this current age of

specialization — and increasing detachment — if the person in question dies in a hospital, it's called a *terminal episode*. Although the insurance company sees it as *negative patient-care outcome*. That one's actually kinda nice, isn't it? And if the negative patient-care outcome was caused by medical malpractice, then it's referred to as a *therapeutic misadventure*. Colorful term. No wonder so many doctors are leaving their practices; it's hard to get therapeutic-misadventure insurance.

But by far the most creative terms we've come up with to comfort ourselves about death are the ones that describe the rituals survivors put themselves through. We owe a lot of this softened language to the funeral business. Or, as they prefer to be known, the *death-care industry*. They have completely transformed the language used to describe what happens following a death.

In years past it went like this: "The *old man died*, so the *undertaker* picked up the *body*, brought it to the *funeral home* and put it in a *casket*. People sent *flowers* and held a *wake*. After the *funeral*, they put the *coffin* in a *hearse* and drove it to the *cemetery*, where the *dead man* was *buried* in a *grave*."

But in these days of heightened sensitivity, the same series of events produces what sounds like a completely different experience: "The *senior citizen passed away*, so the *funeral director* claimed the *remains* of the *decedent*, took them to the *memorial chapel* and placed them in a *burial container*. *Grieving survivors* sent *floral tributes* to be displayed in the *slumber room*, where the *grief coordinator* conducted the *viewing*. Following the *memorial service*, the *funeral coach* transported the *departed* to the *garden of remembrance* where his *human remains* were *interred* in their *final resting place*."

Huh? What's that? Did someone die or something?

I've Got a Train to Catch

This item demonstrates how stupid the average American is. Every ninety minutes someone in this country is hit by a train. A train, okay? Trains are on tracks; they can't come and get you. They can't surprise you when you step off a curb. You have to go to them. Got that?

There are five thousand highway/rail-crossing accidents annually. To counter this problem, the Department of Transportation issued the following rules for people to follow at railroad crossings:

- Don't drive around lowered gates. "Okay, got it."
- Don't cross in front of a train. "Never thought of that."
- Don't walk on the tracks. "Check."
- Be aware that trains can't stop quickly. "Good to know."
- Always expect a train. "This one would probably be tied in to the fact that these are railroad tracks, is that right? Correct me if I'm wrong on this."
- Look for more than one train. "Frankly, this is one I never thought of. Maybe if I remember the others, this one will take care of itself."

Get Down!

Here's something to think about: In the course of history's wars, many battles took place in the woods and the countryside. So, sometimes I picture a soldier waking up on a spring morning, wildflowers growing around his tent, birds singing in the trees, perhaps the comforting sound of a brook trickling by in the near distance. And then a ten-pound cannonball hits him in the face. It's an interesting thought, don't you think?

On My Honor

I wanted to be a Boy Scout, but I had all the wrong traits. Apparently, they were looking for kids who were trustworthy, loyal, helpful, friendly, courteous, kind, obedient, cheerful, thrifty, brave, clean and reverent. Unfortunately, at that time, I was devious, fickle, obstructive, hostile, rude, mean, defiant, glum, extravagant, cowardly, dirty and sacrilegious. So I waited a few years and joined the army.

Pass the Mustard

In New York State, the law says that the ingredients of hot dogs can legally include a certain amount or percentage of insect parts and rat droppings. It's permissible by law. So, in New York, when you eat a hot dog, you more or less have to hope that the hot dog you're eating contains only the most nutritious parts of the insects (not just legs and antennae) and that the rats whose feces you're eating were on good, heart-healthy diets.

You've Got a Nice Voice, Do You Have Insurance?

I've been enjoying a new band from England called So Long, Mate! It's a five-man heavy-metal band, and the reason it's called So Long, Mate! is because at the end of each performance the other four members of the band kill the lead singer. As a result, the music has a certain urgency to it. Also, it keeps the tours nice and short; it's basically one night, and then back they go to L.A. to hold auditions. The band plans to have an album ready in the year 2037.

Danny Needs a Torso

"Hello, this is David Nipplegripper, another insufferable Hollywood movie star who wants you to help some cause or charity merely because I say so. Today, I want to tell you about little Danny Pendejo. Danny needs your help; he was born with no torso. His legs are fine, his arms are fine, and his head is okay except for one really big, caved-in part on top. But he has no torso. Won't you help by being a torso donor? Even a torso that's too big will be better than no torso at all. Thank you. This is David Nipplegripper, reminding you to see my new movie, *Breasts on the Moon*."

Nuts!

Another sign of America's decline: Because a few people are "sensitive to peanuts" and have "allergies" that might "kill them," America's commercial airlines had to stop serving those little bags of peanuts. It wasn't sufficient that the affected people could simply refuse the peanuts when they were offered; the argument was made that the people who did eat the peanuts were putting "peanut dust" in the air, creating a health hazard for the "victims." What a load of shit. If someone is in danger of dying from inhaling peanut dust, why aren't they dead already? Why didn't they die at a baseball game or at the circus? America has gone soft.

Instructions: Follow Carefully

Release the handle by pulling down the strap and tightening the fasteners. Press the button and remove the safety cap, then turn the knob to unleash the spring and wind the excess slack onto the spool. Loosen the screws on the plate lid and insert the tabs into the slots. Rotate the control switch a quarter of a turn before lowering the two levers. Then drop the main crank into a neutral position. Be careful not to unscrew the housing before engaging the catch. Plug in and you're set to go. If smoke fills the room, read the troubleshooting guide at the rear of this manual.

Actors, Not Activists

I like the good actors. The real actors. The ones who keep their lives private. Sean Penn, Harvey Keitel, Alan Arkin, Robert Duvall, Al Pacino, Jack Nicholson, Johnny Depp, Robert De Niro, Gary Oldman, William Hurt, Dustin Hoffman, Gene Hackman,

Gary Sinise, Christopher Walken, Gary Busey. They keep to themselves. You don't see them appearing all the time on TV. They don't cooperate with *Access Hollywood* and *Entertainment Tonight*. They're actors. Not celebrities. They keep to themselves. That's why their work is so good. Good for them.

Dear Ma

Dear Ma,

Even though you're dead, I wanted you to know I'm doing real well. No thanks to you, I might add. I now have my own TV show and it's getting very high ratings. I play the part of a guy whose mother dies but it doesn't really bother him. I know they don't have good reception where you are, so I'm going to send you a tape. Do you think a tape will be okay in the intense heat?

Love, Dirk

Teams Suck!

I don't like ass kissers, flag wavers or team players. I like people who buck the system. Individualists. I often warn kids: "Somewhere along the way, someone is going to tell you, 'There is no "I" in team.' What you should tell them is, 'Maybe not. But there *is* an "I" in independence, individuality and integrity.'"

Avoid teams at all cost. Keep your circle small. Never join a group that has a name. If they say, "We're the So-and-Sos," take a walk. And if, somehow, you must join, if it's unavoidable, such as a union or a trade association, go ahead and join. But don't participate; it will be your death. And if they tell you you're not a team player, just congratulate them on being so observant.

In the Groove

You ever run over a guy with your car? And you kind of panic? So you back up? And run over him a second time? And then you realize you have to get the fuck outta there before the police show up? So you put it in drive again and run over him a third time? What the fuck — might as well. What else you gonna do at that point, drive around him? Anyway, as you drive away, did you ever reflect on the fact that each time you ran over him the crunching sound got fainter and fainter? That's because he already had two good, deep grooves pressed into him that you kept driving through.

Pride Goeth . . .

Parents are such fuckin' doofuses. I saw a bumper sticker that said "Proud parents of a sailor." What the fuck is so special about being a sailor? How about "Proud parents of a tailor"? Isn't a tailor worthy, too? The whole "proud parent" thing is bullshit. Pretty soon I'm expecting to see "Proud parents of a child." Have a little self-respect, will ya? You never see the children with bumper stickers that say "Proud son of Mr. & Mrs. Klayman." That's because Mr. & Mrs. Klayman are such fuckin' doofuses.

I'm in the Moral Minority

I don't think there's really such a thing as morality. I think it's a human construct designed to facilitate the control of people. Values, ethics, legal standards — all of these things are human-generated, and they're lumped under some vague idea called morality. But suppose humans got it wrong? Suppose there's no actual, objective morality? Suppose there's just a natural, worldly, secular, common-sense standard of behavior whose purpose is what's best for getting along and what's best for survival? That would be a good system. Why should a system like that be overlaid with a sense of spooky, mystical, judgmental oversight?

Just Die, Motherfucker

When this Catholic guy, Cardinal Bernardin of Chicago, died, they praised him for accepting death gracefully. Excuse me, but isn't that what you're supposed to do? Accept death gracefully? What's that? You say many people *don't* accept death gracefully? I see. So now we're evaluating people's behavior and praising them based on what other people *don't* do? Wonderful.

I don't think people should ever get credit for doing something they're supposed to do, even if it's rarely done by others. Condemn the ones who don't do it if you like, but don't praise the ones who do it. Only one of the two behaviors is worth commenting on, not both.

True Stuff

You know those broken white lines that separate the lanes on a highway? Have you ever counted them? If you do, you'll find that there are a hundred of them every mile. It's true. Each line is a hundredth of a mile from the next one. Count them for yourself as you track your distance on the odometer. Just count how many there are each tenth of a mile; there should be ten. But while you're counting, don't forget to keep an eye out for that big eighteen-wheeler up ahead, parked sideways in the middle of the road.

Chow Time

"Hi, I'm Ferris Banderhead, another bothersome movie star who tells people to support some charity or other in order to make myself appear concerned and to increase my popularity. Not to mention easing the guilt I feel for having much more than I deserve. But enough about me. April is National Hunger Month. In Beverly Hills, we're having our annual Hunger Banquet and Gala called 'Hors d'oeuvres for Ethiopia.' Send in your dollars today and help us feed people around the world who could certainly use a nice hors d'oeuvre. And remember, the sooner we conquer hunger, the sooner we can start working on upset stomach. Thank you. This is Ferris Banderhead, reminding you to see my new spy movie, *The Snotlocker Papers*."

Mannheim Rehab: Call Today

"I'm Dr. Mannheim of the Mannheim Rehab and Recovery Center. People ask me, 'How can I tell when one of my loved ones needs help with a substance abuse problem?' And I say, 'If you see them lying in a corner, naked, in a puddle of their own filth, it may be time to think about counseling.' Call Mannheim today, and we'll come over and pick them up. But before we get there . . . please clean up the filth."

Uncle Blitzen

Uncle Blitzen was a troubled man. As a child, visiting backstage at a concert, he was fondled by a viola player and lived the rest of his days with an unnatural fear of stringed instruments. He was one of the nine hundred people present at the Jonestown Massacre, but he threw away the Kool-Aid and only pretended to be dead. When everyone stopped moving he looted the corpses. Subsequently, he moved to Stockholm, where he became the town scumbag. Years later, he reemerged in England as a self-proclaimed bishop, roaming the Midlands with a band of rogue altar boys, administering forced communion to lapsed Catholics. He died during Hurricane Shlomo in front of an adult sex shop when the store's sign blew down and he was crushed to death by a giant neon dildo.

Uncle Pinocchio

Uncle Pinocchio had twenty-three separate and distinct personalities; unfortunately, all of them were unpleasant. He believed that Porky Pig cartoons represented actual events, and he once stabbed his dog with a ceremonial Japanese saber in a dispute over a lamb bone. He always wore a three-piece suit. It didn't have a vest, the jacket was just torn in half. He drifted from job to job: balloon vendor, freelance daredevil and stoop laborer among them. He finally settled in his basement, where he lost his mind trying to invent a rectal harmonica. After that, the family kept him tied to a linden tree in the backyard, where they fed him with a slingshot. After six years, they released him on Mussolini's birthday, whereupon he married a passive-aggressive librarian who later beat him to death with a dictionary stand.

Uncle Shadrack

Uncle Shadrack felt he was special because one of his testicles was shaped like a Brazil nut and the other like a cashew. He loved to run up to women, screaming, "You want some mixed nuts?" He told me that in his younger days he was quite a lover and once fucked a girl so hard her freckles fell off. Alas, he didn't marry well. His wife, Chlorine, looked like something that might be found in the Dumpster behind a cloning center. Her PMS was so bad she had a mood swing installed in her backyard. As a child, while watching a gay pride parade, she was run over by a float full of lesbians, and was eventually found dead in a military barracks, having ingested a load of bad sperm. Shadrack was electrocuted by a RadioShack pacemaker he purchased at a thrift shop.

Uncle Shemp

Uncle Shemp was alarmingly unexceptional. He had no detectable lifestyle, and his only accomplishment was the fact that he was a lifelong member of the general public. He started slowly, struggled hard and eventually clawed his way to the back of the pack. Occasionally, he would show a sudden flash of mediocrity, but quickly return to his usual pattern of complete insignificance. He was a man without memories. He didn't have amnesia, he simply had no memories. As he put it, "Nothing big ever really happened." As a result, he wore a Medic-Alert bracelet saying PLEASE LET ME DIE. His only pleasure was his hobby: picking through airline wreckage, looking for children's toys. He died at seventy-five from a head injury suffered as the result of undue glee following a bowel movement.

Tumor Humor:
Guys, Gals & Cancer

Women: The Produce

Department

Mae: I see where Ruthie Garrick went under the knife the other day. She had a tumor on her the size of a grapefruit.

Agnes: Well, that's bigger than Estelle Mealy's tumor. Estelle's was the size of a large navel orange.

Paula: Yeah, but sometimes a large navel orange can be almost as big as a small grapefruit.

Kate: That's true. Especially one of them small Indian River grapefruits. I don't like them. Too sour.

Paula: Me either.

Mae: Listen, girls, this wasn't no small Indian River–size tumor. The doctor said this thing was almost the size of a cantaloupe. He claimed if he'd-a left it alone any longer, it probably woulda wound up as big as a casaba melon.

Agnes: Earlene Miller had a tumor the size of a casaba melon. Actually, her sister claimed it was approaching honeydew proportions.

Paula: Well, I don't know nothin' about no tumors, but when my aunt Ruby died, her liver was the size of a champion watermelon. I got a picture of it somewhere.

Kate: Really? You know, they say that after you die, your liver keeps right on growing.

Paula: Well, I'm thinkin' Ruby's liver had

probably reached its limit. I mean, where do you go from watermelon?

Kate: Beach ball.

Mae: Kate, a beach ball's not a food!

Kate: You want food? I'll give you food. Wait'll you hear this. Ten years ago, when my sister Myra had her gallbladder out, they found twenty gallstones in it. Each one of them was the size — and the shape — of a different type of food: a raisin, a pea, a caper, a grape, a radish, an olive, a pearl onion, a melon ball, a hazelnut, a marshmallow, a Brussels sprout, a bing cherry, a kumquat, a gherkin, a filbert, a small whole boiled potato, a cocktail sausage, a meatball, a lima bean and a dwarf pumpkin.

Paula: They took all of that out of your aunt?

Kate: They sure did.

Paula: Jesus! Did she feel any better?

Kate: She said she was hungry.

Men: The Sports Section

Jim: I see where Petey Whelan died the other day. They say he had a tumor on him the size of a beach ball.

Ed: No kiddin'? That one under his arm? Jesus, it musta grown fast.

Jim: It sure did. I can remember the day I first saw it; it was small, like a marble. Then almost overnight it looked like a golf ball. I couldn't believe it!

Tom: That was the day he showed it to me. By the time I saw it, it looked more like a slightly enlarged handball, maybe just approaching racquetball size. I spent about an hour with him, and as I was leavin', I glanced at it. The damn thing looked like a tennis ball. I don't mean it had fuzz on it or anything. I just mean it was the size of a tennis ball.

Jim: Yeah. That's when he went to the hospital. He said on the way over in the taxi it went from a baseball to a

445

softball, and then, in the waiting room, it reached the size of a small, regulation volleyball. Finally, when he got into the examining room, the doctors were so alarmed at its growth they smashed it with a big fryin' pan, and it temporarily flattened out into an oval shape.

Ed: I remember that. For about an hour it resembled a football.

Tom: Yeah. Then it slowly became round again, but it kept on gettin' bigger. Suddenly, it developed big black spots all over it.

Ed: The soccer-ball stage.

Tom: Yeah. Of course, by that time the situation was hopeless. Pretty soon the thing was up to the size of a basketball, and before you knew it, it had gone right past medicine ball and was headin' for beach-ball status. They finally had to move him out of his room and put him in the gymnasium.

Ed: Appropriate. How did he die, anyway?

Jim: They tried to operate on him, but as soon as they made an incision all the air rushed out of him. Death by deflation.

Tom: Poor guy.

Ed: Yeah.

Tom: Hey, you know what we forgot? Lacrosse and polo.

Soaring and Plunging in the Media

One of my pet pursuits is keeping track of how the news media describe those things in the news that increase or decrease. I can generally rely on the fact that the same verbs will be used repeatedly in the same situations.

One of the first things I noticed is that while certain things *skyrocket*, others tend to *mushroom*. Medical costs *skyrocket*. The national debt doesn't do that; it *mushrooms*. And, experts warn, if present trends continue, both of these things will eventually *go through the roof*.

But *mushrooming* is not the only thing the national debt does; it also *balloons*. There aren't too many things that *balloon*. The annual budget deficit used to *balloon*, then for a while it didn't *balloon*, now it *balloons* again. And, by the way, people can *balloon*, as well. I remember reading in the tabloids once that the actress Delta Burke had *ballooned* to some weight that, apparently, the publication found unacceptable.

So, thus far we've *skyrocketed, mushroomed* and *ballooned*. But let's not forget *snowballing*. You know what snowballs? An investigation. What happens is, an inquiry becomes an *investigation*, and the investigation begins to *snowball*. And what does it *snowball* into? Right! A *full-blown probe*. And if the probe uncovers enough dirt, it could possibly *mushroom* into a *full-blown scandal*.

Then we have the case of *swelled*. During the 1990s, job rolls *swelled*. By the way, I've often wondered if those job rolls are at all similar to the welfare rolls we used to hear so much about. Just between you and me, I've never actually seen welfare rolls, but I'm sure that with a little margarine or jelly they're quite delicious. And it's certainly heartening to see the food stamp program working so effectively.

Getting back to our subject here, I've found that one of the best places to keep an eye on these "up and down" words is Wall Street. Financial reporting. For purposes of this activity, I'll use hypothetical examples of economic activity that don't actually reflect recent conditions. I can't keep adjusting this material according to the whims of the economy. And besides, this is about language, not finance.

Just to review: We've already skyrocketed, mushroomed, ballooned, snowballed and swelled. Now, as we enter the world of Wall Street, we add a few simpler verbs: *climb, surge* and *jump*. "The stock market *climbed* today as prices *surged* on news that housing starts had *jumped* ten percent." Lots of action.

Another big thing on Wall Street is *soaring*. "Stock prices *soared* today, as reports showed earnings were *up sharply*." Or they may have *shot upward*. At any rate, upward is good. I remember one time hearing Lou Dobbs himself telling me that the Dow Jones Industrials had *vaulted upward* two hundred points. And, on the same day, not to be left too far behind, the long bond *inched higher*.

Then we have the very special case of *spiraling*. The nice thing about *spiraling* is that it can go in either direction. "As medical costs have *spiraled upward,* the quality of medical care has *spiraled downward.*" And not only do these two medical numbers *spiral upward* and *downward,* both of them are actually capable of *spiraling out of control.*

Spiraling downward brings us to the verbs for things that are falling. For some reason, downward verbs are more colorful than upward verbs. Downward is where we discover *plunge, plummet* and *nosedive.* You can always tell when a bull market is over, because *housing starts plunge, new-car sales plummet* and *orders for durable goods take a nosedive.* At a time like that, stock prices are usually on the verge of *collapse.*

Or, instead of collapsing, they may simply *tumble, drop sharply* or *go into a tailspin.* And if stock prices are in a *tailspin,* you can be sure it won't be long before they find themselves in a *dizzying free fall.*

Continuing with bear markets, not all days are so dramatic. Occasionally, prices only *dip slightly. Dip slightly* is the opposite of *edge higher.*

And before we leave these words for increasing and decreasing, I would like to make special mention of *beefed up.* I remember reading once that, in anticipation of a visit by Yassir Arafat, security at the United Nations had been *beefed up.*

Arafat being a Muslim, of course, beef would be the preferred meat. You certainly wouldn't want security to be *porked up.* I can think of any number of reasons why we wouldn't want that. And by the way, if you've ever seen some of these security people, you know that the last thing they need is more pork. Or beef. Or food of any kind, for that matter.

Beefed up is one of those terms that has no exact opposite. Nothing ever gets *beefed down.* They never say, "Now that Arafat's visit has concluded, security at the United Nations has been *beefed down.*" Doesn't sound right. Instead, they say *scaled back.* Always remember, anything that's been *beefed up* can be *scaled back.* Although occasionally, for variety's sake, rather than *scaled back* the item may be *pared down.*

Hiked and *trimmed* are two more good "up and down" examples. Quite often, during the same session of Congress, defense spending will be *hiked* while education spending is *trimmed.* And sometimes, if Congress is in a really bad mood, education spending is *slashed,* and defense spending *skyrockets.*

Well, we've gone from *sky-high* to *rock*

bottom and we seem to be *winding down* now, so let me add one last item: I think I may have figured out the difference between *ramping up* and *ratcheting up*. I'm pretty sure that while *ramping up* takes place on a continuum, *ratcheting up* is more a series of increments. But I do find it interesting that, as with the beef situation, I rarely hear of *ramping* or *ratcheting down*.

As for me, I'm at wit's end.

Problems and Issues

As you know, people no longer have *problems* in this country, they have *issues*. This shift grows out of our increasingly desperate need to shade the truth and see things as more positive than they really are. Problems sound negative and ordinary; issues sound important, worthy of attention. People are proud to announce them: "I have issues." They feel superior to others who haven't made the switch: "Poor fuck. He has problems. I have . . . issues!" To feel extra superior they may even pair it with some other trendy upgrade: "He has a *drug problem*, I have *chemical dependency issues*."

As with everything in American culture,

the use of the word spread indiscriminately to the point where it, of course, lost all its usefulness: During the murder case in San Francisco in 2001 in which two dogs mauled a woman to death, one of the neighbors said, "Everyone knew those dogs had issues with females." Commercials picked it up: L'Oreal says, "Mature skin has issues all its own." An adult diaper commercial informs me that "Many women have bladder-control issues."

So now people have all these issues: trust issues, boundary issues, abandonment issues, personal-space issues. Clearly, I have a problem with this word, but *problem* has lost its power, cheapened by the careless use of expressions like, "What's your problem?" "You got a problem with that," "No problem," and, for those truly in a hurry, "No prob."

I needed a new word, and I refuse to say "issues." So, instead, I turned to that ultimate source of creative language-bending, our nation's capital. I heard a prominent senator, when asked if some issue presented a problem for him, say, "Well, it's not a problem, but it is a *concern*." And I thought, Wow, another choice for people who refuse to acknowledge problems. I adopted it immediately. But I hope *concern* doesn't catch on to the point where it becomes a problem. After all this trouble, I'd hate to have to deal with concern issues.

The Secret News
(News ticker sound effect)

Announcer: (whispering)
Good evening, ladies and gentlemen, it's time for the Secret News.

(News ticker gets louder.)

Announcer: Shhhhh!

(Ticker lowers.)

Announcer:
Here is the Secret News:
All people are afraid.
No one knows what they're doing.
Everything is getting worse.
Some people deserve to die.
Your money is worthless.
No one is properly dressed.
At least one of your children will disappoint you.

The system is rigged.
Your house will never be completely clean.
All teachers are incompetent.
There are people who really dislike you.
Nothing is as good as it seems.
Things don't last.
No one is paying attention.
The country is dying.
God doesn't care.
Shhhhh.

The employees of Thorndike Press hope you have enjoyed this Large Print book. All our Thorndike and Wheeler Large Print titles are designed for easy reading, and all our books are made to last. Other Thorndike Press Large Print books are available at your library, through selected bookstores, or directly from us.

For information about titles, please call:

(800) 223-1244

or visit our Web site at:

www.gale.com/thorndike
www.gale.com/wheeler

To share your comments, please write:

Publisher
Thorndike Press
295 Kennedy Memorial Drive
Waterville, ME 04901